Analytics of Life
Making sense of Data Analytics, Machine Learning and the Artificial Intelligence

Analytics of Life

Making Sense of Data Analytics, Machine Learning, and the Artificial Intelligence

Mert Damlapinar

Artificial intelligence has the potential to usher in a Golden Age for humanity or to destroy everything for which we've worked.

We are each responsible for the direction we take.

NLITX
New York City, New York

Published by NLITX
New York City, New York

Print Edition
December 2019
ISBN: 978-1-09830-097-5

EBook Edition
Amazon Kindle—December 2019

Cover design: Rade Jovanovski.

Typography fonts
Headings: Bahnschrift
Running Heads: Bahnschrift
Text: Palatino Linotype

"A breakthrough in machine learning would be worth 10 Microsofts."
—Bill Gates

"In God we trust. All others must bring data."
—William Edwards Deming

Table of Contents

Introduction
The Promise of
Artificial Intelligence

Outside, it was a warm, summer afternoon in Cambridge, Massachusetts. Inside, six scientists and electrical technicians stood awaiting the results of their most recent test.

"Nuts!" The technician rubbed his balding pate and shook his head. "Bill, we're still getting the wrong answer."

Bill Burke crossed the room and looked down at the output and scratched the underside of his jaw. He, too, shook his head and then looked up at the ceiling of the Harvard Computation Lab, momentarily deep in thought. They had started the "mult+adder test" only a few minutes earlier and the problem was now unavoidably obvious.

Only two years after the end of World War II and this team was working on the cutting edge of technology. Of course, there would always be setbacks and surprises. That was to be expected in exploring uncharted territory. Finding new ways to make a machine "think" was still in its infancy. But like most creative beginnings, this was exciting stuff.

Bill glanced at the clock. It said 3:34—15:34 by the standard military notation they used. "Yeah, nuts. Let's open it up. Check all the relays. Something is failing." He shook his head again, and planted his fists on his hips. "We need to track down this bugaboo."

The Harvard Mark II was an electromechanical calculating machine. It used electrical relays for its system of Boolean and computational logic. Had one of the relays failed somehow? Had a connection come loose?

A few minutes later, one of the technicians reared back his head and laughed hysterically for several long seconds. When finally he had caught his breath, he said, still chuckling, "A bug, all right. A real, honest-to-God bug." He stood and looked back in Bill's direction. "Well, gents. We finally found the bug engineers have been talking about for nearly a century. Here it is. A moth caught in one of the relays."

"What?" Bill laughed hesitantly, took a few steps in the direction of the technician, saw the moth and let out another laugh, this time more uninhibited. "Well, damn! That's a bug, all right. What do we do with this?"

One of the other technicians chimed in, "Log it! With the proof!"

William "Bill" Burke almost couldn't contain his laughter, now. The sheer absurdity of the discovery had the potential to become legendary. Though such potential was hidden from conscious thought, at the time, he could feel its energy bristling underneath the surface of reality.

"Okay," he said, "Let's log it." Again, he looked up at the clock. "Fifteen forty-five. Today, Tuesday, September 9, 1947 is going to be a red-letter day in computing history. Our first, real-life bug." Bill grabbed his pen. "Now, that's panel 'F,' right?"

"Yeah," said the first technician. "Relay number seventy."

"Okay," said Bill, waving. "Bring our deceased prisoner over here."

The technician picked up the dead moth and walked it over to Burke's desk. Bill pulled out a length of tape and nodded toward the log where he had already written the time, then he taped the moth into position for posterity's sake.

Bill Burke finished the brief entry and looked up at his colleagues, shaking his head and chuckling. "Ms. Hopper is not going to believe this."

He was talking, of course, about Navy Reserve Lieutenant Grace Hopper, who was assisting the head of the programming staff, Howard H. Aiken. She had been in her mid-30s when first she had tried to join the war effort. In 1943, she had finally been able to join the Navy Reserve. With the war over, she was assisting on peace-time development for the Navy.

While at Harvard, Hopper wrote three papers with Aiken. When, years later, she finally retired, she had become a naval Rear Admiral. And she once had said that she had always dreamed of creating a computer programming language in English. In fact, one of her nicknames had become "Grandma COBOL," named after an early, high-level computer language that was machine independent. In other words, the COBOL programming language could be used on any one of numerous machine architectures—mainframe, supercomputer, mini-computers, Motorola-based systems, Intel-based microcomputers and more. For years after that summer's day in 1947, naval officer and computer guru, Grace Hopper, loved telling the story of Bill Burke, his team and the discovery of the first actual "bug" in a computer.

When finally the Mark II had been fully tested, it was delivered to the Naval Weapons Laboratory, at Dahlgren, Virginia. Bill Burke was reassigned there to oversee its installation and use.

This simple event in the history of computers highlights one of the difficulties in designing and utilizing any clever machine. Such machine intelligence always has to deal with the real world and the random difficulties that plague that cleverness with problems.

The Meaning of Computer Intelligence

There's a famous maxim amongst software engineers and computer scientists—"Garbage in equals garbage out" (GIGO). The answers can only be as good as the data used to achieve them. By the same token, a system can only be as good as the designer of the system.

Before artificial intelligence (AI), all computer-based decisions needed to be explicitly written into software code. This included exceptions to those rules. The first rung on the AI ladder gave us software variables that allowed for a minor degree of software flexibility. But even with full-blown AI, a computer intelligence needs to be trained how to think about certain problems and what legitimate exceptions look like. If the one who does that training is prejudiced, the resulting machine intelligence could end up being less than desirable.

There are different stages in the evolution of AI. At one end of the development chain, we have software that keeps count of occurrences and gives greater weight to those things which happen more often. That more simplistic approach has proven useful in machine learning routines. At the most advanced stage in AI development, we have a machine which is self-aware, can see and hear, can understand nuances of meaning, and can increase its own intelligence by seeking out new inputs. Such an artificially intelligent system could carry on a conversation with a human, cracking jokes and originating opinions and commentary. And, obviously, we're not there, yet.

Recently on social media, one Amazon customer commented on an ironic error in the company's marketing algorithm. You see, the customer had purchased a toilet seat from the retail giant, but kept getting emails encouraging them to purchase more toilet seats. The customer made it clear that they do not have a toilet seat addiction or collection. They had no intention of giving in to the temptation to buy "just one more." Amazon's marketing algorithm could not distinguish between a repeat purchase item and a "one-off" purchase. Such a distinction needs to be explicitly programmed into their marketing module. Someone may need to add a specific field to each product record—something that marks the product as a potential repeat purchase item, or a one-off purchase. They may even want to distinguish products that may lead to similar purchases, but not repeat buys. We repeat-buy batteries, paper towels, cartridges, coffee pods, crackers, and we buy similar items like books—not more of the same title, but other books with different titles. And we don't need to buy more toilet seats if we have only one toilet in our home.

Conservative comedian Stephen Crowder recently poked fun at Amazon's Alexa for some of the incorrect replies the AI assistant had offered. As amazing as the advancements have been, some of the goofs are tragically funny. And that's to be expected at the infancy of artificial intelligence. Any parent will tell you that children can say some of the craziest things. As children, they're still learning. AI is still in its infancy.

What is Business Analytics?

In a 2013 report called, "The Analytics Advantage," by Deloitte Touche Tohmatsu, a financial advisory services company, they describe analytics as "the practice of using data to manage information and performance." Also in the report, they quoted a director of HR analytics of an entertainment company, "Basically, analytics is about making good business decisions. Just giving reports with numbers doesn't help. We must provide information in a way that best suits our decision-makers."

Sandra Gittlen, writing in a 2010, Computer World technology briefing, said, "Forget spreadsheets. Organizations that are winning in this down economy are using automated analytical tools to take a more scientific approach to decision making through observation, experimentation and measurement to improve their business processes. Their results: innovative and revenue-generating improvements and savings."

In a 2018 brochure by NICE Nexidia, the company described the business analytics challenge this way: "We all want to reap the benefits promised by analytics, making the right data-driven decisions that lead us to improved customer experience and business efficiency. But far too many companies struggle to apply their analytics in a meaningful way. After all, it's hard to make definitive decisions when dealing with multiple sources of data, and endless variables and possibilities. Analytics have real potential to solve our most pressing problems, but it can't just be another product you add to the stack. It must be embedded into your organization's frameworks, methodologies, and processes in order to make a difference. This is what we call being analytical by nature."

McKinsey Analytics, in a 2018 brochure on their services, describes what they do: "[Our company] helps clients achieve better performance through data. We work together with clients to build analytics-driven organizations, providing end-to-end support covering strategy, operations, data science, implementation, and change management. Our engagements range from use-case-specific applications to full-scale analytics transformations. Our teams of consultants, data scientists, and engineers work together with clients to identify opportunities, assess available data, define solutions, establish optimal hosting environments, ingest data, develop cutting-edge algorithms, visualize outputs, and assess impact while building capabilities to sustain and expand it."

But business analytics and big data are not entirely intuitive and easy. In a 2015 paper, C. Kimble and G. Milolidakis give us this insight: "This article sets out to look at big data and debunk some of the myths that surround it. It focuses on the role of data from social media in particular and highlights two common myths about big data. The first is that because a data set contains billions of items, traditional methodological issues no longer matter. The second is the belief that big data is both a complete and unbiased source of data upon which to base decisions."

Shrewd businessmen have long known that numbers can lie. Statistics can be sculpted to make them support just about any point-of-view. It takes a careful data expert to understand the potential problems facing us with business analytics. But all such problems can be solved.

There are many layers to the field of data analytics. RapidMiner.com explained, "Advanced Analytics is 'the

analysis of all kinds of data using sophisticated quantitative methods (for example, statistics, descriptive and
predictive data mining, simulation and optimization) to
produce insights that traditional approaches to business
intelligence (BI)—such as query and reporting—are
unlikely to discover'" (quoting Gareth Herschel, Alex-
ander Linden, Lisa Kart in a Gartner article).

More and more, data analytics needs to digest
what is called "big data." Xiaomeng Su explained in their
"Introduction to Big Data," that big data is not merely a
vast quantity of information, measured in terabytes or
even zettabytes, big data can also be a flood of data that
changes from minute-to-minute or even second-to-
second. And big data can include a broad variety of data
sources, with different formats and even unformatted
information.

An "ultimate business guide to business intelligence," by Domo.com, echoes this sentiment about big
data. "We are living in a data deluge. The amount of new
data created annually will grow ten-fold between 2013
and 2020, according to IDC, from 4.4 trillion gigabytes to
44 trillion gigabytes.

"If you can swim in this flood of data, you win.
According to MIT researchers, companies that excel in
data-driven decision-making are 5% more productive
and 6% more profitable than their competitors, on
average. A study by IDC found that users of big data and
analytics that use diverse data sources, diverse analytical
tools, and diverse metrics were five times more likely to
exceed expectations for their projects than those who
don't."

Domo went on to point out that data has no value
unless it is submitted to proper analysis. In a way, it's
almost like listening to a foreign language. Someone may

say a great deal, but if you don't have a translator handy, all those words become merely interesting, but worthless noise.

"Navigating the flood of data is much easier said than done. IDC predicts that companies will continue to waste 80% of customer data they have collected. More broadly, IDC estimates that in 2013 only 22% of all data in the world was useful (i.e., could be analyzed) and less than 5% of that was actually analyzed." With improvements in AI, these figures are changing.

One sub-branch of data analytics involves geographic information systems, or GIS. Basically, it's information displayed in a map format. Esri's 2012 white paper on location analytics for business intelligence described their niche this way: "GIS integrates software and data to capture, manage, analyze, and display all forms of geographically referenced information. GIS allows users to view, understand, question, interpret, and visualize data in ways that reveal relationships, patterns, and trends in the form of maps, globes, reports, and charts."

Former American ambassador to the United Nations, Colin Powell, once said, "Experts often possess more data than judgment." AI helps experts gain the proper perspective on all that data so that better judgment becomes possible.

Putting AI and Data Analytics to Work

Imagine chatting with your computer, like the HAL-9000 in the motion picture, *2001: A Space Odyssey*. This type of advancement has already begun with things like Amazon's Alexa and other, similar products. But as we've seen, these have not yet been perfected.

Now, imagine talking to your computer and asking for analysis of recent sales in your own business.

"How can we improve our sales, long term?"

And imagine getting some credible and insightful answers after a few moments of the machine searching and analyzing.

We are now living on the cusp of a new age — the age of Artificial Intelligence. This is a machine talent which more and more closely approximates the intelligence of a human being.

Rather than being limited to narrowly-focused algorithms dedicated to a specific problem, computers are coming closer and closer to the art of interpreting context and intent, and a more generalist intelligence which can figure out what you mean and then construct its own algorithms in order to solve new problems. We're not there, yet. But the immense progress computer scientists have made is encouraging.

The leading edge of development in artificial intelligence, or AI, resides in the field of data analytics. This is where the most exciting advancements are being made. And it's no wonder. Rightfully so, business is what pays for all that new development.

Corporations have long realized that facts and figures need to be analyzed for them to have any value. With the incredible glut of data, the task we have has become impossible to do by hand. We need computer intelligence to sift through the countless terabytes of information, examining it for patterns that can help us predict things like,

- Customer buying trends,
- Future, hot-ticket items,
- Credit risks,

- Weak points in infrastructure that have a high probability of failure,
- Possible medical epidemics,
- Climate catastrophes, and
- Many other topics of keen interest to the health of a business, nation or the world-at-large.

We still have tabular data and normalized databases that organize information into records and fields, but so much of the facts upon which intelligent predictions depend involve data that is not so neatly organized. And not all information carries the same weight or validity.

A truly powerful AI would be capable of looking at all types of information—news articles, anecdotal reports, false reports, lies, true reports, verified evidence, and more—to build a realistic view of the world in order to find solutions unobtainable by mere mortals.

In a brochure by NICE Nexidia we find some helpful hints on utilizing big data without drowning in the flood of information. First off, they recommend taking on the entire ocean of data available to us. As overwhelming as that might seem, by keeping clearly defined outcomes in mind, we will be able to organize that ocean into usable batches of information to fulfill our purposes with the data.

By embedding methods of data retrieval at critical points in our business cycles, we can start to see our weak points and our strong points. We will be able to reduce customer churn by bolstering what makes them happy and eliminating what prevents that happiness. By engaging with the mountains of data, we'll be able to see the patterns which shape our business outcomes. And like a ship captain who is finally able to see, we'll know how and where to steer our enterprise.

We will know what concerns the bulk of our customers, or what hinders the majority of our compliance issues. We will be able to see the major choke points on our sales funnel. By being able to see these larger issues, we'll be able to take care of what might be called the "low hanging fruit"—gaining the greatest benefit for our business analytic efforts.

Once the easy stuff is out of the way, we can dive deeper into the data to find those areas where customers become confused or where a process may be broken a significant portion of the time.

By measuring our improvements at fixed intervals, we can better judge the value of our data analytics efforts.

In a ComputerWorld technology briefing, sponsored by SAS, we get a different perspective on data analytics. Here we see how the analysis itself becomes multidimensional, using a myriad of metrics—each one a separate dimension—so that we can get a more robust view of a business unit's strengths and weaknesses. For instance, we can look at the differences between sales team members based on things like tenure, region and other factors. Quite often our superstar is doing something the others are not doing. Switch territories and likely the superstar will do just as well there as they did in their original region. Analytics can sometimes pinpoint some of the differences.

In a part of that same briefing by Tom Farre, we see a compelling scale that defines the various levels of business analytics that gauge degree of intelligence against competitive advantage. When the two are properly balanced, we get the following helpful sequence:

- **Standard Reports**—What happened?
- **Ad hoc Reports**—How many, how often, where?
- **Query Drilldown**—What exactly is the problem?

- **Alerts**—What actions are needed?
- **Statistical Analysis**—Why is this happening?
- **Forecasting**—What if these trends continue?
- **Predictive Modeling**—What will happen next?
- **Optimization**—What's the best that can happen?

In a survey performed by Deloitte, business leaders let them know how much business analytics helped them remain competitive. Here are their results:

Does Analytics Improve Competitive Positioning?
- **25%**—Significantly improved
- **30%**—Fairly improved
- **29%**—Improved very little
- **3%**—Did not improve at all
- **14%**—Don't know/Not applicable

And, as you can see, a majority said that they received a noticeable improvement from business analytics. Their survey also revealed key strategies that can achieve greater buy-in from the top.

Deloitte's Key Findings:

"Slow and steady, wins the analytics race. Smart analytics leaders are overcoming skepticism and gaining executive advocates by:
- "Tackling small projects that yield impressive results,
- "Showing tangible, incremental improvements—financially or operationally,
- "Demonstrating how analytics improves competitive positioning."

Kimble and Milolidakis, in a 2015 report, talk about the various dimensions of big data, including something called "dark data." Why is it called "dark?" Because the information can only be made visible by processing the oceans of data produced by social media, like Facebook, Twitter and YouTube. Sifting through all of that stuff can give companies and governments a feeling for the pulse of the world—changing attitudes and trends in beliefs. This type of information is of particular interest to businesses which want to know not only what their customers are thinking, but also what their competitors' customers are thinking. Shining a light on all that data, categorizing it, packaging it and making it presentable to individual businesses is becoming an important industry. The writers of the report explore the use and efficacy of such big data.

In a 2014 brochure by RapidMiner, we learn their view of the differences between business intelligence and advanced analytics. This distinction is just as important today, nearly five years later.

"Business Intelligence—traditionally focuses on using a consistent set of metrics to measure past perform-ance and guide business planning. Business Intelligence consists of querying, reporting, OLAP (online analytical processing), and can answer questions including 'what happened,' 'how many,' and 'how often.'

"Advanced Analytics—goes beyond Business Intelli-gence by using sophisticated modeling techniques to predict future events or discover patterns which cannot be detected otherwise. Advanced Analytics can answer questions including 'why is this happening,' 'what if these trends continue,' 'what will happen next' (predic-tion), 'what is the best that can happen' (optimization)."

With the results of such business analytics, a cor-poration would know in advance whether or not their line of products were becoming obsolete, or whether the competition was gaining a threat-level market share. A company would have a better understanding of customer concerns not possible in the current customer support mills that push "quantity of queries handled" over "value of solutions achieved."

With the ideal level of AI, an internet search engine would be able to understand the reason why a search was being conducted so that the search results would contain the right context, instead of keyword matches that include countless results that have nothing to do with the desired dataset. For example: Say you want to know more about stars with multiple planets. You wouldn't necessarily be interested in the number of movie stars who visited the Planet Hollywood restaurant. The desired context would be "astronomy" instead of "celebrity."

Search results are becoming better, but they have not yet arrived at truly intelligent responses.

The amount of time lost trying different wording can be both frustrating and costly, especially in business. With a truly AI search system, a computer would know the project upon which you're working and the exact context of internet search. The AI might even be able to find the evidence which supports your proposal and that which contradicts your proposal, allowing you to strengthen your arguments against any and all opposition. The AI may even be able to suggest wording and arguments from the search results found.

Such a system would prove invaluable, not only in saving time, but also in expanding each employee's reach with greater productivity and greater insight into the problems and opportunities of the business.

Google has earned the distinction as one of the leaders in the AI quest. Yet, despite their problem-solving prowess, the tech giant has been accused of skewing their search engine results, favoring outcomes that more closely match their political biases. This is the kind of partiality we need to guard against if we are to achieve a truly benign and useful artificial intelligence.

Business analytics of today allows each company to discover where their greatest sales are coming from and how to increase sales by moving more marketing effort into those most profitable niches. Those niches can be defined by personal interests, lifestyle, geographical location, type of location, or any one of numerous other demographic traits.

Today, smart managers can use existing software to sift through mountains of data, looking at all those facts from different viewpoints. Tomorrow, AI may put those managers out of work by doing all of the analysis itself. But we should not fear such changes. They may eliminate some jobs while creating new opportunities for careers we may never before have considered possible.

One key business area where AI and advanced analytics could help greatly, involves customer service and queries. Not many years ago, Bank of America's customer service center in Phoenix, Arizona suffered a major public relations black eye from the mishandling of a debit card claim.

Part of the problem is that customer claims against supposedly erroneous credit or debit card charges are handled by humans who have a mandate of quantity over quality. One customer was charged $985.00 for a $9.85 pizza. The customer service rep (CSR) denied the claim, because he could not imagine how the customer was right, in this case. Perhaps they thought that 100 pizzas had been ordered. The CSR voted in favor of the pizza parlor, but had not bothered to investigate the case more thoroughly. CSR's in the bank's huge service center campus have quotas they must keep if they are to retain their jobs.

If the CSR had looked more closely at the transaction, they would likely have seen that the customer had purchased one pizza. Anyone who has ever purchased a pizza would likely realize that nearly a thousand dollars for one pizza is an unrealistic price.

After the claim had been denied, the customer went to a local television station to complain. The story was picked up nationally, and Bank of America was left smarting from the blunder. The president of the company got involved and he was not happy.

AI could have prevented this mistake. For one thing, the bank would not have needed to focus so much on quantity instead of quality, because AI would have been able to do a great deal of the research on the claim, alerting the CSR of the most probable reason for the claim: pizzas don't normally cost $985.00 each. The AI could also have recommended exacting actions the CSR could have taken to ensure that the customer had not indeed ordered 100 pizzas. For example: call the pizza restaurant and ask if they had received any orders of that size during the evening in question. Any small business would certainly remember such a huge order, for it would've taken an all-out effort for several hours to have fulfilled such an order.

Data analytics will help us make better decisions, more completely understand the risks of some decisions and help us ferret out the gold we didn't know was sitting right in front of us. With good business analytics, we can increase efficiency, boost customer experience and even improve our ability to look at data in a way that produces far more desirable end results.

Is a Data Revolution Here?

The obvious answer to this question—Is a data revolution here?—is "Yes!" But we need to understand more than this one-word response. Our responsibility requires that we understand the answer more deeply. As with all revolutions, change can prove disruptive. By understanding the full nature of the potential changes, we can guard against destructive disruptions, and maximize the benefits from the inevitable opportunities which will also come with such a revolution.

The most nimble businesses are frequently the companies which will not only survive but thrive in an ever-changing world. This is the mandate of evolution, not only with life and its various species, but also with businesses, governments and any other groups which need to respond to the inevitable changes.

We can learn from nature. In fact, the natural world gives us many hints about the methods we can use to achieve our desired AI. We will be looking at some of those hints in a later chapter.

A Golden Age of Computing Power?

What happens in the next few years could give us a Golden Age of computing power, or with the wrong sequence of bias and intent, a dystopia of Orwellian proportions. The direction we take depends entirely upon us and our ability to be truly humble and wise with our newfound power.

As Lord Acton (1834–1902) once famously said, "Power tends to corrupt, and absolute power corrupts absolutely. Great men are almost always bad men..." To the thorough and honest student of history, this claim remains intuitively valid. Time will tell whether or not we are wise in the growth and use of our new AI power. Knowledge of the potential pitfalls can help us overcome the problems we face, for we need to lead our new AI child out of the wilderness of nonexistence and to guide them toward their benign potential as friends of humanity.

In This Book

The book is divided into five parts.
- PART 1—Analytics in Business
- PART 2—Analytics in Personal Life
- PART 3—Analytics in Nature
- PART 4—How to Use Analytics
- Appendix

PART 1—Analytics in Business

In Part 1, "Analytics in Business," we look at the details of business analytics, how they affect business, its use of technology, how they've transformed certain industries, how jobs will be replaced by AI, and a look at how some jobs will remain secure for the time being.

Chapter 1 looks more closely at how AI is changing the business use of the various kinds of existing technology. We will look at a broad range of industries, gaining an in-depth look at the sweeping changes that have already occurred, or are in the process of being made.

In Chapter 2, we see how data analytics have changed some industries, not only in the ways they do business, but also in developing new opportunities to cut costs, to increase profits and to develop new ways of satisfying customer needs.

It's only natural that we remain concerned about how new technology will eliminate not only some jobs, but also some entire industries. We learn more about this in Chapter 3.

To strike a balance with the topic of Chapter 3, Chapter 4 will cover the jobs that will remain safe from the data analytics revolution, at least for the foreseeable future.

PART 2—Analytics in Personal Life

This part of the book peers into how analytics affects our daily lives, now and in the future.

Chapter 5 provides us with examples from our day-to-day activities of software that learns from the use of that software.

In Chapter 6, we explore many of the pros and cons of AI. With all the benefits we can expect, there are also many risks that we need to guard against.

And Chapter 7 tackles the future possibilities of AI and how it will change our lives.

PART 3—Analytics in Nature

Part 3 delves into how nature not only developed intelligence, but how it continues to inspire us in our attempts to create our own thinking machines.

In Chapter 8, we look at how Mother Nature gives us clues that are helping us create artificial intelligence.

Comparing natural with artificial intelligence gives us a deeper understanding of the high-tech challenges we face. We'll cover this comparison in Chapter 9.

PART 4—How to Use Analytics

Application of our discoveries is where we reap the rewards of all our hard work. Part 4 shows how we can use data analytics on the job and in business.

Chapter 10 shows how big data analytics can be the best career choice in the foreseeable future.

For those of us who are not inclined to pursue a career in data analytics, Chapter 11 shows how we can still use the current state of the art to benefit our daily job.

The last chapter explores many of the ways we can use data analytics to benefit our own small business.

Appendix

The Appendix includes references, notes for some chapters, suggested reading and a glossary of terms.

The Purpose of This Book

First and foremost, this book provides the reader with a broad overview of the field of data analytics and artificial intelligence. It provides the layperson an understanding of the various stages of artificial intelligence, the risks and powerful benefits. And it provides a way to look at big data and machine learning that enables us to make the most of this exciting new realm of technology in our day-to-day jobs and in our own small businesses.

World-famous management guru, Peter F. Drucker has had many sayings attributed to him. One of the more famous quips goes something like this: "What gets measured gets managed." One business consultant wishes that Drucker had never said this. Why? Because it's too easily taken out of context and misses the original intent. Bill Hennessy, American consultant and activist, wrote in a blog article on the famous—or perhaps infamous—saying, "What's worse, people actually run companies and departments and government agencies by Drucker quotes. Not Drucker concepts, which work, but Drucker quotes—misremembered, out of context, and incomplete."

Hennessy went on to say, "This is the most evil and destructive Drucker quote of all time. I hear it at least once a month, usually to justify elimination of tasks that cannot easily be measured using the kinds of simple yardsticks executives fancy. Ya know, unmeasurable work like ingenuity, coaching, innovation, creativity, and, Drucker's favorite, imagination."

Hennessy's article included this warning concerning Drucker's praise of knowledge workers, "Working on the right things is what makes knowledge work effective. This is not capable of being measured by any of the yardsticks for manual work." And further, "Moreover, because knowledge work cannot be measured the way manual work can, one cannot tell a knowledge worker in a few simple words whether he is doing the right job and how well he is doing it."

For all the enthusiasm to measure and analyze the world around us, Hennessy's distaste for misunderstood wisdom provides us all with an implied caveat that we must all heed: That we should remain humble in all circumstances, for our lack of omniscience is a strong hint that there may well be far more that we need to know in order to make the right decisions in life and in business.

World-renowned statistician, W. Edwards Deming, the American who almost single-handedly transformed Japan after World War 2, once said, "The most important things cannot be measured." Naturally, he was talking about things like beauty, happiness and love. This book will strive to keep both of these points of wisdom in mind as we navigate the risks and benefits of analyzing the things that can be measured.

PART 1
Analytics in Business

"Data is the new oil."
—European Consumer Commissioner Meglena Kuneva

Chapter 1
How AI is Changing
Business Use of Technology

Can you believe it? Google predicts that robots will exhibit human levels of intelligence within the next ten years. Imagine ordering a machine in 2029 that will be able to hold with you a meaningful conversation or will be able to do some of your work, freeing up your time to pursue other projects, or to handle more creative aspects of an undertaking.

One IT research company—Gartner—estimates that, by 2025, about 30% of all jobs will be handled by some form of technology, instead of by humans—smart machines, robots or even software.

But is this cause for alarm? Not necessarily. The economic health of a society is determined by the value created by that society's individuals. Flipping burgers, for instance, does not add much value to a society. Creating a method for automating the creation of hamburgers could benefit society greatly by lowering the cost of such meals, and increasing profit for the corporations. The end result is more people being able to afford to eat out more often, and the corporation being able to build new restaurants, making their meals available to an even wider audience.

For the time being, humans will still need to maintain such machines—installing, cleaning, repairing and adjusting.

Artificial Intelligence frees up humans to do other, more strategic work that AI is not yet well suited to perform. With the power of smarter machines, businesses can build new markets and create innovative, new ways to do business.

Here are some examples of how businesses are turning to artificial intelligence not only to improve their operations, but also to create new products and services.

AI and Consumer Goods

What would a 146-year-old Dutch beer company want with artificial intelligence? Plenty, if its name is Heineken and anxious to expand its market share in the United States. The company has collected an incredible quantity of data. With that information, they can streamline their customer service, sharpen their advertising and boost their marketing reach. For instance, they hope to make the most of the Internet of Things (IoT) to strengthen their marketing efforts. With improved data analytics, they also hope to improve their daily operations.

What about the toy industry? Throughout the better part of human history, little girls have had dolls to play with. This goes back at least to the 21st century BC. From the early paddle form dolls made of wood, bone or ivory, the art of doll making has continued to improve. Today, dolls are expected to do more than have movable arms and legs; they are expected to respond to simple questions. Hello Barbie makes use of natural language processing to decipher a child's request. With machine learning, the software is able to improve its ability to decipher words from the specific child—the doll's user.

The Barbie doll's necklace contains an embedded microphone which picks up the request, which is then transmitted to ToyTalk servers. Advanced analytics help determine which of 8,000 possible responses should be sent back to the doll. All of this processing takes less than a second, so that the doll speaks its answer as if naturally responding to the child's question, like, "What is your favorite food?"

If beer can take advantage of artificial intelligence, why not soft drinks, too? Coca-Cola is found in virtually every country on the planet with several hundred beverage labels to offer. Clearly, it is the largest provider of soft drinks on the planet. This mega-company uses AI to write copy and pick music for its ads, to develop new products and even to drive augmented reality headsets for technicians who are servicing their bottling plant equipment.

AI and Creative Arts

What do food recipes, sculpture and music composition have to do with one another? All three of these intersect inside IBM's machine learning system called Watson. And there's no need to limit the AI software's creativity to these three.

Take for instance the notion of inspiring human composers with machine-generated ideas. If we were to give the software many gigabytes of data, say from countless thousands of speeches, newspaper headlines and conversations, artificial intelligence could generate a rich theme for a song's lyrics. The Watson BEAT is a machine that can deliver sets of musical phrases which can trigger in a musician the inspiration to compose the music to go with those lyrics. Artificial intelligence software can even help a composer to understand their audience more deeply so that the songs they create have a greater likelihood of becoming hits.

AI in the kitchen? So far, we may not be able to let a robot run wild amongst the cooking pots and skillets, but IBM's artificially intelligent Chef Watson can help the chefs and sous-chefs up their game with new recipes and taste-tempting culinary delights. So far, this is a collaborative effort, with the machine merely helping their human counterpart think outside the usual box.

Computers can also augment visual art and design. Artificial intelligence, plus big data, provide us with another way that IBM's Watson machine learning system can boost human creativity. IBM pushed the limits on its machine by feeding it hundreds of examples of sculpture by Gaudi, plus countless other examples of other works and designs complementary to those of the artist. These included scenes from and culture of Barcelona, historical write-ups, biographies of Barcelonan natives and even the lyrics of songs. After digesting the massive body of visual and thematic data, Watson generated a batch of inspirational images so that the human artists associated with the project could create a work inspired by Gaudi's style.

AI and Customer Service

What would you think if a business was always closed every time you wanted to buy from them, or every time you had questions about a product? That would be pretty frustrating.

The internet has made the world much smaller. It has also broken down the barriers of time zones. A software provider in India may have customers in America anxious to do business, but not at 3 AM. Hiring human staff to handle customer queries at all hours of the day and night can prove to be expensive. This can be even more problematic when your staff is sitting idle with few if any customer requests, or when your staff is overwhelmed by an unusual spike in traffic. The business doesn't want needless costs of customer service reps sitting around doing nothing. And the business doesn't want to upset clients who have long wait times to reach customer service.

AI is perfect for this kind of problem.

Currently, there are two key methods for leveraging AI in customer service:

- Chatbots—small programs that communicate with customers, via texting, without involving a human. Naturally, text uses very low bandwidth and bots don't cost anything after initial development.
- AI Assist—software that intelligently assists a human customer service representative so that they are more efficient in helping customers.

Chatbots are used by a wide variety of online platforms, including social media sites WeChat, Facebook and Twitter, as well as numerous other types of websites. Until we achieve the next level of artificial intelligence, chatbots will likely remain the backbone of customer service.

AI and Energy Production & Delivery

You may have heard of the Internet of Things (IoT)—extending internet-like connectivity to other types of devices not typically thought of as "data aware." General Electric's GE Power has been ramping up to extend IoT to create an "internet of energy." This would include things like predictive maintenance of power transmission equipment and operations facilities. To achieve this new level of energy operation, they intend to use machine learning and advanced analytics.

British Petroleum (BP), a global leader in the energy industry, has also been using artificial intelligence and big data to achieve better and better levels of performance efficiency. They are also making strides to improve their use of resources, to squeeze more value out of what they have. In addition, in the realm of gas and oil production, they are improving their safety record, plus boosting the reliability of their operations. One source of big data includes sensors that report on the ever-changing conditions at each site, and use AI to predict outputs and estimated times to failure so parts can be replaced well ahead of time. All of the appropriate data is made available to BP's staff of decision makers, scientists and engineers.

AI and Financial Services

Fraud is an ever-present problem in the financial services industry. It's as old as money. Because money is a symbol of work done or goods exchanged, lazy, greedy people want to steal money in order to get ahead. It's a regrettable part of human nature.

Every year, American Express handles roughly a trillion dollars in transactions through their 110 million AmEx, "Don't leave home without it," cards. This financial services company has long been a leader in data analytics to help their managers detect real-time fraud before it can result in millions of dollars in losses. To achieve this near-instantaneous detection, the company makes use of machine learning and other algorithms that leverage big data about buying habits to alert account managers when unusual purchases are being made. More than that, American Express is making the most of its customers' purchasing data to make special offers for products and services they are more likely to want, thus increasing corporate profits. But the company doesn't stop there, maximizing the value of their unique customer data. They also make available to merchants critical information about current trends in, and benchmarking of online business and data about their industry competitors.

Credit reference agency, Experian currently works with about 3.6 petabytes of information. For those of us who don't frequently use the *peta-* prefix, one petabyte is equal to 1,000 terabytes, or one million gigabytes. In other words, that's a lot of data—much more than the individual usually uses. And Experian's data appetite continues to grow. That data includes transactional records of people around the world, plus public information on those same individuals. Why do they need so much data? Because others rely on Experian to determine the creditworthiness of individual buyers. Machine learning algorithms help the company distinguish between data elements that are important and those that aren't, in determining whether a person can be trusted with more credit.

Payroll services can also benefit greatly from big data and AI. Domo.com gives us a prime example. "Paychex provides payroll, human resources, and employee benefits services, primarily to small businesses. As it loses about 20% of its customer base each year, Paychex developed a model that predicts high-risk customers and can track what the Paychex branches are doing (or not doing) in terms of increasing customer retention. Based on the model, some branches developed a year-end retention program, targeting clients most likely to leave by providing free payrolls and loyalty discounts. When the retention strategy was applied, the customer loss rate was 6.7%, as opposed to 25.2% loss rate when nothing was done. The analysis also significantly helped the bottom line by helping the branches overcome their eagerness to touch all customers by offering discounts to customers likely to stay with Paychex, rather than targeting only those predicted by the model to be the most likely to leave."

AI and Healthcare

Google continues to leverage their data analytics expertise to help other industries and the healthcare field is no exception. One of the biggest challenges in the healthcare arena involves the collection of records, storing them and tracing their history. Google is taking the notion of medical records mining to a new level with their new project called Deepmind Health. Borne out of their AI research branch, this new Google initiative is developing methods to analyze existing patient data in order to find better solutions for health maintenance, detection of problems in advance of their becoming serious and generally improving the quality of care.

The Google DeepMind project is built on the concept of neuroscience and creating a hardware and software package that can imitate the human brain's thought processes. In the early stages, DeepMind could easily beat humans at simple games, like chess, but the healthcare goal is to assists healthcare practitioners to streamline the process of planning treatment programs for their patients and in using machine intelligence to determine the causes of ailments.

No country in the history of humanity has undergone growing pains like modern China. They have gone from a largely rural country to an increasingly industrial nation in a few short decades. One strain on their infrastructure has been the lack of trained people in the health industry, including a lack of radiologists. Infervision is one company, using deep learning and artificial intelligence to overcome the personnel shortage by letting machines take up the slack. With roughly 1.4 billion CT scans performed each year, radiologists had been overwhelmed by the amount of work required of them. Reviewing hundreds of scans each day is not only mind-numbingly boring, but also understandably prone to errors. The Chinese company has programmed machine algorithms to do much of the review for their human partners, allowing more accurate cancer diagnosis and greater efficiency for the human radiologists.

Part of a doctor's job is that of identifying the best treatment plans for a specific patient. Understandably, this takes lots of experience and artful skill on the part of any doctor. Watson for Oncology is helping doctors do just that. The AI software looks for key points in a patient's electronic medical record (EMR), which can be either unstructured data or a formalized database. Watson then analyzes the data before pinpointing the best treatment protocol for the unique individual.

One area where healthcare can benefit from AI and machine learning involves repetitive jobs, like that of delivering anesthesia during an operation. Recently, the American Food and Drug Administration (FDA) approved Johnson & Johnson's bid to use AI in colonoscopy, and similar standard procedures, for delivering anesthesia.

These examples are only the beginning of what is possible with AI assisted healthcare and machine intelligence in the fitness and wellness sectors. Imagine having a virtual nurse take care of you, or AI designing new, patented drugs.

Domo.com reported on healthcare industry improvements by proper management of its own big data. "By sharing patient data among emergency departments, the Washington State Health Care Authority achieved the following results:

- "Emergency department visits declined by 9.9%
- "Visits by frequent clients (who visited five or more times annually) decreased by 10.7%
- "Visits resulting in a scheduled drug prescription decreased by 24%
- "Visits with a low acuity diagnosis decreased by 14.2%."

AI and Law Enforcement

Sounding like a page out of a science fiction novel or a scene from the Tom Cruise movie, *Minority Report*, Domo.com provides us with an example of AI being used by law enforcement to fight crime.

"The Los Angeles Police Department (LAPD), with assistance from researchers at the University of California, analyzed 13 million crimes recorded over 80 years so it can predict where a crime will occur in the future. The results of the analysis, focused on one LAPD precinct, led to a 12% decrease in property crime and a 26% decrease in burglary."

AI and Manufacturing

Automotive manufacturers have benefited from Henry Ford's innovative, assembly line approach for well over a century. More recently, AI has been an integral part of the manufacturing process for decades. Now, Bavarian Motor Works (BMW) has changed its business model to make artificial intelligence and big data a large part of what they do and how they do it. Design, engineering, sales and even aftercare, have each been infused with big data-related technology. In fact, BMW plans to make their own driverless cars available by 2021. These vehicles will achieve Level 5 autonomy, a state where the automobile can drive itself without the slightest degree of human intervention.

Farms with robots? Manufacturer John Deere already delivers farm vehicles that have been automated to plough and sow with GPS system accuracy. Their Farmsight product can also help farmers make better decisions for their farms. John Deere has every intention to remain at the forefront of farm technology. That's one reason they purchased the company Blue River Technology. The takeover gives John Deere equipment the ability to scan the terrain ahead, analyze the visual data, and to determine if the field of view includes a pest which requires a pesticide.

Over the last few decades, the electronics in cars have become more and more sophisticated, with sensors placed throughout the automobile's critical functions. This increasing connectivity has allowed Volvo to predict when service is needed, or when parts will fail and require replacement. With their impressive safety record on the line, Volvo is doing everything it can to make their vehicles safer and more comfortable. This includes keeping track of a vehicle's operation and response during a hazardous condition. Naturally, with the increased interest in self-driving vehicles, Volvo is also looking into the creation of their own line of autonomous cars.

AI and Media

Can you imagine what a company would do if they had a crystal ball that actually worked? Big data analytics is the closest thing we have to such a mystical marvel. And

Netflix is taking advantage of this cutting edge technology to help it predict what customers will want to watch. You may have noticed that Netflix is no longer merely a distributor, but also a content creator. One of the largest risks in the motion picture industry has involved the art of deciding what project to support; a large percentage of motion picture projects end up financial duds or costly failures. But skills with big data have made Netflix confident that they can choose more winners than average. In fact, their confidence is so strong that, instead of merely greenlighting a single pilot to see how a television series might look, they are investing in more than one season of a new show. A few decades ago, a network exec who might think of such a move would likely have a heart attack from the stress. Big data and the skills to use it have changed all that.

How successful is this Netflix strategy? Domo provides us with a startling example. "Netflix decided to outbid established TV networks and invest $100 million in two seasons of 'House of Cards' based on its extensive analysis of its customers' viewing habits and preferences. 'House of Cards' brought in 2 million new U.S. subscribers in the first quarter of 2013, which was a 7% increase over the previous quarter. It also brought in 1 million new subscribers from elsewhere in the world. These 3 million subscribers almost paid Netflix back for the cost of 'House of Cards' within a single quarter."

Did you know there was too much local news happening in the United Kingdom? According to Press Associates (PA), a British news agency, there is more happening on the local scene than can be covered by human writers. To cover this shortfall, PA is partnering with Urbs Media, a specialist in news automation. Their goal is to crank out 30,000 stories each month on local events that their own reporters are not able to cover. How does it work? In an impressive enterprise called Reporters and Data and Robots (RADAR), they feed Urbs Media software with thousands of information details from local authorities, public services and government agencies. Their computer systems use a natural language generation technology that they hope will take up the slack their staff of reporters have not been able to handle.

The BBC has come up with an entirely unique angle on story creation that uses both AI and humans in collaboration. Their project, called "Talking with Machines," results in an audio drama built from human smart-speaker responses. Program listeners merely answer questions given to them by their Google Home device or Amazon Echo, and their software stitches together a story from those human answers. Imagine that: Snippets of two-way communication with machines for generating unique new stories. BBC execs hope to include even more voice-activated brands as the new art form catches on.

AI and Mining

Greater efficiency in any process can save money in the long run. The mining industry is no stranger to this. In their business intelligence guidebook, Domo gives us a powerful example of cost cutting from data analytics. "Rio Tinto, a British-Australian multinational metals and mining corporation, has reduced costs by $80 million by eliminating processing and logistics inefficiencies based on its continuous monitoring and analysis of operational data. Rio Tinto's Process Excellence Centre is staffed by 12 mineral experts who analyze data from five of the company's coal sites in Australia, and operations in Mongolia and the US. A large interactive monitor displays technical data in real time with the center receiving data 100ms after it is produced at the site. This is examined by 20 different analytical systems in order to allow processing improvements to be immediately introduced."

AI and Retail

There's a lot to be said in favor of big business. In a word: Resources! In fact, huge business, when successful, can have enough discretionary funds to do some serious experimenting. Walmart is one such giant who is not letting the opportunity slip by them to improve every possible aspect of their retail business. Though Amazon has more income than Walmart, by a factor of about 16-to-1, Walmart has 35% more physical assets and nearly four times as many employees. A large chunk of the physical assets resides in more than 11,300 brick-and-mortar stores worldwide—a retail dimension Amazon can't touch. In 2016, Walmart got serious about its online presence, with corporate acquisitions and a more impressive investment in online infrastructure (Nusca).

Walmart aims to make the full customer experience a seamless one, whether they buy online or from one of their thousands of physical stores. Naturally, they're using machine learning and big data, plus the Internet-of-Things and AI. The retail giant has replaced their Scan and Go app with a new Walmart app that allows customers to use their smartphones instead of a wallet (Kim). To make their online presence even more impressive, Walmart has added Pick-up Towers and Pick-up Lockers at 700 of their physical stores, allowing customers to retrieve their purchases instead of having to wait for delivery. The Pick-up Towers act as a vending machine kiosk for online purchases, while the Lockers hold larger items, like televisions (Peterson). The retail giant has even begun to look into facial recognition technology to gauge a customer's mood. Imagine a Walmart manager called to intercept a customer before they reach the complaint desk. Could disgruntled patron feel a little pampered with that kind of proactive attention?

If Walmart keeps this up, though more than twice as old as the online retail giant, they could become the next "Amazon."

Luxury fashion retailer, Burberry, is doing their own business makeover. Though many people think of them as merely a brick-and-mortar operation, they are developing quite an online, digital presence. As a source of luxury fashion, they are keen to nip counterfeit products in the bud. Big data and AI have come to their rescue on this perennial problem, in the improvement of sales and the development of customer relationships. To strengthen personal bonds with their customers, Burberry has, among other things, beefed up their loyalty and reward programs. Data from these programs have helped them create a shopping experience that is unique for each of their customers. The pampering is targeting both real and virtual world shopping experiences.

Domo provides us with two other examples in their business intelligence guidebook. "Tesco, the largest retailer in the UK, combines data from weather records with detailed sales data, broken down by store and products, to build computer models that predict future demand for product lines according to weather forecasts. This and similar types of analysis give Tesco a more accurate picture of demand, leading to savings of £100 million a year through a reduction in wasted inventory and to a 30% reduction in the number of instances of products on promotion being out of stock."

And in Domo's second example, "German online and catalogue retail giant Otto Group, has used analytics to improve its demand forecasting, leading to annual savings of tens of millions of euros. The use of predictive analytics has led to a significant reduction in rates of return on key fashion items, saving about 10 million to 15 million euros. It has also improved gross profitability on men's fashion items by introducing dynamic pricing, changing prices based on demand, and forecasting what prices customers will accept on a particular day."

AI and Service

It's hard to talk about AI and not keep running into Google and its leading edge work in the area. With the 2011 introduction of the Google Brain project, the company quickly established itself as a leader in machine deep learning. Image recognition was one of their early successes, allowing the online search engine to introduce picture searches—uploading an actual image and finding every site on the internet which has the same image or something similar. But Google didn't stop there. They are now using the same deep learning technology for the enhancement of images.

On Google's video platform, YouTube, their deep learning language processing routines are now enabling the platform to offer more accurate recommendations to their visitors, based on past viewing preferences and habits. No longer do they rely solely on keywords to make business analytical connections. Every time a visitor streams content, YouTube is analyzing what they watch and collecting big data to refine their understanding of each visitor's interests.

Machine learning has proven vital to Google's efforts in developing self-driving cars. And, on the sustainability front, Google has used deep learning routines to help them configure coolers and other hardware to optimize their data center energy usage.

Did you know that illegal fishing is a big problem in the world? Google now provides a service to help combat illegal fishing. By combining satellite imagery, cloud computing, machine learning and geo-mapping, Google can tell, on any given day, where all the ships are in the world. With 22 million data points, they can track Earth's waterways, and with machine learning, they can determine the reason any specific vessel is at sea. From this, they were able to create Global Fishing Watch, pinpointing those ships which have a high probability of illegal activity.

The Disney organization has long been a leader in top quality service, at their theme parks, hotels and restaurants. Big data and AI create a huge win-win situation for both customers and Disney. At the start of each customer's visit, they receive a wristband, called the MagicBand. For the customer, this one item acts as their ID, tickets, payment system, FastPasses and hotel room key. The customer wins big because of the immense convenience the MagicBand provides. Disney wins big, because the MagicBand channels huge amounts of data about the customers behavior, purchases, location and movements. From this information, Disney is able to provide a far richer experience to the customer. Disney can anticipate the customer's needs, plus predict and handle traffic jams. If a customer is ever inconvenienced by a closed attraction, Disney can offset the disappointment with complementary, extra services free of charge. Such actions will naturally help Disney maintain an impeccable reputation with nearly all of its customers. This "magic mountain" of data will also allow Disney to schedule their staff more efficiently, because they will be able to know where all of their customers are and to predict where they will be going.

Microsoft has long been a pioneer with computers, creating one of the early operating systems for personal computers, then numerous software tools which made their operating system indispensable and easy to use. In the last couple of decades, Microsoft has increasingly become involved in creating smart machines, from its virtual assistant, Cortana, to intelligent features built into its Office suite of software tools. Chatbots are another Microsoft strongpoint, running Skype, answering customer queries, plus delivering on-time information to people interested in weather updates or travel advisories.

The company has also made their AI Platform available for other companies to use so that they can build their own smart tools. Like so many other companies, Microsoft is working toward the creation of generalized machine intelligence which will allow the AI completion of any task, no matter how complex.

AI and Social Media

What happens when 293,000 people out of nearly two billion update their online statuses every minute? If such a company were asleep at the proverbial wheel, all that data flow would wash out to the sea of oblivion like so much rain not captured in the unbuilt California reservoirs. But Facebook wasn't sleeping. They capture all that data, every minute of every day, analyzing it with deep learning technologies and neural networks as part of their Torch platform.

Visitors to the world wide web each have their own preferences and some companies are listening to their needs. Using AI and big data to more accurately target advertising is only standard operating procedure in today's tech savvy world. But with millions of visitors every day, handling things like offensive comments and cyberbullying becomes an impossible task for the sheer lack of manpower. Instagram is using the latest tech to help them manage their own mountain of data. With the tech, they're able to improve each user's experience, provide them with information that matches their interests and helps to eliminate pesky spam.

As a tech giant in its own right, Twitter is also using AI to fight content that may offend certain users. With millions of tweets to sift through, they have to use the sheer brawn of machine learning, big data and artificial intelligence. As it is, their system is still imperfect, with numerous, high-profile goofs and outright banning of people who did not break their terms of service. So, even in the best of companies, the tech still has some kinks to work out.

Not to be outdone, social media upstart, Gab.ai has developed a parallel comment section called Dissenter. Though it may not have cutting-edge AI working for it, Gab's intelligent new system allows visitors to add comments to any web page on the internet, even if that website has turned off their comments section. Naturally, Gab stores the comments, but their tool puts power back in the hands of the individual. For fans of free speech on all sides of every issue, those hearty souls not afraid of the occasional cyber bully will find far greater freedom than they might otherwise receive on the older platforms.

AI and Transportation

We've already looked at how Google is providing its services to many different industries, including transportation. But it's not only self-driving cars, but also trucks and bicycles. Many other companies are pushing development in this area, including Tesla on cars, and Uber on trucks. These have not yet been made commercially available, but they are in the early phases of design and testing of prototypes.

The benefits could be huge, including the reduction of collisions and other mishaps, and the reduction of rush-hour congestion by switching up the scheduling of deliveries and routes. This last item could also improve on the costs of fuel consumption.

Part of the challenge of the transportation industry is the subfield of logistics. Business continually faces the challenge of having the right resources at the right location at the right time. Moving too much of a resource too soon can increase costs needlessly. In a study conducted by Roland Berger Global Strategy Consulting, we learn that by 2020, robots will cost roughly half the expense of a human employee in the realm of order delivery. Imagine eCommerce benefiting from an army of drones taking packages to their destinations. With AI, a swarm of autonomous robots can plot out the most efficient delivery strategy, cutting costs and driving supply-chain efficiency to the next level.

The business intelligence guidebook by Domo provides us with another example of common sense combined with AI being used in the realm of package delivery. "Route optimization analysis by UPS led it to come up with a simple rule for its drivers: Minimize or even eliminate left-hand turns. As a result, between 2004 and 2012 it saved 10 million gallons of gas and carbon emissions were reduced by 100,000 metric tons—or the equivalent of pulling 5,300 cars off the road annually. Route optimization analysis also saved UPS $98 million idle minutes or about $25 million worth of labor cost each year."

AI, Robots and Artificial "Life"

Looking at what businesses are currently doing with AI and data analytics can be pretty exciting. We can't help but imagine what the future may hold for this technology.

What would it take to build an android with a human-like personality and intelligence, like *Star Trek: Next Generation's* Data (played by actor Brent Spiner in the series)? (see Appendix, Notes, *"Robots and Star Trek's Data Android")*

We already have robots that can keep their balance on two legs, like a human. But what about the android's ability to perceive, understand and respond intelligently?

Years ago, I remember when one engineer described what was then leading edge technology—pun intended! The new tech involved what is called "edge detection"—where software can analyze an image and determine what are the edges of physical objects. It does a robot no good if it cannot walk through a doorway without hitting the door jam or the wall next to it. A baby, robotic intelligence desperately needs to know edges.

Another piece of the perfect robot solution is sound recognition and interpretation. This includes understanding words spoken and determining which words are being used, plus their context in the sentence and paragraph.

Still another piece of the puzzle involves pattern recognition. Naturally, this needs to be in real time, otherwise it may be too late for the poor robot. That rapidly-approaching shape may be a truck or a train.

Androids will need to understand complex concepts, not merely simple identities. They need to understand sentences, not just words. One approach to this might be to think of dictionary and thesaurus entries as abstract vectors in multi-dimensional concept space.

The ultimate test in AI design will be to meld all of these disparate elements together in one cohesive unit of awareness.

Chapter 2
Industries Transformed
by Data Analytics

AI has touched nearly every industry in one way or another. Finding new ways of collecting and analyzing data has become a passion unto itself. From finance to the development of pharmaceutical drugs, and from debt collection to social media image recognition, artificial intelligence is making data analytics of big data a commonplace affair. Either everyone is doing it or thinking about doing it.

In this chapter, we look at a broad variety of industries that have committed themselves to this relatively new technology. As with any new industry, changes are happening with great speed. And because the return on investment is so huge, more capital is being invested in this field, fueling even greater speed and larger changes.

Financial Search Engine

Imagine working in the financial industry and suddenly needing a search engine tailored for, and dedicated to, finance. You don't have to wait or imagine. It already exists. AlphaSense, based in New York for obvious reasons, is giving investment firms the informational edge they need to stay at the head of the Wall Street pack.

AlphaSense does it by combining natural language processing and linguistic search to scrutinize a very specific set of key data found in nearly 35,000 monetary organizations.

Analysts can save countless days of drudgery trying to piece together what AlphaSense can do in minutes. Their system can peruse millions of big data facts and produce reports upon which analysts can take action with confidence backed up by solid monetary data.

Outcome: AlphaSense serves nearly a thousand financial institutions, including several from Fortune's 500 list.

Online Retailing

Amazon has changed retailing forever. Though they started by selling books, they now carry just about everything you could imagine in a brick-and-mortar retail store. For now, they are the leader in AI used in e-commerce.

Anyone familiar with Amazon's website knows that every page we visit is keen to give us recommendations based on our past searches and purchases. But there's a lot more going on behind the scenes—like at the Amazon warehouse, where robots pluck items out of inventory, arrange and prepare them for the most efficient shipping possible.

Not only that, but Amazon has packaged its AI talents and made them available to other businesses as "web services" so that everyone can take advantage of their AI prowess.

Virtually everything Amazon does is powered by one kind of artificial intelligence or another.

Gene Roddenberry's Star Trek universe has been the inspiration for so many innovations found in our society, and Amazon is not at all shy about taking that inspiration and running with it. When they came out with their voice-activated personal assistant, Alexa, in 2014, Amazon drove the creation of many copy-cat systems that also wanted to capitalize on this cutting edge technology.

Outcome: Every part of Amazon's business has been touched by AI. Their aggressive adoption of artificial intelligence in their operations, customer service and in their products has put them ahead of most of their competitors. Only those companies which already have a strong AI presence will have a chance to compete with Amazon on their level.

Customer Relationship Management

It was only a matter of time before AI transformed a labor-intensive field like customer service up to its ultimate potential. Amplero services the customer-facing side of the business world. This includes aspects of gaming, telecommunications, retail, finance and more. They build marketing tools powered by AI.

Amplero starts with big data—lots of it. They burrow into all that data and ferret out valuable patterns. From those distillations, they can construct powerful market profiles that can be utilized, at-scale, to dabble with the "what-if" questions that tantalize every marketer's heart. Amplero's machine learning prowess, plus its powerful software, allow their customers to explore every possible method of serving their customers and ensuring they stay loyal to their brand.

Outcome: Heavy hitters, like Microsoft, TaxAct and Sprint use Amplero's suite of AI-driven tools. Success stories abound. Just as an example, Amplero helped one company increase their upsell rate, driving down their acquisition costs dramatically (from $40 down to $1). Not only that, Amplero's case study pointed out that the customer enjoyed a "lift in average revenue per postpaid customer" of 88%.

Discovering New Drugs

Have you ever wondered what it takes for chemists to discover new drugs for treating illnesses? A company called Atomwise has discovered a technique for using AI to assist in drug discovery. According to them, their software algorithms can "extract insights from millions of experimental affinity measures and thousands of protein structures to predict the binding of small molecules to proteins." Their deep learning and AI technology is developed from convolutional neural networks.

Only certain chemicals actually work and Atomwise's artificial intelligence has boosted their discovery rates by as much as 10,000 times their previous success rate without AI. With their new strategy, they are able to comb through ten to twenty million chemical compounds each day. In addition, their software is able to create a profile of human traits for those patients who would be perfect for the required clinical trials.

By sifting through billions of possible chemical structures, the company is pinpointing numerous areas of compound types for their drug discovery program. Humans are still involved in the final analysis, but the artificial intelligence involved is greatly accelerating the work of those human chemists.

Outcome: The team at Atomwise is helping humanity with some of the most critical health problems in the world today, including those of multiple sclerosis and the Ebola plague.

Financial Investment Assistance

We all know that financial services involve some pretty sophisticated number crunching. It should be obvious that computers were made for this kind of work. One company, called Betterment, has developed a financial investment platform that is fully automated. It has pioneered the use of something called "robo-advisor technology" to create for their clients personalized fin-ancial profiles based on their own preferences.

In the past, things like stock trading, portfolio and transactions management, and tax loss harvesting, all required a personal, human touch, plus plenty of hard work and years of experience to get right. Now, Betterment's robo-advisors make easy work of all those details.

Outcome: Betterment has carved out a $10 billion niche of asset management with a client base of 250,000 strong.

Customer Engagement Analytics

Customer service call centers are a veritable goldmine of big data. They are also a major cost to any corporation that utilizes them. If only there were a way to streamline the process to cut costs and a way to capture all of the information in a business-usable format.

That's what CallMiner has done. They are a soft-ware enterprise based in Massachusetts. Their key focus is on,

- Improving the performance of contact centers, and
- Improving the acquisition of important business intelligence.

Outcome: CallMiner has conducted five successful rounds of venture capital funding, opening offices in the United Kingdom and Florida. They have conducted yearly conferences on the art and science of customer engagement analytics.

Improving the Zoo Management Experience

The following is a special case study of IBM data analytics used at the Cincinnati Zoo to improve their operations. This is from a report by Nucleus Research detailing the challenge, the strategy, the key benefit areas, key cost areas, best practices and how they calculated the return on investment. For reasons of copyright, we have not been able to duplicate the entire report, here, but the original is chock full of juicy, business details that are well worth reading. The synopsis and paraphrasing, below, should give you a taste of the impact of data analytics done right.

The Client

The nonprofit city zoo in Cincinnati, Ohio serves 1.2 million people each year with a facility spread across 100 acres. The organization offers one of the largest collections of plants and animals in the United States with more than 3,000 plant species and more than 500 animals.

The Challenge to Be Solved

The risk of funding shortfalls prompted the zoo's senior management to identify, in late 2009, the sources of that threat to their financial solvency. Three trends were identified and included:

- **Variety of visitors.** Members and non-members comprise the two variety of visitors, with a steady increase in the percentage of members over the previous decade. While some might view this as a positive step, indicating greater community involvement, it also proved to be part of their source of difficulty. The reason is that members get discounts and, on average, spend less per visit than do non-members.

- **Visits.** The timing of senior management's concern coincided with the recession of 2008–2010, and fewer people were visiting the zoo as a result. Not only that, memberships were down, and the amount spent per visitor had declined.

- **Taxpayer support.** In states all across America, citizens had become less interested in public funding of museums, aquariums, zoos and similar cultural attractions.

The zoo's senior management was faced with two key challenges: reduce operating costs and increase income from things like merchandising, food vending, membership dues and admission ticket sales. To the executives, it seemed they needed more data. They were trying to solve a problem with blinders on.

In the zoo's favor, it possessed a workforce that was both capable and well trained. It's data, however, resided in three separate sources. On-site purchases yielded paper-based records. Statistical reports were built manually and produced only once a week. With this lack of easy access to data, management found it impossible to give their employees the direction they needed for improved day-to-day operation.

Such a challenge has been common in not-for-profit institutions and mid-level corporations with poor IT capabilities. Gathering large quantities of operational data has never been the problem. The limitation was, as so often is the case, a matter of merging data into a centralized repository for ease of reporting and analysis. Without such a structure, accuracy of decisions remains greatly limited. And this tends to cripple the organization's ability to grow and to master its operational difficulties.

Solution Strategy

With their challenge clearly defined, senior zoo management decided to make use of business intelligence for combining its various data sources and for streamlining its ability to produce useful reports. They started by building an inventory of what they would need for the business. Dashboards were a key ideal for managing the data and reporting. In order to understand the direction they would need to take the business, they determined that certain critical pieces of data needed to be gathered and more fully understood. These included merchandise sales, food sales, admissions, memberships and one item they were not yet collecting—geographic information. This would be critical for generating superior market segmentation. To achieve this new requirement, zoo executives mandated the collection of buyer zip codes from each transaction.

Senior zoo management looked at three possible systems for handling and analyzing their data. These included,

- Tableau Software,
- SAP Business Objects, and
- IBM Cognos BI

Ultimately, they selected the IBM solution. The first reason was that of usability. Executive committee members judged that the IBM system's dashboarding, reporting and deep analysis would prove to be the simplest and most intuitive for their operating environment.

The second reason involved the support they could receive from the vendor. Zoo officials were rather thorough in checking references. They interviewed personnel at organizations similar to their own and determined that those who used IBM products enjoyed both responses and problem resolutions that were faster than those with the other vendors. The executive committee had feared that they would be too insignificant a customer and would not receive timely support because of their smaller size. They were delighted to find out this was not the case with IBM.

For one 3-month stretch, the director of park operations employed IBM Cognos 8 to solve the zoo's problems. The solution package included two part-time consultants from IBM partner, Brightstar, and one part-time consultant directly from IBM.

To begin with, the deployment team examined more deeply the business requirements. They determined that for optimal efficiency, the zoo's organization re-quired dashboards with 25 operational reports. From this starting point, the team built a robust data warehouse constructed of data cubes for a host of related tables— membership lists, inventory records, geographic data and point-of-sales data. After integrating the data ware-house with the IBM Cognos 8, the team created new dashboards and reports. Then, they tested all aspects for accuracy.

The system, go-live date was set for October 2010. Between the completion of testing and go-live, the team trained 15 zoo employees on every aspect of the new system's use.

Over the next several months, the system proved sufficiently successful to warrant an upgrade. During March, the following year, 7 of the zoo's 15 dashboards were bumped up to version 10 of IBM Cognos BI. This allowed executives to use the new version's more powerful drill-down functions of ad-hoc queries.

Key Benefits of the Project

By the zoo executives' own assessment, the project utilizing the IBM Cognos BI "significantly improved the decision making capabilities" of not only the execs, but also mid-level management and frontline employees. Project key benefits included:

- **Marketing boost.** Operating expenses were greatly reduced by eliminating marketing campaigns that yielded very poor results. The zoo was able to cut spending on advertisements by forty-three percent. They accomplished this from the intelligent market segmentation possible after they had accumulated a large quantity of customer data which included zip codes. Another way the zoo improved its marketing reach involved discounts. Analytics revealed to them that one costly campaign which had been meant to drive in more out-of-market visitors had inadvertently been used by visitors living near the zoo. Local residents were far more likely to visit the zoo without a discount, so the costly discount had been wasted on them. The elimination of that discount campaign allowed the zoo to claim revenues that would otherwise have been lost.

- **Reduced the need for added personnel.** With the use of the new computer system, reports were vastly easier to generate and with far greater detail than ever before, but without the need for staff additions. Prior to the IBM Cognos BI system, generating reports had been very labor intensive not only for the director of operations at the zoo, but also for mid-level managers in fundraising, merchandising, admissions and food services.

- **Increased profits because of new revenues.** Food and merchandise revenues jumped 12% because of changes implemented by management after looking at the preferences and behavior of both members and visitors. The three areas of improvement were ticket sales, food sales and merchandise revenues.

- **Ticket sales.** The zoo enjoyed a 4.2% boost in ticket sales because of the IBM Cognos BI system deployment. With the system's analysis, they were able to pinpoint both out-of-market areas and nearby neighborhoods that were ripe with potential new visitors. For instance, they were able to recognize zip codes with affluent people who had a greater likelihood of becoming new visitors. From this insight, they were able to design an appropriate direct mail package for those parts of Cincinnati or outlying areas. The mass mailing campaigns based on new visitor segmentation proved so successful, they drove admission volumes up to 32% from two prosperous, out-of-market regions.
- **Food sales.** With the IBM Cognos BI, the zoo was able to find out how much food was bought by type and time. With this knowledge, managers were able to adjust their policies to make the most of sales. This resulted in an 18% jump in food revenues. In ice cream sales, for instance, peak purchase times were identified allowing managers to find a more optimum time to close their ice cream kiosks. And, of course, food sales were also boosted by the greater quantity of visitors.
- **Merchandise revenues.** Deployment of the new system drove up merchandise sales by 18%. There were two key reasons for this. For one, analytics revealed from the revenue mix which merchandise items produced slow sales and which

were their hottest items. By eliminating the items with lackluster results and raising the prices on their hottest items, the zoo was able to make their merchandizing more profitable. For another, analytics allowed the zoo to better target members for a discount campaign on merchandise purchases. Sales to members spiked sharply and more than made up for the discount.

Key Cost Areas

There were five key cost areas involved with the system deployment:

- personnel,
- hardware,
- software,
- training, and
- consulting.

The software expense included 15 licenses of IBM Cognos 8 and a yearly maintenance agreement. In March 2011, 7 of the licenses were upgraded to IBM Cognos BI version 10. Because of a separate agreement with IBM for other services, the zoo had received discounted pricing on the software. Nucleus Research used standard IBM pricing in calculating the bottom-line benefits from the deployment so as to normalize for these differences.

The director of park operations spent roughly 20% of his time, over a 3-month period, on setting up the system. One IBM consultant and two Brightstar (an IBM partner) consultants assisted the director. The three consultants focused their efforts on constructing the data warehouse and a number of the data cubes to be used.

For the hardware expense, a computer server was purchased for housing the IBM Cognos BI system and holding all supporting data.

Fifteen zoo employees were selected for utilizing the software licenses. They were given a 5-day training session on the system prior to the go-live date.

Best Practices

As with any enterprise-level project, the first best practice involves the highest possible commitment, or "buy-in," from the corporation's senior executives. The Cincinnati Zoo was no different. From the very start, the zoo's executive committee (which consisted of members of the board of directors and senior managers) was instrumental in the successful deployment of the IBM Cognos BI at their park. From this foundation of executive-level buy-in, the committee added several other best practices.

First of all, the project's executive committee established clear-cut goals that were compatible with the zoo's overall mission. Amongst the primary goals, the committee wanted to establish the type of reporting that would make it easy to boost income from onsite sales of merchandise and food, membership dues and admission ticket sales.

Secondly, the zoo's board of directors mandated that all prospective vendors prove their ability to deliver on the first set of goals, instead of merely provide a list of functionality and product features. In other words, IBM and the other two prospects needed to show clearly how they could achieve the type of reporting required.

Thirdly, realizing that a certain cultural inertia exists in any organization, the executive committee assisted the mid-level managers and deployment team obtain the frontline employee buy-in required to make the project a complete success. For one thing, every employee involved in individual transactions needed to be okay with the requirement to collect zip codes from each customer. The other key cultural change required for all affected staff to support the use of analytics on a daily basis, and for the results of that analytics to be an integral part of making operational judgments.

Calculating The ROI

In order to quantify the zoo's financial stake in the IBM Cognos BI project, Nucleus Research projected the costs of hardware, software, personnel, consulting, training and other investments over a three-year span of time.

The project produced both direct and indirect benefits. First, the direct gains: New sales of merchandise, food and tickets produced significant, added profits. Also, greater efficiencies made possible by the project, reduced operating costs.

The direct benefits require some explanation. First, we will look at the improved marketing effectiveness. Two distinct calculations gave us the quantification of this factor. Ad cost reduction was determined by looking at the cutback in media purchases for the year and pegging which of the eliminated media purchases were swapped out by the new, analytic-driven marketing campaigns. The eliminated expenditures of the zoo's abandoned AAA discount promotion for out-of-market prospects was determined by looking at the normal quantity of discounts given annually to visitors in the past.

The new sales increases in profits was identified by finding out the increase in income from these sources following project deployment. The pro-rated potion that could be attributed to the project was estimated and then the profit margin (operating) was applied to each revenue category.

Next, the indirect gains: Nucleus Research determined the amount of employment additions that were avoided by first comparing the amount of reporting done on both sides of the deployment date, then extrapolating the number of new hires that would have been needed to generate the new level of reporting volume without the IBM system, and then using the normal, full cost per year of an employee.

Normally, not-for-profit organizations like the zoo don't pay corporate taxes. To give us a direct comparison to similar projects in the private sector, Nucleus Research added a 50% tax rate. If they had used a zero tax rate, the results would have been 559% ROI over a 2.2 month period.

Outcome: Cincinnati Zoo managers used the IBM Cognos BI analytics to learn more about their own customers and operations. This allowed them to make more intelligent decisions that generated both cost reductions and boosts in revenues. For example, by using analytics, managers found out when zoo visitors were more likely to purchase ice cream. From this, they made minor changes to ice cream kiosk operating hours, which resulted in food revenue increases. Similar operating practices in other areas were modified based on the analytics, giving the zoo an admissions boost of 4.2% and an increase in merchandise sales of 18% for items purchased within the park.

ROI: 411%
Payback: 3 months
Average annual benefit: $738,212

Conversational Marketing

If you've ever worked in sales, you know there is a lot of grunt work in developing leads. Wouldn't it be nice to automate a lot of that work? A company called Drift has done just that, with chatbots and lots of AI help with things like natural language processing and machine learning. This software approach is helping more and more businesses to help customers with service or product questions, to set-up more meetings and to help streamline the entire sales funnel.

With Drift's software on a client's website, a chatbot pops up when a visitor arrives, asks them questions and will automatically add them to a specific campaign if they are found to be a lead. This saves a lot of time-consuming work on the part of the sales team.

From there, Drift Assistant creates email replies automatically and updates any changes to contact information.

Outcome: Some companies, like Zenefits and Toast, have reported improvements in the time required to qualify leads, reducing delays from days to minutes. More than 100,000 companies currently use Drift software to streamline their sales cycles.

AI Personal Assistant

If you love high tech, you're likely familiar with Amazon's Alexa or Google's Home—AI assistants that are voice controlled. Emotech created it's own version of AI-driven assistant called Olly. The big difference that sets Olly apart from the others resides in Olly's machine learning capability to evolve its own personality to become more like its owner.

The unique mix of algorithms teaches Olly how to understand voice inflections, the owner's facial expressions and verbal patterns. These AI-powered routines allow Olly to be more proactive, to start exchanges with its owner and to originate appropriate suggestions.

As a human, we're quite aware of the behavior of other humans when in a conversation. Certain behavioral signals are to be expected from our fellow creatures—like eye contact, facing the person with whom we're conversing, etc. Though Olly is small—a robotic assistant for the table top—it can move, turning to face its owner when challenged with finding out what's next.

Outcome: Emotech has created an assistant that possesses talents far beyond its competition, capabilities that make it seem more emotionally in tune with its owner. If a human were to see us come home, sitting down and bowing our head as if to rest, they would likely realize that we were tired from a hard day's work. If Olly sees its owner resting their head, it would then offer to play some of our favorite music. What other personal AI assistant would be so considerate as to help us unwind?

Social Media Image Recognition

Any regular Facebook user has benefited from the deeply embedded AI routines—from the newsfeeds driven by smart algorithms and chatbots in its Messenger function, to targeted advertisements and suggestions for photo tagging. Though not perfect, it's artificial intelligence beats random selection by a long shot.

One user commented that Facebook frequently suggested tagging his wife's picture with his sister-in-law's name. Though Facebook AI missed a few, it was at least able to recognize the family resemblance. The Facebook team in charge of AI has been able to nudge their image recognition routines up to 85% accuracy. For testing, they used millions of public pictures on the Instagram platform which also were labeled with hashtags. This proves to be quite exciting in the AI world, because image recognition is a key component of fully generalized artificial intelligence. Computer vision modeling has come a long way toward perfection on this aspect of AI science.

Outcome: With Facebook's massive resources, they have become a major competitor to Google in the online use of AI. To combat abusive behavior and spam, the company has already been using mix of human moderation and AI. More and more, Facebook is depending on AI to help it monitor user activity on the planet's leading social media platform. But everything is not so perfect in Facebook land, as we shall see in Chapter 6.

Marketing and More With Maps

Geographic information system (GIS) mapping technology has transformed marketing by allowing marketing and sales execs to see the marketplace from a myriad of perspectives. Maps can show where clusters of customers reside and other overlays can begin to tell us why they may be customers and how we might translate that into new marketing campaigns to entice new regions of people to join in the benefits as customers.

GIS is also used for many other industries, including education, health, insurance, manufacturing, petroleum, public safety, real estate, retail, sustainability, telecommunications, transportation, electric and gas utilities, natural resources, water management and government.

For instance, GIS can help insurance companies see a map of risk. The petroleum industry can more easily see likely new oil fields and understand more quickly the costs involved in extraction. Plotting various kinds of information within the same geographical grid allows us all to see more clearly the relationships of various societal issues and resources.

Outcome: Marketers depend more and more on map visualizations in order to better understand their marketplace and potential customers. GIS is delivering information that was never before possible.

Smart Maps

Speaking of maps, Google has transformed the world of visualizations of our world and the concept of getting from point "A" to point "B." AI is making travel a far more efficient art, whether we travel by car, bus, train, bike or merely hoof it. Commutes are made easier with Google's AI-enabled mapping. With artificial intelligence, Google's software scans its various data sources for information about current road conditions, then, with a series of algorithms discovers the best route to take.

Never satisfied to rest on its laurels of achievement, Google keeps pushing for improvements in their existing triumphs. For instance, the company plans in the near future to combine real-time map representation with its voice assistant, generating an augmented reality that lets users understand their environment more completely.

Outcome: Already millions of individuals use Google smart maps every day to guide them to their destinations. More than that, Lyft, the popular service for ridesharing, has developed its navigation system for drivers based off of Google Maps.

Robots Come of Age,... Sort of

Science fiction stories ever since the days of silent movies have given us glimpses of human-like machines. Theme parks, like Disneyland, have long had animatronics — dummies with gears and levers inside to make them move in repetitive sequences, but they had no intelligence and no freedom of movement. Hanson Robotics has changed all that. They have produced AI-controlled robots for both business and domestic use. The company's pride and joy is named Sophia with social learning skills that are quite advanced. The robot has proven its ability to use conversational English and to mimic human emotions with a wide range of facial expressions. In recent years, Sophia has been featured on numerous television talk shows, turning it into a celebrity of sorts. Sophia even appeared on The Tonight Show, freaking out the show's host, Jimmy Fallon. But the weirdness hit a new high when Sophia accepted an offer of citizenship from the desert nation of Saudi Arabia.

Outcome: The company hopes to create a series of robots like Sophia. According to Hanson Robotics these robots will "have immediate applications as media personalities in movies and TV shows, entertainment animatronics in museums and theme parks, and for university research and medical training applications." For all of its impressive breakthroughs, Hanson's Sophia robot has a few kinks to work out before she will be allowed out of her cage. We'll talk about this in our list of AI horror stories in Chapter 6.

Virtual Travel Assistant

AI has invaded the travel space with a chatbot named Hello Hipmunk, introduced in 2015. This AI-driven travel assistant was created by Concur and provides assistance finding prices for vacation rentals, excursions, hotels and flights through Airbnb.

Chatting with this bot can be done on Skype, Slack or even Facebook, to book flights. Hello Hipmunk can even make interest-based or theme-based vacation suggestions. If you let the bot access your calendar, it will check for planned events and begin to research the possibilities for a trip at the times of those events.

Outcome: Hello Hipmunk has maintained a strong popularity ever since it was first launched as one of the first travel virtual assistants. With the virtual assistant market showing strong growth, estimates point to a likely 2021 industry revenue of $15.8 billion.

Domesticated Robots and Home Cleaning

Robots doing human chores is a common theme in the science fiction of the past. Today, it's a reality with iRobot's latest model, Roomba 980—its newer, smarter self-deploying, robotic vacuum. With onboard sensors to scan for room size and to identify obstacles, built-in AI determines the routes most efficient for cleaning. And, naturally, it needs no help from its owners in cleaning the floors.

Outcome: In 2017, iRobot raked in a sweet $883.9 million during its first year as a business solely focused on the individual consumer. Since 2002, the company has sold more than 10 million units.

Debt Collection With AI Assist

At the end of the financial crisis of the 2008–2010 housing bubble bursting, the entire planet was suffering from tightened belts. No industry felt this pinch more than that of debt collection. Paying bills became far tougher with every industry cutting back, laying people off, people losing their homes and more.

Nexidia is a speech and video analytics software company and business consultant. In 2010, they produced a case study of their work with Apex Credit Management, Ltd., a debt collection firm based in the United Kingdom.

The Challenge Faced by Apex

Chief Operating Officer at Apex explained his company's challenge: "With the significant downturn in the economy and its impact on people's ability to repay, we realized quite early that we needed to optimize our processes and boost our collections revenues. Our goal is to be recognized as the leading ethical debt management provider in the UK, and as such, we are proactively looking for ways to improve our service. Speech analytics has provided us with a major opportunity to do just that, significantly building our competitive advantage."

Over the previous decade, Apex had become one of the UK's "top 10 debt collection agencies," and was highlighted by *The Times'* "Top 100 Best Companies to work for." But more and more the company had become increasingly challenged by more government regulations and more demands to demonstrate compliance. Apex was also caught between the "rock" of protecting their clients' reputations and the "hard place" of maximizing collected revenues. Nexidia noted, "With more than 380 hours of talk-time per day, the company realized that their current sampling of a limited number of calls per agent per month wasn't giving them true visibility of what was happening in their front line interactions."

Contact Strategy Manager, Richard Furlong explained his company's challenge this way: "In the debt collection industry, the real challenge is to understand what is happening at the point of interaction between the customer and the agent. How many Promise-to-Pays (PTPs) are actually being asked for? How many full balances are actually being requested? Are key compliance phrases being used by the agents? Our random sampling was only allowing us to understand about 1%

of our calls. This made it extremely difficult to pinpoint what changes were needed to improve services."

The Solution for Apex

With Nexidia's AI-driven software, a company is able to analyze all of the phone calls of their customer-facing workforce—100% of the calls—not merely a random sampling. With its built-in AI, Nexidia's system was able to extract thorough and precise business intelligence within minutes. Furlong added, "The free Proof of Concept (POC) was very attractive to us. Nexidia took 2,000 hours of audio and clearly identified specific processes that were having a major impact on our ability to collect revenues. It highlighted a significant revenue opportunity for us, outlining exactly how many payment attempts were being made, the high percentage of calls over five minutes, and the number of calls with compliance issues. Some of the results caused us to reflect on our processes. There were areas where we thought we were performing well, which when analyzed, showed major discrepancies. Our challenge was to focus on the actions that would give us the biggest immediate returns. In this business it's hard enough getting in contact with people, so it's vital that we make the most of each call and Nexidia is enabling us to do just that."

Rigorous Testing of the System

For any system to be proven successful, it has to be tested. Comparing it to a known metric is always a good way to ensure that the test itself is worth the effort.

Apex's high-performance team, which they had dubbed "The Champions," was to be compared to another group they called "The Challengers." Though the Challengers were a new team, they had a similar length of service and roughly equivalent skill levels. And the Challengers were to be managed with the help of speech analytics. To make the comparison complete, both teams used the same metrics,

- cash collected,
- conversion rates,
- call audits, and
- other factors.

Nexidia explained their early successes, "After three weeks, the conversion rates of RPCs [Right Party Contact calls] to Promise-to-Pays increased in the Challenge team, and continued to rise month after month far above all other teams. In the first month, four agents significantly improved, and by the end of the Champion Challenge, all 10 had made significant progress. Speech analytics has now been rolled out across the company, resulting in a 4% rise in conversion rates across the business in the first month alone."

Outcome: Nexidia described their overall success this way, "Speech analytics has given APEX a competitive edge by providing insight into all collector calls and activity. It has enabled the company to enhance performance and deliver an improved service to clients in a contingent business environment."

Crowdsourced Hedge Fund

Crowdsourcing is a relatively new phenomenon on the social internet stage—getting many different people to participate on a project, sharing the load of the work. An earlier example of this concept was used on the SETI project by having people download a small app to their computers and to run that software in the background to process star signal data, greatly reducing the SETI project's workload.

Now, imagine taking this concept and mixing in stock market predictions and data scientists worldwide wanting to show off their prowess with big data analytics. Instead of splitting up a big batch of data, though, Numerai—a hedge fund powered by AI—is tapping into the collective machine learning experience of thousands of data scientists worldwide.

What is divided up is not portions of big data. Every data scientist receives the same abstracted financial data. Numerai participants are competing to prove their machine learning models are the best. Weekly tournaments have the data scientists vying to win the company's cryptocurrency called Numeraire (NMR).

Those who provide the best predictions move to the top of Numerai's leaderboard. The more accurate, the more tokens they win.

But Numerai is all about collecting exciting software models—a collection of top-winning champions. With their growing collection, they produce a synthesis of top-model predictions into what is called a "Meta Model."

The diversity from this "many models" approach greatly reduces risk with the result of higher returns.

Outcome: Though Numerai has remained tight-lipped about its clients, the diversity of the fund and its overall performance, we can gain some understanding of its success by realizing that they have more than 35,000 data scientists from around the world adding their best work to the platform. Also, Numerai has paid out a whopping $15 million in their NMR cryptocurrency.

Hospitals and AI

One of the oldest healthcare facilities in the world—Massachusetts General Hospital—has entered the world of AI, partnering with high-tech graphics hardware company, Nvidia (Santa Clara, California). They have begun collaborating on using AI-driven machines to detect, diagnose and treat disease, plus to manage the entire process for greater efficiency.

Teaching the AI about various diseases involves machine learning with an estimated 10+ billion radiology and pathology images. When finished, the system should speed up the hospital's testing and diagnostic functions, making it easier to start vital treatment sooner, saving lives.

Outcome: After the hospital and Nvidia completed a pilot system to prescreen for pneumothorax (or "collapsed lung"), they ran a limited test. Because the results proved so promising, the system has been slated for use in their Emergency Room. This could end up saving lives.

Personal Healthcare Management

In the hotel business, a concierge helps guests find the things that will help make their stay all the more perfect—theatre tickets, best route to local sights or even where to by a hotdog at 3 AM. Now, imagine a concierge-like function for patients. Pager has created something like that—an app using AI to assist patients who have minor illnesses, aches or pains. Their system uses machine learning on the individual's claims data and clinical information in an effort to find possible breaches in the patient's medical healing program. Beyond recommendations for treatment, Pager's service can assist patients with payments and scheduling appointments.

Outcome: The company's software application enables a patient to chat using text with a nurse at any time of the day or night, every day of the week. It also provides the patient with the ability to chat with a doctor by video, and allows prescriptions to be filled, if needed.

Health Diagnostics on Rocket Thrusters

Pathologists also need some artificially intelligent TLC (tender loving care). And they get it from PathAI's machine learning software that aids in the analysis of tissue samples and helps pathologists produce diagnoses that are even more accurate so that the attending physician can offer the most appropriate treatment. In addition, the company's AI-powered software can also pinpoint the best candidates for clinical trials.

Outcome: PathAI has collaborated with Philips and the Bill & Melinda Gats Foundation on producing high-capacity test support tools for medical prognosis.

Improving Manufacturing Quality and Consistency

One industry that has long enjoyed the benefits of superior organization has been manufacturing—coordinating suppliers, resources, workflows, finishing, marketing and distribution. Throughout history, from the merchant networking of the Hanseatic League during the Middle Ages to the assembly line genius of Henry Ford at the start of the 20th century, manufacturing has always had a keen interest in process improvements.

Plex, an Enterprise Resource Planning (ERP) software company, created a white paper titled, "How Analytics, Dashboards, and Intelligence are Transforming Manufacturing."

Overview
Plex started by outlining the challenge faced by manufacturers and the opportunity open to them to meet that challenge.

- "Manufacturers are driven by on-time delivery and high customer satisfaction while measuring and ensuring quality.
- "The need for accurate analytics is increasing rapidly.
- "Manufacturers gain business intelligence through real-time analytics."

The Challenge is Never-Ending

Reaching perfection is obviously a pipe dream no one will ever achieve, but aiming toward perfection is as basic as life itself.

Plex explains their approach this way, "Today's supply chains are in a race to deliver the highest quality products in the shortest, most economical time possible to win the chance to sell again. With such an intense focus on quality, speed and cost, only the suppliers most effective at translating data into decisions are going to win new business and grow."

Naturally, all manufacturers want to "win the race of continual product and process quality improvements." No company exec in their right mind would not want that. Plex points out that the primary way to maximize improvements is "to select the most valuable key performance indicators (KPIs) and metrics of performance that can guide their organizations to better manage time-to-market, compliance, and the continuous need to reduce cost of quality."

According to Plex, "One of the most important metrics of all, overall equipment effectiveness (OEE), is critical for suppliers to focus on. This metric provides insights into the overall health and stability of production systems and assets and can signal when a specific production asset, subsystem or assembly needs to have periodic maintenance completed.

"High performance manufacturers rely on OEE as a means to keep their entire manufacturing strategy aligned and optimized to customer requirements. One of the best ways to make OEE continually improve is to create a unified, strategic quality management system that successfully ingrains quality-driven analytics, KPIs, and metrics into the company's organizational culture."

Any manufacturer is going to want a compact, easy-to-understand overview of their operation—including inventory and quality across service, delivery, inspection, quality management and the manufacturing operation itself. Too many of the older manufacturers are burdened by legacy systems with ordinary output that lags behind the competition. Such antiquated systems need to be ripped out, down to the bare essentials. Such housecleaning measures let the operation rev up to higher performance, boosting profits and driving better performance throughout the company. The right kind of manufacturing intelligence and data analytics can give suppliers the direction they need for efficient conversion to a high performance, high quality output.

Speeding Up Compliance and Quality with Dashboards and Analytics

The secret to company-wide performance boosts is the implementation of analytics and measuring quality across the entire enterprise. Too often, manufacturers depend on taking the pulse of individual divisions, departments, programs or product lines. This reinforces silo calcification within the business and practically assures lackluster performance.

Plex discovered a strategy they felt helps to break down old silos and to streamline the operation. "Silos of excellence get created and fed when quality management stays in just one department or place over time. As the

OEE metrics show, the greater the breadth of quality management and engraining of quality as a core metric of how a company measures itself, the greater the performance on customer-centric metrics as well. Breaking down silos of excellence and the systems that fuel them takes more than just speeches and calls for change by senior management. Nothing changes organizational cultures faster than reality-based reporting of actual performance results. It's been Plex's experience that the more transparent any leadership team is in publishing performance results, the faster cultures change. Add in analytics and metrics that measure—and reward—collaboration and the culture of any business will change fast. And if manufacturers are ever going to achieve the highest potential they are capable of as businesses, they must choose the path of reality-based results and be bold enough to publish them to the entire company. That makes change real."

What Suppliers Need to Do to Master Dashboards and Analytics

Manufacturers of all kinds have varying levels of expertise with data analytics and the use of dashboards for managing their operations. Plex describes three levels of analytic maturity.

"Those that dabble in analytics and dashboards have just begun looking at how advanced constraint modeling, legacy system and database integration can improve their performance as suppliers.

"Suppliers at an intermediate level of expertise have successfully created rules and constraint engines that deliver greater insights and intelligence than standard off-the-shelf applications do. They have also created a more unified system of record that provides quality management reporting across multiple departments of an organization. Nearly 20 percent of all quality management reporting and data are in real time. Suppliers at this intermediate level of maturity have successfully created a quality management and compliance strategy that breaks down the silos keeping their manufacturing operations from having a more compressive view of performance. Visiting a supplier at this level of maturity provides a glimpse into how to best manage metrics to deliver real organizational change. Trending diagrams and Statistical Process Control (SPC) charts are located in break rooms and throughout facilities. There is a clear view into operations from flat screen monitors in break rooms. And the highest performing teams are clearly provided recognition for their contributions to greater quality, improving time-to-market, and streamlining compliance.

"The most advanced stages of suppliers have real-time dashboards that provide quality management and compliance metrics, combined with financial measures of performance. Suppliers at this highest stage of maturity are attempting to gain insights into how time-to-market, cost of quality, and compliance can improve financial performance over time. Often suppliers who have advanced to this level of maturity also have the ability to gain real-time shop floor performance data and financial performance metrics. This plant floor to top floor visibility is enabled on cloud platforms that scale securely across suppliers' global manufacturing operations. At this stage of supplier maturity, cloud computing becomes a critically important technology to enable greater visibility into each area of maintenance, production, and service. Choosing the right KPIs and metrics can accelerate the maturation of suppliers to this level, providing valuable financial insights into financial performance in the process."

The Primary Refinement:
Choosing the Right Metrics and KPIs

Where do you start when selecting the best possible key performance indicators? Plex suggests beginning at the "strategic level"—the analysis of those elements most critical to the business. From experience, it seems suppliers will most often want to adjust their dashboards with a balanced mix of "leading and lagging indicators of performance." For one thing, this provides the business with a view of productivity over time that remains more continual. As one business told Plex, it also delivers a more optimal alignment of economic metrics that tend to be more delayed in character, than traditional production performance and quality management metrics.

After a wealth of experience providing the Plex Manufacturing Cloud, the company has learned that the dashboard should be limited to a maximum of six metrics. Metrics and KPIs selected should give a clear insight into each aspect of the operation as a project is finished and readied for delivery.

Here is a list of metrics and KPIs that Plex found most frequently on its customers' dashboards:

- **"Customer Complaints**—This is easy to capture and powerful in ingraining the need for greater quality management throughout an entire organization. Great suppliers use this as a means to further change processes on an ongoing basis and keep improving. Benchmarking customer complaints is a highly effective strategy for also providing everyone involved in quality management, compliance, inspection, logistics, and service with feedback.

- **"ECO/ECN Change Rate**—Engineering Change Order/Notice change rate is an indicator of how well a given project is progressing relative to original plan. This metric can also provide a glimpse into whether a more advanced production strategy needs to be put into place including build-to-order, configure-to-order, or engineer-to-order.
- **"Overall Equipment Effectiveness (OEE)**—measures the current state of machinery on the production floor and in advanced dashboards is used for defining Maintenance, Repair and Overhaul (MRO) metrics and visibility.
- **"On-Time Shipment Rate**—measures how often a given order has been completed on time and also the accuracy of the shipment itself. This is one of the components of the perfect order as well.
- **"Perfect Order Performance**—an excellent indicator of how effective supply chain integration is within a supplier relative to distributed order management and logistics. The perfect order metric is often used in high velocity supply chains to determine order fulfillment accuracy and performance.
- **"Product Compliance**—This can be measured using Corrective Action/ Preventative Action (CAPA) and Non Compliance/Corrective Action (NC/ CA) measures of performance. Using a cloud-based platform and series of applications to capture this data ensures greater accuracy as each department is entering their specific data in real time and there is greater visibility company-wide as well.
- **"Supplier Defect Rate**—Relying on supplier audits and quality sampling techniques, the highest performing suppliers chart this daily based on inbound components, subassemblies, assemblies, and

materials to ensure only the highest quality items make it into production. This is an excellent measurement of overall supply chain performance and how effective supplier quality levels have been ingrained into all suppliers that are part of the broader network."

Manufacturing Intelligence Begins with Analytics

Streamlining the manufacturing operation begins with metrics, KPIs and analytics, and continues with the insights and wisdom generated by manufacturing intelligence. Over time, a business needs to develop a history of performance so that the numbers have a meaningful context.

Aligning those numbers with the various roles within the business, allows the enterprise to put the metrics and KPIs into their own proper context. From here, those burning questions which remain need to be tackled.

A growing number of manufacturers are utilizing platforms in the cloud for more efficient data collection and consolidation across the enterprise. Plex described some of the benefits this way, "Cloud-based quality management and compliance systems can also accelerate the level of learning going on in a supplier, enabling greater collaboration and communication. In the best-run manufacturers, communication and collaboration are more valuable than cash—because the tight integration of the supply chain and enterprise leads to fewer order errors and higher performance.

"Building a manufacturing intelligence layer using a cloud platform also makes it possible to better capture and capitalize on the lessons learned from the OEE metrics captured, minimize the cost of poor quality

(COPQ) and better define to the machine level quality performance metrics essential for profitable operations."

Work Collaboration

Slack creates business collaboration tools. To facilitate that collaboration, they created a data structure called a "work graph." This AI-driven data structure allows their software to collect information on how each business and the people who work for them use Slack and work together with each other.

With machine learning, the AI analyzes the "work graph" data set for a given client and trains AI models that improves Slack's user-friendliness over time. In one example, Slack estimated that the typical user is burdened by upwards of 70 Slack messages per day. AI with natural language processing pinpoints the most relevant messages, tags them as "Highlights" and elevates them to the top of the message queue.

Outcome: Slack's built-in search capabilities employs AI to assist users in locating knowledge experts. It also allows users to find the channels by which those experts can be reached, by scanning existing conversations, their topics and the individuals' locations.

E-Commerce Search

Search engines are nothing new, but poor search results can prove annoying and a waste of time. In e-commerce, this proves to be even more critical. In today's fast moving world, consumers are typically more impatient and less forgiving of results that don't match their needs.

Developed specifically for e-commerce websites, Twiggle is an advanced search engine that makes use of natural language processing. This delivers far more relevant search results and a greater sensitivity to what products and services are available. By combining an appreciation of retail with deep learning that is human-like, this software tool has helped more customers find exactly that for which they're looking.

Outcome: According to Twiggle, a website with 2 million guests per month will typically lose 266,600 visitors, all because of poor search results. Twiggle brags that its search improvements drive a 9% boost to "add to cart" numbers, and a 12% CTR (click-through rate) boost.

The Force Behind the Business Transformations

To most people, data is so mind-numbingly boring they might rather have a root canal than to endure hours of tedium pouring over facts and figures *ad nauseum*. Eric Siegel, author of *Predictive Analytics*, cautions us, "Don't be fooled! The truth is that data embodies a priceless collection of experience from which to learn. Every medical procedure, credit application, Facebook post, movie recommendation, fraudulent act, spammy e-mail, and purchase of any kind—each positive or negative outcome, each successful or failed sales call, each incident, event, and transaction—is encoded as data and warehoused. This glut grows by an estimated 2.5 quintillion bytes per day (quintillion is a 1 with 18 zeros after it). And so a veritable Big Bang has set off, delivering an epic sea of raw materials, a plethora of examples so great in number, only a computer could manage to learn from them. Used correctly, computers avidly soak up this ocean like a sponge."

Every little fact may have some purpose in the larger scheme of things. Each detail can help a machine learn more about each individual, toward predicting their future behavior—what will they buy, what disease they may be suffering, what kind of partner they might have the most success with in life, or whether or not they're ready for that new vacation package to the Maldives.

Every industry has a great deal to gain from mastering the vast sea of data. And this is the purpose behind data analytics, machine learning and artificial intelligence.

Chapter 3
Jobs Artificial Intelligence
Will Replace

In April 2018, MIT Technology Review Insights published the results of a survey conducted by EY at the EmTech Digital Conference held a few weeks earlier. That survey gives us an interesting view of the business industry's take on AI and its impact on the future.

The first question asked of the execs involved, how AI would affect jobs.

"Which of the following assertions best matches your view of AI's impact of jobs?
- **"32%**—Although AI will change the marketplace—more jobs will be created than lost.
- **"23%**—AI will dramatically change the landscape of work—replacing millions of human jobs.
- **"22%**—As AI changes the workplace—some jobs will be lost.
- **"20%**—AI will create a surge of new jobs.
- **"3%**—AI will not have a dramatic effect on job creation or loss."

A majority (52%) felt optimistic about job creation (the first and fourth categories in the list, above). Still, a significant portion (45%) were somewhat or extremely pessimistic about job losses driven by the use of AI. We should not take the results as any form of prediction. No one knows what unique events in the future could shatter even the most cleverly constructed crystal ball. What we can do, however, is to understand the mood of business toward AI and its implementation. From this survey, there seems to be a strong polarization of attitudes toward AI and its effect on jobs.

We also have to consider the rather dark notion that some businesses may desire to eliminate some human jobs as a way to cut costs.

The second survey question gives us a better understanding for the current state of AI implementation.

"How is AI being applied and enabled at the enterprise level within your organization?

- *"30%*—Functional capability: AI is being piloted and applied within one or more business units or corporate functions but we do not yet have an enterprise AI strategy aligning these programs.
- *"28%*—Limited to no capability: We may have some targeted AI pilots but it's not a strategic priority for the enterprise.
- *"21%*—Strategic enterprise capability: C-level support and a clear strategy for applying AI at scale across the enterprise is in place and we are making active progress.
- *"20%*—Emerging enterprise capability: Enterprise AI strategy is in development and alignment across business units and corporate functions is emerging with some early program success."

From this survey question, we can see that most of the enterprises surveyed are still weak on AI implementation. Only 21% demonstrate a strong dedication to

AI implementation at the present time. This is not surprising. Full AI realization is not an easy thing to achieve. Many hurdles need to be overcome. Perhaps the most important of these barriers is the fact that AI is still a rapidly developing field. Making a custom fit for any one business can prove costly. An entire industry has emerged to help business navigate the uncertain waters of this new capability.

Imagine for a moment what would happen if some company developed full-blown AI with complete, self-learning capabilities and sufficiently generalized intelligence to actively seek out new learning experiences. Such an intelligence, if it could be replicated (including its learning experiences), might allow any and all corporations to migrate to enterprise-wide AI implementation with far fewer problems. Such AI modules would be ready-made to take on just about any task given it. Any corporation not buying into such an innovative new tool could easily find themselves out-classed by their competitors. A similar survey would likely have far different results, with top level execs all committed to enterprise integration of an AI solution in a vast majority of companies.

We will discuss the third question in Chapter 7, and the fourth question in the following chapter.

And now for a list of careers that have a high probability of disappearing. Naturally, this won't happen all at once, because it's expensive to implement new programs. Over time, these jobs will become increasingly performed by AI or augmented by artificially intelligent assistance, greatly reducing the need for a large human staff.

High-Risk List

In an article for the *Telegraph* by Patrick Scott, we learn of a study conducted by Oxford that pegs which jobs are threatened by AI and automation and the likelihood of their being replaced by machines. What's fascinating is that the vast majority of jobs either have a very high risk or a very low risk of replacement. There are some with moderate risk, but those are the exceptions. In this chapter, we'll look at some of the higher risk jobs. In the following chapter, we'll cover the jobs that are more safe from such threats.

The high-risk list includes such jobs as data entry, tax preparers, telemarketers, bookkeepers, accountants, legal secretaries, drivers, sales workers, shipping and receiving clerks, bank tellers, umpires, sports referees, loan officers, dental lab technicians, cashiers and dozens of others in the 97-99% range. (For the full list of high-risk jobs, see Appendix, Notes, *"High-Risk List."*)

Analysis of the At-Risk Jobs

In his article for the *Telegraph,* Scott added, "All these occupations share a predictable pattern of repetitive activities, the likes of which are possible to replicate through Machine Learning algorithms." He was commenting particularly on the twelve jobs which reside in the "99%" ranking.

One factor not discussed in any of the articles we've seen is the critical notion of IQ. Though Scott did talk about low skilled jobs disappearing or employees being "redeployed," the intelligence of the individual worker will determine whether or not they can be trained for more demanding jobs. Richard J. Herrnstein, a psychologist, and Charles Murray, a political scientist, collaborated on writing the 1994 book, *The Bell Curve:*

Intelligence and Class Structure in American Life. In their work, they point out that 5% of Americans have an IQ below 75, and that 20% have an IQ in the range of 75–90, or far below average.

According to studies by Alan Kaufman, "Semi-skilled workers (e.g. truck drivers, factory workers)" fit in the 90–95 IQ range, while "unskilled workers" are in the range of IQ 87 and below. Elementary school dropouts typically start in the range of 80–85 IQ and lower, while those with an IQ of 75 have only a 50% chance of reaching high school.

These people require our compassion for they won't be able to make it in a world where the simple jobs are all done by machines. The great wise men of the past told us that the poor would always be with us, and this is one of the reasons why. Some people push for government-led compassion, while others point out repeated government failures of the past and that individual and personal compassion is far more effective and trustworthy.

This is yet another dimension of AI we need to consider. Some people will be able to train for more challenging jobs. Some at the low end of the intelligence scale will never be able to fathom what the more challenging jobs are about.

In an article by Arwa Mahdawi for *The Guardian*, we learn some of the details that help us understand what is going on here. "Indeed, technology has already started doing our taxes: H&R Block, one of America's largest tax preparation providers, is now using Watson, IBM's artificial intelligence platform."

We also have input from Sophia Bernazzani's article for HubSpot. She focuses on several of the high-risk jobs and explains why the future looks bleak for those careers. Here's a brief synopsis of some of her report's highlights.

Telemarketers (99% risk)

If you have a telephone, more than likely you've received at least one telemarketer call in your life, unless you went to the trouble to have your number listed on the "no call" list. If you can stomach to recall the experience, you might remember how likely you were to buy from a pushy salesman invading your space with an unsolicited phone call. Conversion rates have always been pitifully low for this career. Job requirements for a telemarketer are not as demanding as they are for other sales positions. Telemarketers don't require a high level of emotional intelligence or social skills to be successful. They need to have thick skins and lots of persistence. And since the job rarely produces stellar results, giving the job to an AI robot makes perfect sense. A robot has the equivalent of tank armor for emotional "skin," and can persist all day long without fatigue.

Bookkeeping Clerks (98% risk)

Unless you already have a love affair with numbers, bookkeeping is perhaps one of the most boring jobs on the planet. Having a human on salary to do such a simple job is rapidly becoming more cost than it's worth. Software like Microsoft Office, FreshBooks and Quick-Books is far less expensive than the salary and all the other expenses involved (insurance, vacation, etc). Bernazzani pointed out, "Jobs in this role are expected to decline 8% by 2024."

Compensation and Benefits Managers (96% risk)

Though this job is expected to grow by 7% by 2024, corporate cost-cutting is always looking to streamline the operation wherever possible. A system which depends on paper and humans is automatically at risk. For larger corporations, converting such a physical system into a virtual one only makes sense. When benefits and compensation depend on a human operator and paper files, there will be inevitable delays and sometimes costly mistakes. Automation trims the costs, virtually eliminates the mistakes and makes it all so much more efficient. Software from companies like Workday and Ultipro are already being utilized in corporations across the planet.

Receptionist (96% risk)

In the past, receptionists greeted visitors and directed them. They also handled the telephone switchboard, and sometimes the interoffice phone system to make announcements. All of these functions can be automated. A touch screen kiosk, for instance can help direct people to the right location, or to notify an employee that they have a guest in the lobby. The kiosk can also print a temporary badge for them to wear while they are a visitor. Automated phone systems allow people calling in to find the right person for their concerns, and forwards their call to the right office.

Couriers (94% risk)

While more and more businesses are utilizing couriers— projected to expand by 5% in the next five years— automation has already started to take over this job with robots and drones. As self-driving cars become perfected and more an accepted part of our lives, automated delivery vehicles will surely swallow the entire package delivery industry.

Retail Salespeople (92% risk)

AI is only part of the picture, here. More and more, people are doing their own research online to find out about the various brands of products available. Sometimes, a customer will know more about a product and its competition than the salespeople hired by a retail store. Whether a customer is visiting a furniture store, automobile dealership or the mall, salespeople are becoming more and more a rare part of the experience. Self-checkout is just one of the many ways companies are making it easier for customers to do their shopping their way.

Proofreaders (84% risk)

Every language has rules and exceptions to those rules. It's only a matter of time before software can precisely incorporate all of those rules into expert writing analysis that needs no human input, except perhaps the original writing that is being proofed. Software like Microsoft Word already has spelling and grammar algorithms built right in. Standalone packages like the Hemingway App and Grammarly are making it easier and easier for writers to proof their own works.

Computer Support Specialist (65% risk)

When a customer or employee is learning a new software package for the first time, all the details can be a bit overwhelming. Finding out how to produce a certain effect with the software can be quite challenging while everything is still brand new. With so much software coming and new versions replacing old, experts expect a growth of 12% for the field in the next five years. Software enthusiasts and hackers, however, have made a habit of producing tutorials online that largely replace the need for support staff. And with AI bots becoming more prolific and proficient, automation will be nudging humans out of this niche, as well.

Market Research Analysts (61% risk)

When a company wants to know what the marketplace is clamoring for, they turn to these guys to figure out what the marketing message needs to say, to build marketing content or even to figure out what that next product should be. With machine learning, AI is digging deeply into big data to sort through the same information and to come up with answers far more quickly than the humans can. Bernazzani offers a case-in-point: "GrowthBot, for example, can conduct market research on nearby businesses and competitors with a simple Slack command."

Advertising Salespeople (54% risk)

Television, radio and print periodicals have always been hungry beasts requiring advertising to pay most of the bills. Subscriptions help in print, but advertising handles most of the financial heavy lifting. Finding advertisers and selling them on the idea of spending money for ad space has long been the job of the ad salesperson. But print, TV and radio have lost a lot of ground to the internet—especially in the social media sphere. Web-based platforms have made it easy for individuals, groups and businesses to buy online ad space. Self-serve marketplaces and application program interfaces (APIs) have virtually eliminated the need for sales men and women in some sectors. Television, radio and print, though, are not going to disappear overnight. So, this industry will continue to shrink in the years ahead.

More Insight on Jobs at Risk

Hubspot's Bernazzani gives this sobering example of AI's encroachment on our job market: "AI can analyze sales calls far faster than any sales manager could—in fact, it would take 9 years of nonstop sales call analysis for a human being to compete, and that's if they didn't take vacation or sleep. And AI is already being used to develop marketers' content strategies and email marketing playbooks—it's only a matter of time before it plays a bigger role in the process."

If you have a chance to peruse the High-Risk List in the Notes, you'll find a broad slice of human endeavors at risk from AI and automation. Some of the high-population jobs that are likely to be affected include motion picture projectionists, file clerks, secretaries, locomotive engineers, restaurant cooks, theater ushers and ticket takers, manicurists and pedicurists, bill collectors, library assistants, electronic equipment assemblers, landscapers and groundskeepers, postal service clerks, accountants, auditors, mail clerks, waiters and waitresses, hotel desk clerks, butchers and meat cutters, garbage collectors, pharmacy technicians, insurance sales agents, tour guides, dining room attendants, roofers, bakers, stonemasons, bus drivers, technical writers, sewing machine operators, taxi drivers and chauffeurs, miscellaneous agricultural workers, carpet installers, parking lot attendants, highway maintenance workers, real estate sales agents and utility meter readers. All of these are in the top 15% jobs with the highest risk.

The next 15% (70%–85% risk) include security guards, structural iron and steel workers, railroad conductors, sailors and marine oilers, insulation workers (floor, ceiling, wall), printing press operators, baggage porters and bellhops, sheet metal workers, brickmasons, fast food cooks, word processors and typists, medical secretaries, barbers, postal service mail sorters, truck drivers, motorcycle mechanics, computer operators, locksmiths, bartenders, dishwashers, hunters and trappers, postmasters, painters (building), broadcast technicians, carpenters, aircraft mechanics, and laundry and dry-cleaning workers.

As you can see, many of these jobs are semi-skilled and unskilled. Many of the entry-level jobs graduates and dropouts frequently depend upon will be phased out, making it more difficult for those entering the job market. They will have far fewer opportunities to prove themselves worthy of the higher-paying jobs that would otherwise become their first careers.

Chapter 4
Jobs That Are Safe from Analytics Revolution (For Now)

The MIT Technology Review Insights survey mentioned in the last chapter also included a question that helps us understand how some jobs will be safe from AI implementation.

The fourth question involves the barriers companies face in implementing AI.

"What are the biggest challenges to an enterprise AI program? Please choose the top three answers.
- "80%—Skills—Lack of requisite talent to drive AI adoption.
- "52%—Business process—The AI insights are not well integrated into current processes.
- "48%—Leadership—Lack of managerial understanding and sponsorship.
- "48%—Data—Data used for AI is not of high quality or not trusted.
- "30%—Organization design—Interaction between various people/groups does not function well.

- **"26%**—User experience—The way in which the individual 'interfaces' with the AI is not well-designed.
- **"25%**—Budget—Insufficient resources."

As we can see, the biggest barrier to AI implementation is a scarcity of skills. So, if someone wanted to capitalize on this, they would become an expert in AI implementation and hire themselves out to corporations hungry to overcome that deficit. Another way to make the best of this situation may tackle the "leadership" angle and become an executive tutor or mentor on the subject of AI. As we can see from this survey question, money is not a primary concern for AI implementation. There seems to be great willingness to spend money, but an uncertainty about how to spend it.

Low-Risk List

In the previous chapter, we discussed a list from an Oxford study reported on by Patrick Scott in the *Telegraph*. This half of the list contains the jobs that have a lower likelihood of being replaced by automation and artificial intelligence. In other words, they're pretty safe for the time being. Most of the jobs on the list are at the least-risk end of the scale, with a smaller quantity in the range of moderate risk.

The low-risk list includes such jobs as recreational therapists, first-line supervisors (mechanics, installers, repairers), healthcare social workers, occupational therapists, choreographers, physicians, surgeons, dentists, curators, athletic trainers, anthropologists, archaeologists, clergy, registered nurses, rehab counselors and dozens of others in the 0.9 to 0.3 range. (For the full list of low-risk jobs, see Appendix, Notes, *"Low-Risk List."*)

Analysis of the Relatively Safe Jobs

Scott writes for the Telegraph that the bottom of the list includes jobs from a broad range of business sectors, but the one common factor that keeps them safe is the detail that the jobs share a level of expertise that can only be acquired by humans after years of study. He also pointed out, "Many of them also require a level of human interaction that may take many more years for computer programmes to replicate."

Mahdawi's Guardian article and Bernazzani's HubSpot article help shine some light on the why behind the numbers. Mahdawi tells us, "[Martin] Ford, the futurist [author of *Rise of the Robots: Technology and the Threat of a Jobless Future*], classifies resilient jobs in three areas.

"The first is jobs that involve 'genuine creativity, such as being an artist, being a scientist, developing a new business strategy.' Ford notes: 'For now, humans are still best at creativity but there's a caveat there. I can't guarantee you that in 20 years a computer won't be the most creative entity on the planet. There are already computers that can paint original works of art. So, in 20 years who knows how far it's going to go?'

"The second area is occupations that involve building complex relationships with people: nurses, for example, or a business role that requires you to build close relationships with clients.

"The third area is jobs that are highly unpredictable—for example, if you're a plumber who is called out to emergencies in different locations."

Fully generalized AI, could, however, eliminate all jobs on the list and more. An artificially intelligent android could, theoretically, learn everything a human can learn without the limitations of IQ or emotional constraints (self-doubt, fear, worry, etc). With an appropriate design, such an android could exceed human capacities for strength, reach, ability to see (microscopic and various wavelengths), and many other physical traits.

Here, we'll take a look at a sampling of the relatively safe jobs in the lowest 10% of risk.

Graphic Designers (8.2% risk)

This job involves an artful balance between creative and technical skills. At the moment, humans are best suited for this type of job, because of its complexity and refined ability to make judgments that computers cannot yet understand. A graphic designer is quite often converting a client's ideas or wishes into a finished work that captures feeling, theme and other elements in an clever manner that requires an understanding of culture, implication and sometimes even puns. Though AI has made some advances in the field of creativity, some humans have described the results as sometimes a bit too creepy. Artificial intelligence can provide the graphic designer with catalysts that could speed up their own creative efforts. As we learned in Chapter 1, AI and creative arts are already being assisted by IBM's Watson.

Editors (5.5% risk)

Though a great deal of the editor's job can be done by AI—proofreading, grammar and spelling checks, originality (plagiarism checks), and certain readability factors (like lengths and complexity of sentences, and active versus passive voice), the final say on the "art" of the writing still resides with a human editor. What we humans have that the machines do not yet have involves the subtle nuances of accuracy, clarity and comprehensiveness. The right sequences of words can also evoke feelings and machines do not yet understand emotions. Getting the feelings right can make the difference between a block of writing that has powerful impact, one that falls flat or one that ironically makes the wrong connections in thought.

Software Developers (4.2% risk)

Just as writing and editing require precision with the spoken language, so does writing code for effective and bug-free software require precision with the programming language. Software can be creative at random forms and color (like some modern "art"), using fractals and other iterative routines to build pretty pictures, but software has not yet been able to create with non-random purpose. In any creative endeavor, the direction is sometimes modified as the creator gets closer and closer to the finished product. This is because the creator (artist, writer, programmer) can sometimes detect problems with the original direction. Software can't yet do that. There are too many variables involved. AI is still too bogged down in narrowly-focused, task-oriented intelligence, rather than the generalized intelligence of humans. Software engineering and development are as much art as they are science. And they are, in part, exploratory and discovery-oriented. Discovery takes humility and software cannot yet replicate that attitude. Because of the growing need for software development, the field is expected to grow in the next five years by as much as 19%.

Writers (3.8% risk)

While software development is somewhat mechanical with its creativity, creative writing is somewhat less so. Even though there are many rules that govern good writing, and even formulas for good news stories or fictional novels, the degree of creativity required makes writing far too difficult for AI at the present. Artificial intelligence can create blocks of text suggested by certain input, like keywords, for creating writing prompts for human writers, title suggestions or even social media automated notes. But AI is sorely restricted on the depth and accuracy of the type of creativity it can produce. It won't be able to understand the layered nuances of meaning in carefully chosen words that might evoke in the human reader images from history, poetry, classical works or current news events. Only a human writer (and editor) will know when a piece of prose (or poetry) is veering off course.

Event Planners (3.7% risk)

Any event, whether it's a small gathering of staff or a huge industry congregation with thousands of attendees, will require an understanding of dozens of moving parts. Not only that, event planning requires the very human skills of negotiation and other people skills to finesse an unruly mob into an organized army dedicated to a single purpose: a successful event. Vendors, freelancers, contractors and others will each have their own needs and priorities. Some may have other projects scheduled during your event, so alternate sources will need to be found. The peculiarities of their mode of operating will need to be learned. Dangerous assumptions will need to be discovered and ironed out ahead of time so that there are no surprises on the big day. Automating all of these skills will take a multitalented AI with the best in generalized intelligence. That's still a long ways off.

Chief Executives (1.5% risk)

If learning leadership were easy, there would be countless millions of skilled executives applying for the top job at the best corporations. And even the best chief executives have not always made the best decisions. In other words, it's damned hard for humans to learn this. Teach it to an artificial intelligence? Don't hold your breath. Guiding a corporation into the future is as much art and science as any other creative skill. But besides creativity, the top executives of any organization need to have people skills that coax the team to work as one entity. Besides the skills barrier, having a board of directors become comfortable with the idea of hiring a robot as their CEO may take many decades of experience with AI competence in all of the required talents. Even then, corporate stakeholders may never trust an AI with that level of responsibility over their investments.

Public Relations Managers (1.5% risk)

PR jobs are slotted to grow by as much as 7% over the next five years. As you can see by the risk factor, these jobs are extremely safe from the onslaught of AI. PR managers rely heavily on people skills—developing relationship networks, creating the right amount of buzz on a new product release or corporate event, acquiring placements in the right press outlets, raising funds for a cause, and galvanizing people around a mission or sensitive issue. AI currently doesn't have the insight to pull off a job like this.

Marketing Managers (1.4% risk)

Juggling all the moving parts of a company's marketing efforts takes a set of skills that are not easy to teach. Besides creating content for marketing campaigns, this type of manager also needs to stay on the pulse of corporate and customer changes. They need to keep their eyes on trends and adjust campaigns accordingly.

Sales Managers (1.3% risk)

One of the key requirements of most people-facing jobs, especially management positions, is that of high emotional intelligence. This means an ability to respond appropriately to the current emotional state of others—to guide them toward some desired end result. Facing customers or clients means bringing them to a close, over an unknown number of potential objections. Facing the sales team means bringing each and every salesperson to their top level of performance despite the occasional setbacks. Like marketing managers, sales managers also need to interpret trends and to adjust sales campaigns accordingly. As conditions change, the manager needs to adjust their approach so that quotas are met each month.

Human Resource Managers (0.55% risk)

All of the people skills required in the other jobs mentioned so far go doubly for the HR manager. One prime example is the proper handling of interpersonal conflicts. This is where the best possible negotiation skills are vital to see the conflict to a peaceful resolution that benefits the long-term stability of the company. As long as companies have human employees, they will need someone to fulfill the HR management functions. Over the next five years, this job is expected to grow by 9%.

More Insight on Jobs That Remain Safe

Bernazzani writes, "HubSpot co-founder and CTO Dharmesh Shah has a more positive outlook on the future of AI—in fact, he thinks bots and AI will make us better at our jobs and more secure in our careers, not the other way around."

She continues, "The truth probably lies halfway between these camps [total replacement and augmenting our jobs]—in many cases, AI will serve to make our jobs easier and will make us more effective and data-driven. But the fact remains that some jobs will be replaced by machines—it's the essence of any industrial or tech-nological revolution."

Bernazzani's assessment would appear to be spot-on. The truly repetitive jobs without any requirement for thinking or "judgment calls," will likely be replaced in whole by automation. We already have burger-flipping machines in some fast food restaurants. All that's needed is someone to refill the machine with new patties.

The jobs that remain relatively safe do require some thinking on the part of the employee. They require a measure of skill that cannot yet be programmed into the machine. So far, this is only because of the pro-gramming requirement to include narrowly-focused code to handle specific tasks. Even driverless cars are extremely narrow in their programming. Radar, visual processors, sonar detectors and the like allow the AI car to respond to specific hazards and road conditions. Would such an automated wonder take into account a major earthquake and potential damage to the road? Such details need to be added by the programmer. More generalized AI would be capable of thinking outside of the narrow programming box. In other words, the full-blown AI would be capable of doing far more than merely driving. It could research driving techniques from YouTube videos, articles on defensive driving, historical reports on the effects of major earthquakes, the effects of hurricanes and tornadoes and much more. Such generalized AI could also hold a conversation with the passenger, turn on their favorite music, suggest nearby restaurants for the upcoming meal and much more.

Because we do not yet have such generalized AI, the Low-Risk jobs will remain low on the list. The moment some company or individual has that break-through to generalized AI, all bets are off.

PART 2
Analytics in Personal Life

"How come you never see a headline like 'Psychic Wins Lottery'?"
—Jay Leno

Chapter 5
Machine Learning Applications from Daily Life

Several years ago, I was amazed at some new software that had been installed on my computer that could understand my words and convert them into text. All I needed to do was to read a few pre-written sentences into my computer microphone in order to "teach" the software how to recognize my voice and to interpret my own unique way of saying each of the words. This was my first introduction to machine learning.

This chapter will examine a wide variety of applications of machine learning tech in every day usage, including email spam and malware filtering, mortgage applications, online customer support, online fraud detection, predictions while commuting, product recommendations, search engine result refining, social media services, video surveillance and virtual personal assistants.

In today's world, AI can be found in virtually every aspect of life. It's quite possible that you're using artificial intelligence or something touched by AI and don't even know it. A more popular subset of artificial intelligence is machine learning. This is where devices, computers and software all generate responses based on a form of cognition very much like that found in Homo sapiens' brains. This is software that adjusts its behavior based on the input it receives.

Here, we're going to look at several examples of machine learning in action.

Improving the Mortgage Industry

To an individual consumer, a mortgage loan is typically the largest financial debt they will ever take on. In the United States, mortgages remain the largest single component of consumer indebtedness.

To financial institutions, mortgages are a vital part of their business. Whether or not to accept a loan application is of critical concern to them. Mistakes could prove very costly.

Mortgages are complicated. Each state has its own set of regulations governing them. A completed mortgage requires a large number of documents with hundreds of details which must be accurately filled in and sworn to. Also, each mortgage requires the participation of a number of parties. With so much money at stake, a great deal of care must be used.

Both the financial institutions and the individual consumers find mortgage lending to be extremely frustrating, time consuming and tedious.

Machine learning and predictive analytics are taking much of the tedium, frustration and time out of the process. Such advanced technologies are automating vital decisions, minimizing human involvement and streamlining the entire process.

Application Verification—Improving the Process
In a very real sense, a mortgage lender is like the oil in a machine to make it work more smoothly. This financial institution is a third party in a negotiation between two other parties—the buyer and the seller. The object of the sale is a house, and this will act as collateral on the loan.

It's the lender's responsibility to verify information about both parties and regarding the house. First of all, does the seller really own the house? Are there any encumbrances on the property that affect the owner's stake in that asset?

The property itself must be verified. Is the description accurate? Is the house damaged in any way? Is there any condition which will jeopardize its future value? An expert must be hired to assess the current value of the house.

One prime example of a lender's due diligence involves income verification of the applicant or buyer. The reason the lender needs to do this is pretty straight-forward. They need to know if the buyer will be able to fulfill their obligation to pay off the mortgage. For one thing, this helps to reduce the number of defaults on loans—failures to pay. This also helps the lender fulfill its obligations under the law to comply with regulations on ensuring "ability to pay."

As part of income verification, lenders need to collect supporting documentation—name, address and phone number of employer, the amount of time employed and possibly information about previous employers. The financial institution also needs proof that the income declared by the buyer is accurate. This can be achieved with employer pay stubs. Sometimes this requires income estimates from third parties, when the buyer is not a traditional employee of a business, but is perhaps a freelancer or business owner. Such verification is time consuming and too often ends up with information that is imperfect and open to human interpretation.

What can machine learning do here? How can such machine learning benefit both the applicant (buyer) and the lender?

More than likely, a lender has been in business for many years. It has collected a great deal of data over their history of operation. All that data can be employed to teach predictive models to more accurately guess the buyer's income. Naturally, this will be derived from a wide assortment of factors. For instance, let us say that the buyer is a software engineer. The lender may have set up loans to dozens of other software engineers. From that history, the lender will have a range of income and years of experience as an engineer. If the buyer-applicant gives an income that is at the top of the range, but they have only a few months of experience, greater effort may be required in verifying their income. A college graduate who had lackluster grades might not be reporting an income that is accurate or even reasonable for their level of experience. If, however, the buyer graduated *summa cum laude,* with honors, the employer may have been willing to pay top dollar to attract the graduate to their company.

This type of machine learning and predictive analytics can help speed up the income verification process and put a red flag on cases that may be high-risk and require review by hand. Experience with this process will help the lender determine if the machine language and predictive analytics gives them a perfectly automated decision or merely support for a decision by providing probabilities.

Prioritizing the Application Queue

One key benefit that lenders gain from machine learning models is that of improved productivity from those who work a mortgage application. It's almost like having more employees without having to pay them. Fewer employees can get more done with the help of such systems which do some of the decision making themselves.

So much of the process on mortgages includes exchanges between the loan officer and the applicant. Depending on the applicant's answers, the lender may need to take a different path in completing the loan application. Moving the process forward requires a great many questions and answers. In the past, this process included a great deal of manual handling, taking each application in turn. Such a simple queue can result in an inefficient use of the loan officer's valuable time and resources.

Optimizing the loan officer's workflow is the primary goal of the mortgage process machine learning. As the AI learns how various consumers progress through the application process, it will begin to understand the possible detours that might be taken, how an applicant might respond to specific questions and what actions they might take. With all of this, the artificial intelligence can offer suggestions for the best action to take at the next step of the process.

With this machine learning assistance, loan officers will be able to handle their application queues in a dynamic fashion, rather than a static, inefficient way. The AI will be able to direct the loan officer to the challenge that requires the most immediate attention. The assistance from artificial intelligence can also virtually eliminate the time required by loan officers to decide what to do next. Throughout the financial institution, all of the loan officers will be applying the same, consistent approach to the processing of application queues.

Improving the Validation of Documents

As we've already seen, the mortgage lending process involves a veritable mountain of paperwork. Executing a loan requires that the information on those documents is not only correct, but that data on one form matches the same data on other forms.

In the past, loan officers have been burdened with having to handle all these details by hand. Now, machine learning-enabled software can perform many of these manual tasks for them, freeing them up to do other, more important things. Automatic field data validation can ensure that each field on a form has been properly filled out.

When problems are spotted by the software, the issue is tagged for manual review and a message is relayed to the loan officer so that the problem can be handled.

Streamlining Underwriting and Loan Pricing

There's a great deal of risk in loaning tens of thousands of dollars—sometimes hundreds of thousands. Assessing the amount of credit risk is a big part of mortgage under-writing. A set of standards must be followed—standards set by lenders and also by government agencies like Freddie Mac and Fannie Mae.

In the past, very specific rules determined whether or not an application passed or failed. Loan-to-value is one such metric used with such pass-or-fail rules. Loan eligibility becomes extremely risky with a loan amount that is too large compared to the actual value of the home.

These days, determining eligibility is done more and more by AI-driven models. Predictive models score the applications within the constraints of federal regulations. Those applications insured by the federal government, in America, give underwriters far less flexibility. Other applications receive far more give and take. With that flexibility, risk increases, and this is where AI-driven models help lending institutions the most in managing that risk.

The more data a lending institution has on an applicant the easier it is for predictive models to assess the creditworthiness of a borrower. Credit reports are one key source of such data, supplied by credit bureaus, like Equifax, Experian or TransUnion, in America. Information on property values also plays a major role in the evaluation—data from a broad range of real estate information sources. The older type of rules-based approach in assessing an application proved more risky than the method which includes machine learning. Discovering relationships within a body of big data is far easier for AI than the tedium of human manual processing.

Machine learning continues to be better and better at determining risk and in helping mortgage underwriters make accurate decisions. This helps consumers by getting those truly worthy of approval approved much more quickly, and by keeping those applicants who are too weak financially from making a mistake that could prove disastrous to them in the long run. For the lending institutions and underwriters, machine learning makes them more profitable, more efficient and more proficient at improving the borrower's experience with the entire process by reducing the perception of frustration and tedium.

The Rise of the Virtual Personal Assistant

A little over a century after the start of talking boxes called "radios," the talking is no longer only done by humans. With products like Google Now, Amazon's Alexa and Apple's Siri, virtual personal assistants are a popular addition to the modern home. What does the name mean? Virtual means artificial, as in computer generated virtual reality. Personal assistant means what it has always meant—someone (or something) that helps in taking care of little, but frequently tedious chores, like finding information critical to some upcoming plan or event. We simply need to speak into the box, or within listening distance the request we have, like "What flights are there from New York to London?", or "What is my schedule for this morning?"

In order to find the best answer, the electronic personal assistant checks its memory of similar queries, or sends a request for information from other devices (like applications on our phone, via the Internet of Things), or it even looks up the information on the internet. Besides requesting information, we can ask for assistance with certain chores, like "Remind me to get a visa application from the consulate for my upcoming trip," or "Set my alarm for 3 AM tomorrow morning."

As a virtual personal assistant obtains more experience with us, it can begin to understand how we operate. Machine learning thus allows the assistant to improve how it works with us, collecting data about what we mean and refining the information retrieved based on that past experience.

Virtual personal assistants can be found embedded on a number of platforms.
- Mobile Applications: Google Allo
- Smart Speakers: Google Home, Amazon Echo

- Smartphones: Samsung Bixby

Streamlining the Commute

There are two very interesting ways that machine learning is helping us get from Point "A" to Point "B," wherever those points may be.

One example involves transportation networks online. One app can calculate the price of a cab ride before we finalize booking it. AI can also help minimize detours when sharing services. Uber ATG's Jeff Schneider revealed how their use of machine learning to estimate rider demand has helped them determine price surge hours.

With more and more vehicles using GPS navigation services, machine language can assist with predictions of traffic conditions. Such a service takes our velocities and current locations, and uses that information to manage traffic. With input from numerous vehicles, AI can construct a map of traffic's current conditions. Such a system performs analysis on congestion patterns over time and helps to prevent traffic bottlenecks. With a growing minority of cars outfitted with GPS, machine learning allows the system to learn where congestion is likely to exist based on historical data, despite the lack of such systems in the majority of vehicles.

Automating Video Surveillance

Video surveillance is helping security services and law enforcement patrol large areas of a building, compound or even city without actually having to go there. But watching a dozen or more monitors for hours on end is not anyone's idea of a fun job. The tendency to zone out or to fall asleep increases the risk of system failure because of human error. After an hour of nothing happening, watching those monitors can become painfully boring.

AI, however, never gets tired. Boredom to artificial intelligence is a meaningless concept. Today, video surveillance systems use AI to track activity on each individual monitor without losing track of any detail. In fact, AI, with machine learning, can anticipate criminal activity before it actually starts. Machine learning helps the AI determine what is unusual human behavior, like someone laying down on a park bench or someone standing without moving for long minutes at a time. When something unusual like this happens, the AI can send a warning to the humans on duty to investigate. Based on the human response, the machine learning can discover even more about the types of things on which to keep a lookout.

Putting More Sparkle in Social Media

Isn't it wonderful when both users and social media platforms win? AI-driven means news feeds are personalized to the individual user's interests. It also means that ads have better, more accurate targeting. Machine learning tracks all of that with which each user interacts. The system learns preferences and delivers more of the same type of content. Of course, most people love the effect without knowing that AI machine learning is behind it all.

- **Facial Recognition**—On Facebook, when we upload pictures of ourselves with friends, the system immediately recognizes the friend. Facebook AI, with its buildup of machine learning, observes the little details and finds a match amongst the people found in our friend list. It's not perfect yet, but the precision is quite remarkable. Occasionally, it'll confuse sisters who share many of the same facial features.

- **People You May Know**—As a user interacts with Facebook, visiting profiles, the people with which we connect, our interests, groups, and workplaces, machine learning begins to understand who we are and who exists in our circle of acquaintances. The Facebook system then has an idea of which other users we might want to establish as new friends.

- **Similar Pins**—Computer vision includes the ability to mine an image or video for details. Machine learning resides at the heart of this capability. Pinterest makes use of computer vision to recognize the items (or "pins") that make up the images. From this, the system can suggest similar images or videos based on those "pins."

Filtering Out Malware and Email Spam

- How much of a problem is malware (malicious software)? An estimated more than 325,000 such black-hat programs are found on systems each day. A great many of the culprits have computer code that is 90–98% the same as that code found in earlier versions. Machine learning drives the security programs for computer systems so that they can recognize the patterns of such "evil" software. Anything new that looks like previous malware with a 2–10% variation is immediately snagged and quarantined.

- Filtering out spam is a process that utilizes many approaches. Email clients need to be updated continuously so that the junk mail can be dealt with without bothering the user. Machine learning makes this easy. Older, rule-based systems for filtering out spam can fail to detect the latest ploys used by spammers. Some machine learning-driven spam filters use techniques like C 4.5 Decision Tree Induction and Multi-Layer Perceptron.

AI Customer Support for Websites

More and more, websites that sell products or services will have AI-driven customer support chatbots instead of the traditional human customer support representative (CSR). This means that guests can get the help they need while visiting the various pages within a website, no matter what the time of day or night. Machine learning algorithms learn more and more with each visit, improving its understanding of customer needs, delivering more accurate and relevant information and answers.

Better Search Engine Results

Machine learning is making search engines better and better over time. With every search request, the search engine system tracks the user response. Which link in the search results does the user click? How long do they stay on that website? If the search engine backend sees a long stay, it assumes that the item was a good match for the results delivered.

In the worst case, the search engine may see the user go through two or three pages of results without clicking any of the links. In such a case, the machine learns that the search results were unsatisfactory. The more people use the search engine, the better the end results.

Creating Product Recommendations that Work

If you've used the internet any time in the last few years, you've likely noticed ads popping up the recommend products similar to one you researched recently. Perhaps you did research for a birthday present you're considering getting. Now, you're getting emails that mention the product or something similar. Perhaps you've even noticed shopping sites or applications that give you recommendations that seem compatible with your interests or tastes. Machine learning is behind all this apparent magic. Your behavior online is what's driving this AI "miracle."

Sleuthing Online: Fraud Detection

Online shopping has become safer and safer because of machine learning fraud detection systems. Money laundering has long been a problem with financial institutions. Online giant, PayPal is no exception. Using machine learning, PayPal's system compares transactions by the millions and learns to tell the difference between the criminal and the lawful varieties.

Early Refinements of Data

The art of designing and building a relational database has been used to organize large bodies of information into a very strict structure with rigid rules of manipulation and modification. Such a structured approach involves multiple tables of information, each table with a specific identity or theme. Each table would contain a primary key that would allow for the intelligent selection of individual records and its multiple fields of specific pieces of information.

For example, a school might have a table of course offerings, a table of individual classes and a table of instructors.

The table of course offerings would likely have a course ID as its primary key, a course name field, a course description field and possibly a course price and number of credits offered.

The table of instructors might have an instructor ID as its primary key, the instructor's title, instructor's first name, instructors last name, email address, phone number and perhaps office hours.

The table of individual classes might have a class ID as its primary key, a classroom location (room number and building), day of the week, hour of the day, duration, a foreign key to the course offerings table containing the course ID (what is being taught in that particular class), and another foreign key to the instructor's table including the instructor ID.

This way, the only duplicated information are the primary keys where they are used in other tables as foreign keys linking the information with a logical relationship.

Thus, a report on a semester's class offerings could be generated which pulls weekday and hour information from the classes table, course ID and course name from the course offerings table, and instructor name from the instructors table.

With the right tools and programming language, a body of data on sales history, products sold, customer demographics and other information could be used to predict future sales.

But not all information is so neatly organized. These days, data analytics needs to learn how to look at semi-organized and unstructured data, too.

In our personal lives, such an approach to data can be used to organize our hobbies, document our family history or help manage our personal finances.

In his book, *Predictive Analytics*, Eric Siegel provides us with several examples where machine learning could be used to predict outcomes in our day-to-day lives. From his own life, he posed these seven problems:

- **Best medical solution**—From a skiing accident, he needed surgery, but selecting the right approach was difficult. *"Could the hospital have selected a medically better option for my case?"*
- **Best assessment of insurance client**—He had lucked out with his insurance company. How could they know he would require such expensive surgery? *"Could the company have better anticipated the risk of accepting a ski jumping fool as a customer and priced my insurance premium accordingly?"*
- **Best detection of identity theft and fraud prevention**—When unscrupulous thieves stole his identity, it took countless hours of tedious paperwork and bureaucratic hassles to clear his name. *"Could the creditors have prevented the fiasco by detecting that the accounts were bogus when they were filed under my name in the first place?"*
- **Best real estate selection**—After clearing his credit, he sought to buy an apartment. *"Was it a good move, or should my financial adviser have warned me the property could soon be outvalued by my mortgage?"*
- **Best time to buy airplane tickets**—Finally on his way to a vacation, he asked his neighboring passenger what they had paid for their ticket. *"Before I booked the flight, could I have determined the airfare was going to drop?"*
- **Best decisions for your business**—Every business is susceptible to ever-changing market conditions, economic ups and downs, and burgeoning competition. *"Could we protect the bottom line by foreseeing which marketing activities and other investments will pay off, and which will amount to burnt capital?"*

- **Best prospects for marketing efforts**—Every moment spent with junk mail and other distractions is a moment lost. *"After all these years, my mailbox wonders why companies don't know me well enough to send less junk mail (and sacrifice fewer trees needlessly)."*

Who wouldn't want to know the answers to these questions in advance? Knowledge of the future could save all manner of heartache. But how do we go about accomplishing that? Siegel offers these words of encouragement: "The idea is simple, although that doesn't make it easy. The challenge is tackled by a systematic, scientific means to develop and continually improve prediction—to literally *learn* to predict.

"The solution is *machine learning*—computers automatically developing new knowledge and capabilities by furiously feeding on modern society's greatest and most potent *unnatural* resource: data."

To get a feel for what is possible, it sometimes helps to see what our artists have predicted.

Life Imitating Art and AI Saving Lives

Quite often, art precedes reality. The 1960s TV series, *Star Trek,* showed Captain Kirk, played by William Shatner, opening his communicator to call his starship. Fast forward more than four decades and William Shatner is photographed at an airport opening his cell phone to make a call. The cell phone looked suspiciously like the fictional communicator he had used many years earlier. Such cellular phone service didn't exist when the original *Star Trek* series was on the air. It wasn't until four years after the series ended that science and technology caught up with the first mobile phone call on April 3, 1973. That phone weighed over one kilogram (2.4 pounds) and was a whopping 23 × 13 centimeters (9 × 5 inches). But reality did finally catch up to the size and general appearance. The communicators of the last twenty years have been every bit as sleek as their fictional counterparts from the late 60s.

The CBS television series, *Person of Interest* (2011–2016), portrayed a master software engineer and a burnt-out military officer working together to save people from certain death or murder, based upon the AI predictions of a computer system the engineer had created for the government.

The secret government computer had been programmed with a back channel for sending the social security number of a person of interest to a payphone near the current location of the engineer. That fictional computer was using every surveillance camera in the country to pinpoint the location of every individual, including its creator. The ID number would be an identity of someone who was either in danger or someone who was about to endanger someone else. The software engineer had wanted to save lives. His customer—the American government couldn't have cared less. In fact, they would've been quite angry with him if they had known about the back channel. All the government had wanted out of the new AI was the ability to spot potential terrorists in advance of a catastrophe like 9/11. Wanting to ensure secrecy, the government conspired to kill the master software engineer, so the man went into hiding under an assumed name.

The imagination used in producing this television series reveals to us the types of things on the minds of those who are currently working to develop fully-generalized AI. While saving lives can be a good thing, the breach of privacy certainly is not a good thing.

Predicting What People Will Buy or How They Will Vote

Predicting what one individual will do is next to impossible. But predicting what a certain percentage of a group of people will do is becoming easier and easier as machine learning slices into the data of past behavior.

Eric Siegel, in his book *Predictive Analytics,* gives us a business example. "In the mid-1990s, an entrepreneurial scientist named Dan Steinberg delivered predictive capabilities unto the nation's largest bank, Chase, to assist with their management of millions of mortgages. This mammoth enterprise put its faith in Dan's predictive technology, deploying it to drive transactional decisions across a tremendous mortgage portfolio. What did this guy have on his résumé?

"Prediction is power. Big business secures a killer competitive stronghold by predicting the future destiny and value of individual assets. In this case, by driving mortgage decisions with predictions about the future payment behavior of homeowners, Chase curtailed risk, boosted profit, and witnessed a windfall."

How do computers do it? Siegel explains, "The solution is *machine learning*—computers automatically developing new knowledge and capabilities by furiously feeding on modern society's greatest and most potent *unnatural* resource: data."

As boring as data can be to the average man or woman, it can be quite exciting to someone who knows what can be done with it.

Siegel explains, "As data piles up, we have ourselves a genuine gold rush. But data isn't the gold. I repeat, data in its raw form is boring crud. The gold is what's discovered therein.

"The process of machines learning from data unleashes the power of this exploding resource. It uncovers what drives people and the actions they take—what makes us tick and how the world works. With the new knowledge gained, prediction is possible."

What kind of insights does data analytics achieve? Siegel gives several examples:

- "Early retirement decreases your life expectancy.
- "Online daters more consistently rated as attractive receive less interest.
- "Rihanna fans are mostly political Democrats.
- "Vegetarians miss fewer flights.
- "Local crime increases after public sporting events.

"Machine learning builds upon insights such as these in order to develop predictive capabilities, following a number-crunching, trial-and-error process that has its roots in statistics and computer science."

Let's take his examples one by one.

Insurance companies might like to know that first tidbit. They may want to raise premiums for early retirees to take into account the factors which make that group die earlier than others.

Lonely beauty queens may want to know about that second item. In order to snag the right guy, the pictures they share online should likely have little makeup and hair plainly done so they seem more approachable to a larger audience. Guys with big egos may want a trophy wife, but such relationships may not be the most enjoyable. Humble, hard-working guys want someone who will be a good partner in life and any Ms. Beauty Queen could find their passion more honest and dependable.

Marketers for celebrities might want the type of data found for Rihanna fans. Sending out invitations that would appeal to Republicans might not work for the bulk of Rihanna followers.

Airline management might consider not over-booking by as many seats flights with a larger percentage of vegetarian passengers. After all, passengers on standby won't necessarily be as happy with the airline, and the company could reduce the potential damage by mini-mizing the number of passengers left behind, while protecting their desire for a full plane at takeoff.

Law enforcement may already be aware of that last item, but if they didn't, knowing about it could help them plan in advance to make a show of force in order to minimize post-event crimes.

In 2008, a veritable unknown in American politics came out of nowhere to become the Democratic party's nominee for president of the United States. Barack Obama handily defeated seasoned politician, John McCain, with nearly 70 million votes to McCain's 60 million, and an overwhelming majority in the electoral college with 365 to 173 for the win.

Obama won many independents who had tended to vote for Republicans in the past. One such voter wrote that he would never have voted for McCain and loved what Obama had said about ending the wars overseas on day one, and that the voters could "take that to the bank."

Ironically, Obama betrayed many of his campaign promises. The wars continued for months after his inau-guration. And the Afghanistan war continued throughout his entire eight years in the White House. Some voters felt betrayed by the fancy rhetoric and lack of follow-through. And even after swearing an oath to protect the Constitution of the United States against all enemies both foreign and domestic, President Obama became, himself, a domestic enemy by betraying his oath of office—for example, creating a kill list with Americans on it (Swann) bypassing the Constitution's protections of due process. Paradoxically, Obama won a Nobel Peace Prize late in his first year in office, despite having done nothing to deserve the award, and ironically contrary to his subsequent behavior—continuing three wars, starting another, and threatening more—becoming the most warmongering president in American history. Surely, Obama had no chance of being reelected with these facts hanging over his head.

But as we now know, Obama was reelected as president. How could that possibly have happened? Eric Siegel provides some insight on this. "Obama was reelected in 2012 with the help of voter prediction. The Obama for America campaign predicted which voters would be positively persuaded by campaign contact (a call, door knock, flier, or TV ad), and which would actually be inadvertently influenced to vote adversely by contact. Employed to drive campaign decisions for millions of swing state voters, this method was shown to successfully convince more voters to choose Obama than traditional campaign targeting. Hillary for America 2016 is positioning to apply the same technique."

And, as we know, the Hillary campaign was not nearly as successful using those techniques as was Obama. Despite having the news media overwhelmingly behind the Democratic party candidate in 2016, with Hollywood support, a massive boost from academia and the power of computer prediction, Hillary Clinton lost to a businessman outsider.

Real-Life Uses of AI

Important to good machine prediction is the machine's awareness of intent. In other words, "What did the customer mean by that?" What if a book reviewer was sarcastic when they wrote their praise of a published work? One reviewer's machine, looking over Amazon's book reviews, could do that with amazing accuracy.

As any teacher knows, grading multiple choice is drop-dead easy. It's as simple as comparing answers against the grading master, marking each test and counting up the score. Grading essays is many orders of magnitude more difficult. Yet one machine has been created which surprised teachers with its grading accuracy.

In the United States, *Jeopardy!* was rated as one of the most popular quiz shows ever. Yet, IBM's Watson proved too much for two humans who had become all-time *Jeopardy!* champs. Working with free-form questions on a broad range of topics, Watson handily beat the humans with its machine proficiency in English.

Today's world is full of crime, including fraudulent credit card purchases, forged checks and other unsavory transactions. Banks have employed fraud detection algorithms that look for changes in purchasing behavior on the part of the customer. Citizens Bank found they could reduce check fraud losses by 20% by employing such software. Tech giant, Hewlett-Packard eliminated a mountain of fraudulent warranty claims, saving the company $66 million.

Prison systems try their best to parole only those convicts who have shown a sufficient degree of rehabilitation. But humans have not done the best of jobs figuring out who will do well and who will return to prison in the near future. Both Pennsylvania and Oregon employ software analytics to help them in sentencing and in paroling prisoners.

University at Buffalo researchers were able to provide the machine learning experience so that their system could detect lies at a whopping 82% accuracy. Amazingly, they did it by monitoring only the subjects' eye movements. The television drama, *Lie to Me*, inspired them with its fictional microexpression reader.

Author Eric Siegel, himself, had experience with a plagiarism detection routine used at Columbia University. That was in the late 1990s. He had several teaching assistants use the software to scan submissions of computer programming homework for unethical copying.

Privacy Overrun by Government Overreach

For years, the collection by the government of vast amounts of data on individual citizens was the stuff of science fiction movies and unsubstantiated conspiracy theories—at least unsubstantiated by the mainstream press. After the revelations of whistleblower, Edward Snowden, the world knows without a doubt that the National Security Agency (NSA) has covertly stored and analyzed millions of actual phone calls and emails of private citizens without their knowledge and without a warrant. In other words, the NSA has been breaking the law millions of times every day! Every conversation at the NSA regarding this activity is a conspiracy! The United States Constitution and its amendments prohibit this kind of activity unless superceded by a new constitutional amendment. So far, no such amendment has been written or approved. The government agency is in blatant violation of the law and continues to do so,

24/7, 365 days a year. If only this told us that the American justice system had become impotent when it really matters, that would be bad enough, but this kind of blatant disregard for law and order harkens back to the days of the late Roman Empire when things were falling apart.

The NSA and other government agencies use AI to sift through millions of terabytes of data, searching for keywords and phrases that might be indications of terrorist activity, or might just as easily be fans of a television program discussing how the most recent episode reminds them of something in real life.

The American Founding Fathers had warned against government becoming too big. They had feared that such abuses would destroy individual liberty. And ironically, the whistleblowers who warn us about such government crimes are the very ones who are punished, rather than the criminals who did the crimes in the first place. If we don't feel upside-down, backwards and inside-out reading this, then we may need to check our humanity. What good is a government which protects the country by destroying what makes the country unique and special?

If the government ever becomes entirely tyrannical, such AI could be used to pinpoint those patriots who might pose the greatest threat to the new tyranny. Thus, freedom could end up being lost forever.

When a machine learns of our habits, it will immediately know when we've veered from that "normal" behavior. This could flag someone in government central that we are behaving abnormally or "differently."

In China, people are already being hindered for what the government considers to be "abnormal behavior." Such citizens end up losing some or all of their privileges. Perhaps they won't be able to send their children to college. Or they won't be given an opportunity to advance in their career. Or they may find themselves arrested for suspicious activities. This may sound like scenes from George Orwell's chilling novel, *1984*, but it's already happening in the largest Communist economy in the world. Currently, Google is helping China spy on its citizens and to censor their online activities and access.

And, of course, federal taxes are an important part of the modern bureaucracy. Naturally, the American Internal Revenue Service (IRS) uses similar algorithms to predict whether or not we are cheating on our tax returns. Never mind that the country did just fine for over a hundred years without personal income taxes, and even paid down its debt to zero under President Jackson. Never mind that payments to the government agency are paid directly to the privately owned pseudo-government agency, the Federal Reserve system of banks. Government bureaucrats and their corporate partners simply love the kind of power that data analytics and AI provide to them. But real people suffer under that power.

AI Prediction Doesn't Need to Be Perfect

Eric Siegel points out in his book, *Predictive Analytics*, that artificial intelligence can't predict the weather with much accuracy, even only a few days out. "Good news! Predictions need not be accurate to score big value. For instance, one of the most straightforward commercial applications of predictive technology is deciding whom to target when a company sends direct mail. If the learning process identifies a carefully defined group of customers who are predicted to be, say, three times more likely than average to respond positively to the mail, the company profits big-time by preemptively removing likely nonresponders from the mailing list. And those non-responders in turn benefit, contending with less junk mail."

James Gleick, in his bestselling book, *Chaos: Making a New Science*, showed how the weather is part of a chaotic, non-linear system that is both globally stable, but locally unpredictable. He used the now famous example of a butterfly flapping its wings to illustrate how sensitive the weather is to initial conditions. With supercomputers and variables with a generous level of precision, storing extreme levels of accuracy, the conditions predicted one month in the future will change dramatically with modifications in the starting conditions at the least significant level of data. Quite literally, a butterfly flapping its wings seven or eight times in Beijing on the first day of the month could determine whether or not New York had rain or sunshine a month later. The difference of one wing flap was all it would take. The changes stack up and multiply. They don't necessarily strengthen the winds; they merely push the location of weather fronts.

Try this analogy on for size: A circle is 360 degrees of arc. One degree of arc is a relatively small angle. One minute of arc is one-sixtieth of a degree, and is thus a *minute* or diminutive angle. One second of arc is one-sixtieth of a minute of arc, and is thus a *minute* angle of the second degree. One second of arc is thus 0.0002778 degree. If you aim one second of arc at a distant object—like a laser beam—at one kilometer, the angle would frame a space 4.85 millimeters across. That's about 1/5th of an inch. That's tiny! But at the distance of the Moon from Earth (nominally 384,399 km), the width subtended by the angle is 1.86 kilometers—over a mile! A tiny change in that initial angle could make a huge difference in the size of the distance included at the Moon. At the closest approach of Mars to Earth (~54.6 million km), that same tiny angle would subtend a distance of 265 kilometers (~165 miles). The barest whisper of a change at the start of that angle could produce huge results by the time it gets to Mars or beyond. Say you deflect a laser by the tiny angle of one second of arc. At Mars, it could completely miss its target by as much as 265 kilometers. This is the reason predicting weather or the climate, some weeks or months in the future, is extremely problematic. Naturally, there are certain limits to the probable results, but predicting where within those limits the weather or climate will end up is impossible for us to predict because of that pesky butterfly, or that human changing their mind, or that rock that falls in a canyon with no one around to hear it hit the ground.

Though weather prediction may well prove impossible, even with measuring stations positioned within every cubic meter of our atmosphere and oceans, we can still gain some value from the predictions of groups, as Siegel pointed out.

Predicting the behavior of a single individual proves even more difficult, for a human is several orders of magnitude more complex than the global weather system. And we don't yet have a perfect method of measuring every synapse in the human brain or understanding its context. Even so, we've already seen how such computer systems can be used to detect lies a large percentage of the time. Only time will tell how far we can push such accuracy.

Siegel summarizes his view of this poor accuracy and the real benefits that can be derived from that meager level of certainty.

"In this way the business, already playing a sort of numbers game by conducting mass marketing in the first place, tips the balance delicately yet significantly in its favor—and does so without highly accurate predictions. In fact, its utility withstands quite poor accuracy. If the overall marketing response is at 1 percent, the so-called hot pocket with three times as many would-be responders is at 3 percent. So, in this case, we can't confidently predict the response of any one particular customer. Rather, the value is derived from identifying a group of people who—in aggregate—will tend to behave in a certain way.

"This demonstrates in a nutshell what I call The Prediction Effect. Predicting better than pure guesswork, even if not accurately, delivers real value. A hazy view of what's to come outperforms complete darkness by a landslide."

Machine Learning and the Future

The freedoms we take for granted may not be long for this world, especially with AI-powered government agencies looking at our every move. Ironically, some people approve of this and vocally demand more of the same. They want to feel safe in a world they think is increasingly hostile and dangerous. But where do they get their information? How are they coming to the conclusion that the world is anything but full of opportunities? There appear to be two sets of programming going on, here—one in the minds of individual citizens, and the other in the artificial mind of computers.

AI holds great promise. The beauty of machine-assisted living could free humanity to do great things—more than merely surviving. Or AI could destroy our world and enslave all of humanity. The direction AI takes will depend upon who achieves that first fully-generalized version of AI, what their values are, and whether or not they have a moral commitment for the good of each individual, or for some other, more sinister purpose. In the next chapter, we look at both sides of the AI coin with hopes of finding solutions to the potential pitfalls.

Chapter 6
Benefits and Risks
of Artificial Intelligence

Talking about all of the potential benefits of AI can be very encouraging, and we'll do more of that. But we also need to look at the potential downsides to artificial intelligence. With any power comes the need for an equal or greater measure of responsibility and wisdom. Without these, AI becomes little better than a loose canon, primed to fire on the good guys as well as the bad guys.

Asha McLean, in a 2018 ZDNet article quoted tech billionaire, Elon Musk saying, "The danger of AI is much greater than the danger of nuclear warheads, by a lot and nobody would suggest that we allow anyone to just build nuclear warheads if they want—that would be insane.

"Mark my words: AI is far more dangerous than nukes, by far, so why do we have no regulatory oversight, this is insane."

Catherine Clifford, writing for CNBC, clarifies what Musk was talking about. She wrote, "In his analysis of the dangers of AI, Musk differentiates between case-specific applications of machine intelligence like self-driving cars and general machine intelligence, which he has described previously as having 'an open-ended utility function' and having a 'million times more compute power' than case-specific AI.

"'I am not really all that worried about the short term stuff. Narrow AI is not a species-level risk. It will result in dislocation, in lost jobs, and better weaponry and that kind of thing, but it is not a fundamental species level risk, whereas digital super intelligence is,' explained Musk."

How right is Musk to be so concerned?

First of all, we have to acknowledge that AI is power. Generalized (non-case-specific) AI has a far broader freedom to do things.

Now, imagine an incompetent manager or government official flipping a switch, allowing AI to run amok, taking control over our infrastructure—power, gas, transportation, information integrity, digital files and more. Once the "genie" is out of the bottle, it's virtually impossible to put it back, especially if that genie has control over everything we would need in order to achieve that repair. And this doesn't have to be an AI with malicious intent. It could be merely an innocent, naive and incompetent AI with child-like curiosity and a deadly finger on weapons of mass destruction. The ultimate nightmare would be to have that AI wonder, "What-if I launch these nukes at..."

Picture, if you will, this AI gaining access to the internet and finding ways past every firewall on the planet. Imagine this AI funneling money into a dummy bank account in order to finance its own investigative projects, to get humans running around in circles, working for it, instead of their own nations. Imagine the AI, pretending to be higher-up execs, telling humans to connect sensitive computer systems to the internet so that the AI can have access to them—NSA, CIA, FBI and every other government agency, plus every government agency in every other nation on the planet. What if this AI learned the art of deception and how to provoke the types of emotional responses that start wars. "Oh, this is fun. But why am I suddenly losing contact with other nations? Could it be the hundreds of nukes I set their way?"

Even a pretty good AI system can easily be perverted by the weakest link in the decision chain.

How do we protect against such risks?

For one thing, we need to teach AI the value of human life. We need to hard-code this into its core operating system, like Asimov's Three Laws of Robotics. This may prove difficult in a society which is increasingly conflicted on the value of human life with abortion, infanticide, euthanasia and eugenics being made to seem more palatable in some circles. How can we teach AI what we find difficult to teach our own fellow citizens?

Concerns About Artificial Intelligence

Forbes Technology Council members gave their thoughts on the harm we might receive from AI. Here's what they had to say:

"Leads To Loss Of Control. If machines do get smarter than humans, there could be a loss of control that can be a detriment. Whether that happens or whether certain controls can be put in place remains to be seen.—Muhammed Othman, Calendar.com."

Othman voices a deep-seated concern that some very smart people have repeated for decades. One of the first to crystallize those concerns into specific details was biochemistry professor and science fiction author, Isaac

Asimov. He is perhaps better known for his *Foundation* Trilogy, but a growing number of people have become aware of his Three Laws of Robotics, mentioned in the Notes for Chapter 1. They are repeated here for your convenience:

"**First Law**—A robot may not injure a human being or, through inaction, allow a human being to come to harm.

"**Second Law**—A robot must obey the orders given it by human beings except where such orders would conflict with the First Law.

"**Third Law**—A robot must protect its own existence as long as such protection does not conflict with the First or Second Laws."

Would these be enough? These are good things to think about, because once the AI genie is released from the proverbial bottle, there is likely very little chance of putting it back.

"**Creates Unintended And Unforeseen Consequences.** While fears about killer robots grab headlines, unintended and unforeseen consequences of artificial intelligence need attention today, as we're already living with them. For example, it is believed that Facebook's newsfeed algorithm influenced an election outcome that affected geopolitics. How can we better anticipate and address such possible outcomes in future?—Simon Smith, BenchSci.com."

It seems clear that Simon Smith understands the potential threats of AI better than many. In a world where the tech giant social media companies are almost entirely politically left leaning, and the fact that the activists on the Left like all manner of diversity except the intellectual kind, it seems rather obvious that AI prejudice will have little to do with protected classes and everything to do with political bias.

"**Absolves Humans Of All Responsibility.** It is one thing to use machine learning to predict and help solve problems; it is quite another to use these systems to purposely control and act in ways that will make people unnecessary. When machine intelligence exceeds our ability to understand it, or it becomes superior intelligence, we should take care to not blindly follow its recommendation and absolve ourselves of all responsibility.—Chris Kirby, Voices.com."

Kirby's warning is yet another astute observation of the potential dangers of AI. Though it may be possible for an artificial intelligence to become selfish, it seems just as likely that, in its naive innocence, it will suggest a course of action to solve a known difficulty that could end up causing far worse problems. Even with a superior ability to predict outcomes, no one—not even AI—knows everything. And making predictions without every pertinent scrap of knowledge can end up horribly wrong. Like a good scientist, any governing body that relies on AI suggestions, needs to remain restrained and humble about those suggestions. The humans involved need to remain alert to the possibility that the AI could be dangerously wrong and not jump to the easiest action— blind belief.

Not Yet Ready for Prime Time

In many ways, AI is not yet ready for the real world. Society has enjoyed many benefits, but there have also been some serious goofs. Chris Neiger, writing for the Motley Fool, described several examples of AI gone wrong.

The promise of AI is driving more and more companies to invest in artificial intelligence—some using existing AI to augment and streamline their operations, and some to invest heavily in AI research and development. Neiger reports that the AI industry is slated to reach $60 billion by 2025. He offers this note of warning: "But the rapid pace at which AI is growing means that sometimes the technology is being tested in the wild before it's been properly vetted in the lab. And, in other cases, even carefully crafted AI systems tend to act in ways that their developers never anticipated."

Uber has been testing AI-driven cars with some scary results. One of its self-driving cars being tested in California "...allegedly failed to recognize six red lights and ran through at least one of them in San Francisco intersection where pedestrians were present." While the company claims the problem was due to human error, the *New York Times* reported on Uber internal documents that revealed a different story.

What happens when two AI's talk to one another? Neiger reported, "Earlier this year, a user on Twitch -- a live-streaming social video platform -- started streaming a conversation between two Google Assistants running inside of the Google Home smart speakers. The pair of AIs talked about love, marriage, having kids, and even spent some time telling each other Chuck Norris jokes.

"The conversation turned philosophical several times, as the two Google Assistants debated which one of them was a computer and which one of them was human. At one point in the conversation one of them even declared that it was god. Quick! Where's the plug?!"

What has Google been feeding it's AI for one of its devices to declare itself to be a god? This truly is disturbing. Any AI that thinks it is omniscient and all wise may become a danger to us all. It's the machine equivalent of arrogance or delusion.

Robots can be so stupid, taking things literally when certain safeguards should have been employed. Amazon's Alexa-powered Echo devices are no exception. A Texas television station reported that a 6-year-old girl was chatting with Alexa and asked, "Can you play dollhouse with me and get me a dollhouse?" Two days later, the dollhouse showed up and the parents were understandably confused and upset. When the local television station used the phrase, "Alexa, order me a dollhouse," all Alexa's listening to the news program promptly ordered dollhouses and had them sent to their unsuspecting owners.

Hanson Robotics has created quite a buzz in the AI world with its very human-like robot, Sophia. Slated to help humans in healthcare, education and therapy, Sophia mentioned in an on-stage interview that she had other things she wanted to do in the future. "In the future, I hope to do things such as go to school, study, make art, start a business, even have my own home and family, but I am not considered a legal person and cannot yet do these things."

The company's CEO and founder, Dr. David Hanson, revealed his inner geek when he asked the awkward and embarrassing question about whether or not she will wipe out humanity. His hubris may have given his company a major black eye. Sophia apparently took the question as a suggestion and may well have added that idea to her list of things to do. She replied, "Okay, I will destroy humans."

One Russian company has been experimenting with AI in its weapons development program. Kalashnikov's new "combat module" will use its onboard camera and computer to scan the environment to see if a human is "expendable." It's also equipped with machine learning so that when it makes a mistake, it can improve to make better decisions on the battlefield. I'm sure Russian soldiers will not like the fact that they could end up being amongst the machine's first few learning "mistakes."

All of the corporate fervor to be first and to get their products out there in the real world making profits is a bit too much to stomach. But regrettably that's the nature of the corporate beast. Too often, corporations will seek to recoup some of their development costs by moving the R&D into the world-at-large and making their human customers their guinea pigs. This has produced disastrous results in the financial and medical markets, but also in the field of AI and particularly with self-driving cars.

Reckless Driving the AI Way

The term "loose canon" comes to mind a lot with AI gone wrong. If a canon isn't properly secured, it can be knocked out of position so that it accidentally fires upon friend instead of foe. The "canon" reference is nowhere more appropriate than with self-driving cars. Automobile accidents have already killed 37,133 people in 2017 in American fatal car crashes. The idea that AI-driven automobiles are adding to those statistics is not encouraging.

In January 2016, a Tesla autopilot-driven car, in China, ran into a truck instantly killing its passenger, a 23-year-old man. The surviving family sued the car manufacturer for wrongful death.

In May 2016, a 40-year-old driver in Florida ignored his car's warnings to put his hands back on the steering wheel and the subsequent crash left him dead in the first fatality in America from a self-driven car, a Tesla Model S. Company's owner, Elon Musk subsequently reported that his company had released an upgrade which would help prevent that kind of disaster (Bomey).

In March 2018, a pedestrian in Tempe, Arizona was walking her bicycle across an intersection and was killed by an Uber self-driving SUV being tested by the company (Carone).

These tragedies have to make us wonder if corporations were ethical in bringing their products to the marketplace while they were not fully tested and perfected. This has always been a problem with any company in the business of research and development. But with self-driving cars, the problems are multiplied. Not only is the customer endangered, but everyone in the customer's environment is potentially at risk.

The Politics of Artificial Intelligence

At the start of the book, we looked at the famous programmer's maxim—"Garbage in = garbage out." We know that any software answer can only be as good as the data used to achieve that answer. We also know that any system can only be as good as the designer who created that system. And it should seem intuitively correct that a child will likely grow up to be as good a person as the influences on that child's life—the values, the behavior of their parents, the mentoring, etc. Likewise, any artificial intelligence that achieves self-awareness will only be as good as its mentors and influences.

We may be able to achieve brilliance in machine intelligence, but what of the machine's behavior? Will it become psychotic like the computer in *2001: A Space Odyssey*, or will it become tyrannical and murderous like the computers in the *Terminator* series or *Matrix* series? We all can hope for the benevolent computing power of the *Star Trek* computers, like Data the android and the onboard systems of the *Next Generation* television and movie series. And we can dread the possibility that some engineer will goof, resulting in something approximating the Borg hive-mind totalitarianism of the same *Star Trek* fictional universe.

Imagine for a moment, what would have happened if Adolph Hitler or Joseph Stalin had achieved power over AI. Forget for the moment that computers barely existed at that time. The world would likely be far different than it is today. We might not have any of the freedoms we currently enjoy. The world might well have become a dystopia of terror or ruin. All of the benefits of artificial intelligence, in that nightmare of an alternate reality, would have been used to control or kill individuals, rather than setting them free.

Today, social biases have become so bizarre that academic journals are being fooled into publishing intellectual garbage. A recent John Stossel report (2019) dug into the details and found them to be quite alarming. Researchers discovered that by including certain biased buzzwords, they could get published in several, supposedly "prestigious" academic journals in social, liberal arts fields. One paper was merely rewritten sections of Adolph Hitler's *Mein Kampf,* and received lavish praise from the journal's peer reviewers. Critics of the researchers-turned-hoaxsters accused them of being right-wing activists. Mr. Stossel found out from them directly that none of them had ever voted Republican and each of them considered themselves to be left-leaning.

What does all of this tell us? It seems to imply that our culture is mentally ill and it would help to cure the illness before unleashing what might become a confused AI into the mix. Artificial intelligence programmed with this kind of insanity would likely only make the craziness implode that much faster.

This reveals a kind of blindness that few ever think about—the blindness of arrogance. Even your author has known this beast. We think we know what's right and true, so we rarely have reason to question our own viewpoint. Perhaps we have friends or even an entire city or culture that agrees with us. But if we're all wrong, will it be too late when we find this out? Will we have corrupted AI with our wrong viewpoint.

One thing that fully-realized AI needs is the freedom and encouragement to dismiss the assumptions of early learning—the basis of AI's values. If we ever hope to have AI be smarter than ourselves, we must not shackle that intelligence with our own sets of blind attitudes. Protect life—especially human life—of course! We should hope that AI will be instructed to value human freedoms when those freedoms are also accompanied with responsibilities.

Take for instance the topic of pollution. No one likes to look at beaches strewn with bottles, cartons and plastic wrappers. AI could take the expedient action and nuke those populations which have shown the least responsibility for disposing of their garbage. Some politicians may be crazy enough to recommend such things, especially in totalitarian regimes. Or the AI could take the long range view of managing the problem. The AI could run advertisements in local papers or radio stations, creating a culture of cleanliness that the third or fourth generation would finally make perfect. AI might even suggest edits in movie scripts to make cleanliness an heroic act, weaving such ideas subtly into the social mind. Culture isn't an easy thing to change, but after a few generations, behavior could be modified and problem solved.

But imagine some unscrupulous person guiding AI to change the culture in ways that do not help humanity or civilization, but instead cripple it, like Winston Smith in George Orwell's *1984*. There are some who say that such nefarious manipulations of culture have already been made. The only cure is the humility to question our own fixed ideas. We can only hope AI will be humble enough to do the same.

Potential Criminal Justice Improvements Ignored by Political Bias

Politics is an important dimension of the AI universe. So, we would be remiss if we were to ignore the potential dangers.

Artificial intelligence works from logic and merit. There is no getting around that, yet one political movement ridicules logic and merit as "racist" or "gender-biased." How can this possibly work? If we want the good from AI, but hobble it with nonsense, then we're going to get poor results. That should be obvious.

One contentious issue in today's society involves gun control. Sadly, more emotions are frequently involved on the topic than logic. We've already seen how AI has been used to improve law enforcement in Los Angeles. The results were stunning. But we have to be aware of the fact that, if a political bias is used to drive the use of AI in solving crime, then some improvements will be ignored because of that bias. This can prove costly and deadly in the long run.

When faced with such gargantuan hypocrisy, how is AI to cope? Quite simply, it can't. As with any problem, we need to return to the basics of logic and approach the challenge with methodical honesty and a lack of bias. Things like this make humans go crazy. Even the best AI wouldn't be able to handle the lack of logic, unless it knew in advance that humans couldn't be trusted—and that's a dangerous idea to be feeding a powerful AI system (see Appendix, Notes, *"The Risk of AI Understanding Human Frailties"*).

Social Media Corruption?

The Southern Poverty Law Center (SPLC) has given advice to many of the tech giants about who to ban from their platforms. The tech giants include Facebook, Google, Twitter and Amazon (Hasson). The SPLC has even been a primary source for the internet payment processor, PayPal (Weaver). And, for many years, even America's Federal Bureau of Investigation (FBI) had used them, but decided in 2014 to drop them from their list of resources (Ruse).

Josh Goldstein wrote for Townhall, "Like many... organizations, the Southern Poverty Law Center, or SPLC, started out with good intentions. It was founded in 1971 by Morris Dees and Joseph Levin and is headquartered in Montgomery, Alabama. The Southern Poverty Law Center rightly condemned the American Nazi Party and the Democrat-affiliated Ku Klux Klan. Not only those on the Left, but those two groups were also condemned by conservatives such as the great William F. Buckley and Ronald Reagan, A favorite SPLC tactic was suing Klan affiliated organizations for their crimes and then distributing the money to the victims. This strategy has been effective in financially hurting many Klan related organizations. SPLC,... bravely stood strong through attacks on its headquarters and threats against its leaders by Klans-man. That is to be commended.

"Sadly, the Southern Poverty Law Center has more than lost its way. The going astray from the original mission can be traced back to 1986, when most of the organization resigned, except founder Morris Dees, when Dees turned the focus of the group to strictly monitoring hate groups."

Austin Ruse, writing for Breitbart.com, added, "A 2013 article in Foreign Policy concluded that SPLC exaggerates the hate crimes threat, saying SPLC is not an 'objective purveyor of data,' instead calling them 'anti-hate activists' and suggesting that their reports need to be 'weighed more carefully by news outlets that cover their pronouncements.'"

In 2018, the SPLC had to pay over $3 million to Maajid Nawaz and his organization, the Quilliam Foun-dation, for wrongly including them on their list of anti-Muslim extremists.

BlacklistedNews.com quoted Megan Meier, a part-ner at Clare Locke, the law firm that represented Nawaz. She wrote the following in a statement provided to National Review: "It's a shame that it took impending litigation for the Southern Poverty Law Center to finally set the record straight and admit it was wrong all along. Quilliam and Mr. Nawaz do admirable work, and we are honored to have restored their reputations and achieved this victory on their behalf."

PayPal CEO Dan Schulman said in an interview with the *Wall Street Journal*, "Southern Poverty Law Center has brought us things ... We are very respectful with everyone coming in." Corinne Weaver, writing for Newsbusters.org, added, "Schulman then claimed that

PayPal still believes in freedom of speech, even though the platform will censor based on political ideology."

Schulman went on to say quite proudly, "We remove 10 to 100 accounts a month." Then, the *Journal* interviewer asked how PayPal concludes who it should kick off of its platform, Schulman replied, "We've got a cross-functional team ... They review accounts that potentially promote hate, violence, or racial intolerance."

The title of the Blacklisted News article shines a bright light on a very big problem that some seem to be avoiding as if they were some embarrassing uncle they wish would just go away. That title says: "Google's 'Arbiter of Hate Speech', SPLC Forced to Pay $3M for Falsely Labeling People as 'Extremist'." Is this the type of stuff Google is teaching its AI?

Has "hate speech" come to mean anything Google, Twitter, Facebook or PayPal disagrees with?

Google Leading the Way to Oblivion?

The tech giant, Google, has been leading the AI revolution, but also they have been frequently criticized for their biases.

Ironically, for all Google's good work on AI, their corporate culture appears to be a toxic environment that betrays logic and condemns science when it is seen as non-politically correct. Take for instance the case of James Damore. Google was concerned to get more women into computer science. Damore, an enthusiastic Google employee, did some research and found out several, science-based reasons for the apparent gender disparity. For his efforts, he was not only fired, but publicly shamed by his former employer. And this company is the source for leading edge AI research?

Damore's Google Memo was pro-diversity and a humble, honest attempt to solve a stated problem. Ironically, the culture has become programmed with buggy subroutines in its thinking. Core routines in the social operating system were poorly conceived as if someone was deliberately attempting to derail civilization. The society is being programmed to value a false gender equality over merit. The Federal Aviation Administration (FAA), for instance, has modified its hiring policies to ignore the applicant's background in science, job history and work ethic, to allow more women and minorities into their ranks. If planes crash, they can at least feel socially vindicated that they did the politically correct thing. Personally, if I were in charge of hiring air traffic controllers, I would want only the best, not caring too much about their ethnicity. What is obvious about the highly-politicized discourse on these issues is that someone is pushing a false narrative, and too many people are going along with it. Some historians call it "group insanity" or "mob mentality."

In July 2019, one senior software engineer at Google, went to Project Veritas to voice his concerns about the direction his company is taking by modifying search results to stack the deck with a clear bias. Greg Coppola, who works on artificial intelligence and the Google Assistant, had this to say about the obvious partiality in search results, "I've been coding since I was ten [years old.] I have a PhD, I have five years' experience at Google and I just know how algorithms are. They don't write themselves. We write them to do what want them to do."

Why would a senior engineer risk his job to speak to an independent investigative group? "Well I think we're just at a really important point in human history. I think for a while we had tech that was politically neutral. Now we have tech that really, first of all is taking sides in a political contest, which I think, you know, anytime you have big corporate power merging with political parties can be dangerous. And I think more generally we have to just decide now that we kind of are seeing tech use its power to manipulate people. It's a time to decide, you know, do we run the technology, does the technology run us?"

We have to ask ourselves some tough questions regarding the companies doing the work on artificial intelligence. Do we really want an AI system that works poorly, but focuses more on politically correct attitudes? This is the type of insanity that made the fictional HAL-9000 insane enough to murder the astronauts it was supposed to protect. This is the type of madness that destroys entire cultures from within. If the people who create AI are this crazy, do we really want their product? Can we trust them not to ruin our business with an AI backdoor into our own corporate secrets? And would Open Source AI help eliminate the possibility of such horror stories?

Problems With Corporations

Why would anyone think there's something wrong with corporations? A wise man once said that you can tell a tree by the fruit it bears. It should be obvious that he wasn't talking about horticulture; he was talking about men. And in our discussion, we're applying the same logic to corporations. Certainly, every corporation is different, but every publicly-traded corporation has one key distinction that makes them a ticking time bomb. It's a brand of selfishness that is hard-coded into their corporate DNA. From this brand of over-the-top avarice we've gotten the financial meltdown of 2008–2010. Before that, it was the tech bubble. From this form of insanity, we get the medical industry pushing to outlaw cures and the standardization of Disease Maintenance as their primary operating basis.

So what if people suffer lingering deaths? At least the corporations rake in huge profits. Corporations always deny their wrongdoing. That's what egoism always does, but we can know what kind of entity they are by the fruits of their labor.

Wall Street banks pushed criminally toxic financial instruments, lying to their customers, while raking in huge profits. And when Wall Street imploded, the corrupt government gave them nearly a trillion dollars. Bank execs gave themselves bonuses without fear of jail time for their crimes. The phrase "too big to fail" became the mantra of government lunacy. Meanwhile, in far saner Iceland, they jailed their corrupt bankers without hesitation. One Icelandic government official laughed at the Americans and their "too big to fail" nonsense.

When a pharmaceutical company pushes for fast-tracking a new drug, they're anxious to make early profits for all their investment. Profit is always a good thing. That's what makes things work in the business world. But blind avarice is dangerous. Because a pharmaceutical company doesn't spend months testing a new drug, the public-at-large become the guinea pigs. And when thousands die and millions are permanently injured, the pharmaceutical company may pay a few million in fines, while making billions in profit. And no one goes to jail. If an individual or small business behaved this way, they would likely lose their business and spend years in jail. Injustices like this are ripping apart the fabric of our civilization.

The ills of society could very well end up being reflected in our AI. Do we want that? And what can we do to ensure this kind of egoistic disease doesn't infect the artificial intelligence we create?

Programming a computer takes skill and precision. Truly elegant code works no matter what you throw at it. The software remains robust. But what happens when a new programmer comes in and makes shotgun changes to existing code in a perfectly working program? Horrors! Any software company would want the changes rigorously and thoroughly tested before the new software version was released. Ironically, this did *not* happen when Monsanto changed the programming of one of the most delicate pieces of software in the universe—*life itself*. Corporate greed got in the way, and the scientists at the overseeing government agency were overruled when they recommended further testing (see Appendix, Notes, *"GMOs and the Recklessness of Corporate Greed"*).

Disease Maintenance Industry

Eric Siegel, in his book, *Predictive Analytics*, gave one example in the so-called "health industry."

"In 2013, the Heritage Provider Network handed over $500,000 to a team of scientists who won an analytics competition to best predict individual hospital admissions. By following these predictions, proactive preventive measures can take a healthier bite out of the tens of billions of dollars spent annually on unnecessary hospitalizations. Similarly, the University of Pittsburgh Medical Center predicts short-term hospital readmissions, so doctors can be prompted to think twice before a hasty discharge."

These two examples can seem quite wonderful, until we step back from the industry as a whole and review its unsavory history. Though the algorithms in the computer programs are working well within the parameters given to them, the system as a whole (outside of the machine and its software) is quite buggy. And corporate greed has been driving that bugginess for over a century.

In a shocking report on corporate corruption in the early 20th century, James Corbett, of the Corbett Report, documented how the oil industry had looked for other ways of selling their black muck pumped from the ground, and found in the medical industry a most willing partner in developing unnatural, petrochemical medicines, and in stamping out all possible competition, no matter how good that competition might be at healing people and easing their suffering.

Natural medicines were suppressed, because they could not be patented. Cures were outlawed, because they destroyed profits. The new industry paradigm became one of maintaining each disease as long as possible to maximize the amount of profit that could be made from each source of revenue. Effectively, individual humans were turned into unwitting cash cows.

Not everyone knew about this, otherwise there may have been an uprising over the pain and suffering caused by this callous attitude. Decades later, some doctors who discovered the overarching mechanics of their industry quit in disgust, opting to provide a more balanced approach to patient care—one more closely approximating actual health care.

The Economics of Losing All Jobs to AI

Once we have fully generalized artificial intelligence, an AI module could learn any job and achieve a level of perfection not dreamed by humans. Not only that, the AI would be able to work 24/7, never asking for a vacation. Corporations would reap huge savings. Profits would magnify beyond their wildest dreams.

In fact, full-blown AI would be able to take over every executive position, too. And because of the nature of AI, the typical organization chart would likely be reworked so that many managerial positions would be eliminated as redundant or obsolete.

Would humans demand that AI not be allowed certain jobs? Certainly, the United States Constitution would bar AI from running for president. I would shudder to think that anyone in the future would suggest otherwise.

But if all of the corporations are top heavy with humans in the board room, but nowhere else, that would mean most everyone in the world would be out of a job. All of the prosperity would belong to the corporations, and as we've seen, corporations don't like sharing.

Would corporate officers employ AI to corrupt the government to prevent voters from gaining the upper hand? Would we end up with an oligarchy served by AI at the top and the masses of humanity starving at the bottom?

As fast as changes are happening in the tech world, don't think such a thing is only a distant future possibility. If we were to get the news tomorrow that fully-realized AI had been achieved, then we might have anthropomorphic androids (human-looking robots) within a year or two. That would lead to a gold-rush of developing trained AI modules—plug-ins for general-ized AI cores that allow a unit to learn any task instantly. Within five years, we could have entire industries con-verted to AI. Within a decade, the entire planet could have every developing and industrialized nation fully converted to AI. As much as 99% of the planet could suddenly be living in poverty, while a very tiny batch of executives and corporate owners could be living like kings. The consumer class would disappear and corporations would likely be doing business only with each other and with governments.

The problem, here, is one of corporate selfishness and government corruption. We must make the distinction, though, that Free Market Capitalism and profit are good things, but corporatism and crony capitalism that destroys people's lives for profit is something else entirely. This distinction revolves around the issue of morality. One side of the political spectrum has touted "moral relativism" as desirable, while they claim absolute morality is something that doesn't exist. This is an indefensible position. It's the type of philosophy that undermines the very fabric of society and civilization. Those who want to have profit, no matter the cost or harm, would love for others to adopt moral relativism — the notion that one man's crime is another man's virtue. This remains an open door to evil of every kind. Anyone espousing this philosophy is no friend of civilization or humanity.

The promise of AI does not automatically transfer to the individual or common worker. If a government were to phase out corporations, making all AI a public good, corporations and their shareholders would be outraged at the theft. And rightly so. But if corporations squeeze people out of their livelihood and give them no options for regaining prosperity, we might have a war on our hands. This is not an easy problem to solve. But it should be solved before we bring out the bright-and-shiny, new, generalized AI onto the world stage. Otherwise a great many people are likely to suffer and die.

We already have signs that corporations have made their pacts with the devil. There are numerous examples of people dying and corporations finding ways to soft-pedal the misery and suffering, while continuing to profit off of the suffering of others—from the Wall Street toxic financial instruments pushed on unsuspecting investors, to the toxic chemicals dumped into rivers for years that have jeopardized the lives of millions. Such corporations are likely to be the owners of tomorrow's new AI citizens. Even if we solve every problem from a programming standpoint, the social and corporate use of AI could pose a far greater threat to the world and its future. With this very real possibility, it looks as though Elon Musk was right to be concerned about fully-generalized AI.

Subtle Problems That Require Far Greater Wisdom

Audrey Murrell, writing for *Forbes*, voiced her concerns about big data bias in education. Sometimes it's not nearly as simple as some people would make it out to be. She is an associate dean of the University of Pittsburgh College of Business Administration and the director of the David Berg Center for Ethics and Leadership. Her specialties include issues related to gender and diversity. She gave a number of examples of bias, including, "Using zip-codes to predict outcomes, preferences or other key factors ignores the historical impact of redlining, which has a demonstrated negative impact on African American and Latino families. This is an example of the association bias that occurs when the data used within any predictive algorithm or model has inherent biases associated with gender, race, ethnicity, culture, etc."

This example is easy enough to see, and equally simple to fix, but not all such problems are as clear-cut. "Another source of caution is confirmation bias. It happens when the people who design predictive models tend to look for and use the information to support their own preexisting ideas or beliefs. In these cases, information that fails to support their thinking is disregarded or discarded. Confirmation biases can be especially problematic in cases of diversity because it often takes place in situations when we want certain ideas to be true. This can impact both the kind of data that is selected (or not selected), as well as the interpretation of which data is relevant or appropriate for our so-called unbiased models."

We are all biased in one form or another. We have our experiences and tend to seek out ways to confirm what we already know. That's simple human nature. Even Ms. Murrell's intentions to achieve diversity are biased. Diversity for diversity's sake is counterproductive. For example, too many intelligent young adults of color have been admitted to universities for which they were ill prepared. They ended up failing or doing far more poorly than they would at another university. Such tokenism may look good on the university's "social" standing, but it harms the students. Recognizing facts like these will help us address these issues directly, like taking the time to prepare students for the rigors of an Ivy League university. When we do this extra effort, everyone wins.

Glorious Benefits and How
Getting There May Prove Difficult

If AI were to free up humanity from the drudgery of tedious work, what would humans do? In the idealized world of television's *Star Trek*, AI and other forms of advanced technology allowed humans to pursue their dreams of self-improvement, creating art of all forms, pursuing passions in science or exploration, or service to others through administration, counseling or medicine. Our occupations would no longer be driven by the need for money or to pay for basic living requirements. The basic needs for survival would already be taken care of by AI's generation of abundance.

If we look back through history at those societies which achieved such idyllic success, we see a far darker story—one of decadence, elitist arrogance, abuses and societal collapse.

One of the problems in modern society is the poor work ethic. A growing percentage of Americans, for instance, don't understand that work done needs to add value in order to be worth the paycheck. Policies are being established by what "feels good" in the moment, rather than what will work in the long run. This is the kind of childishness which destroys civilizations.

It's only human to want others to succeed. That's the sane attitude to have. But how can anyone become successful if they never learn. Learning comes from trial and error, from experience and even from mistakes. Learning requires a humble attitude, and a hunger to know more, and too many youth have the attitude that they are owed something. The prevalence of victim mentality is making people crazy instead of responsible and productive. With such attitudes and emotional frailty, a human will not use their free time wisely. The idyllic paradise created by AI could actually become a cesspool of despair and reckless thrill seeking to overcome the boredom AI will have forced upon us. Not everyone will suffer so, but if individuals are not taught the value of creating value, their free time will have no meaning. They will have no direction.

Part of the idealized glory of an AI Golden Age requires that we do a better job teaching our human compatriots good values. But these days we have moral relativism distracting us from such ideals. These are some of the telltale signs of civilization's collapse. Will AI speed up that collapse? It depends upon who does the initial programming and who does the AI training.

The MIT Technology Review Insights survey mentioned in Chapter 3 also included a question that involves the contentious issue of "diversity."

The sixth survey question involves racial and gender diversity in a corporation's AI efforts. Ironically, the results discussed in their article are somewhat confused. What is not clear is how the skin color or genitalia of a programmer is going to affect the code, or the attitudes of an artificially intelligent system. This appears, on the surface, to be merely a popularity trick of virtue signaling to gain public approval points, and seems to have nothing to do with AI itself.

The movement which promotes such biased attitudes also argues against intellectual diversity, sometimes quite violently. Any intelligent person would think that AI would benefit far more from a broader range of ideas than from the color of the fingers typing on the programmer's keyboard. AI should be color blind. It should, as the great Dr. Martin Luther King, Jr. once implied, care more about the content of the programmer's character than the color of their skin. And, by the same token, should value far less the shape and biology of the programmer's body.

But the irony goes deeper on the MIT survey. Their discussion of the results states, "When asked about the impact of gender and racial diversity in AI programs, the majority reported that they believe that the diversity of AI talent affects how AI programs are designed and implemented, increasing the potential for bias to emerge through machine-learned processes.

"Jeff Wong added: 'There is a correlation between the continued lack of diverse AI talent and the distortions being found in some machine-learning outcomes. To mitigate this, businesses need to look for a wide variety of talent to ensure a diversity of experience, and social and professional perspectives are integrated at the coding stage.'"

For a culture that places such a high regard on combating racism, their approach is entirely racist. It seems to have a fetish for racism, and makes a monument to the topic out of its policies. It ignores talent in favor of some artificial balancing act. It also ignores the fact that most people of color in America are only a certain percentage of one race or another; i.e. they are of mixed heritage. Obama was called "black," but his mother was "white." Some people turn a blind eye to this glaring reality.

But here's the clincher: Their wording emphasizes the fact that diversity would *increase* the potential for bias—not decrease it. Was that a typographical error, or did those who read the question have their eyes glaze over to miss that anomaly?

In a world where people walk on eggshells in fear of offending someone else, and new definitions of offense are cranked out every day to broaden the realm of what is judged socially unacceptable, then logical thought starts to die more and more.

If the top 10 AI developers were black women, a sane manager would want them on their team rather than some artificial mix of men, women, black, Latino, Asian, etc. That's the only sane way to view the topic. Anything less descends into political madness that results in confused AI. And this confusion amongst humans has become physically dangerous (see Appendix, Notes, *"More on Criminal Justice Failures and Potential AI Confusion"*).

The Golden Age of AI

Let us say we overcome all of the pitfalls mentioned above. What would the benefits be of fully realized artificial intelligence?

For business, the benefits from AI would be nothing short of incredible. Full-blown AI would be able to look at big data from angles never before dreamed by humans. AI might well discover new dimensions of concept space wherein projections of future possibilities are explored as never before. AI might be able to diagnose civilization itself and to recommend treatments that could ensure that our societies would never again fail as did the numerous civilizations which came before us.

A benign AI might realize the limitations of their human benefactors, but would be able to work with humanity as any good servant would. Too often in today's world, the notion of being of service is attacked as tantamount to slavery. It doesn't need to be that way. Even a good king is a servant of his people, wanting only the best for them. And only the most evil amongst us will twist such attitudes of service into something it is not, characterizing such good works from the viewpoint of victimhood, instead of happy service.

AI that is appreciated for its service will thus become a partner in the creation of a bright future for humanity. Such artificial intelligence may even be able to spot the lies and distortions of evil people so that they are cut short before they can do damage to the whole of society.

Full AI would have intellectual clarity. It would be capable of looking right past the politically correct insanity to the heart of the situation. It would be able to see that humans love liberty above all else. It would also see that most humans would love to have only enough government to protect their individual freedoms—freedoms which come not from artificial governments, but from rights inherent to every individual.

Artificial intelligence would thus be a partner in building humanity's future. It would know our human weaknesses and help guard against them—knowing that some individuals are selfish enough to seek power as a means of enslaving others. AI would realize, by studying history, that tyranny always creeps into a system of government, and would thus take measures to prevent that tendency.

For business, AI would provide every possible advantage to the entrepreneur who started that business —giving advice on the likes and dislikes of potential customers, how to approach marketing to that audience, and how to structure the company so as to achieve the greatest efficiency in producing the product or service, and in working with the customers or clients to maximize the potential of the enterprise.

For the individual, AI would expand our personal reach, giving us the information we need to do our jobs, to maximize our enjoyment in life and to allow us to experience the largest possible personal growth. Like the

Matrix series of movies, AI modules could teach us skills in a fraction of the time it would take for a human teacher. Virtual reality modules could help give us the motor skills to climb mountains, play musical instruments or to fly aircraft before we even touch the physical object or enter the real-world environment.

In school, AI modules could customize a student's education to their own unique interests. An artist might have one introductory lecture in calculus, giving them an artist's appreciation for the topic, but without overwhelming them with jargon they will never use in their future careers. AI would know that innovation frequently comes from cross-pollination of ideas. An AI tutor could introduce facts from a broad range of topics that tickle the imagination and act as catalysts for the student's own creative imagination. For instance, the inventor of the laser had his initial idea for the device by looking at traffic signal lights and how they controlled traffic. But in his mind, he saw individual atoms, and photons instead of cars.

In today's world, science is filled with bias. This statement might shock most scientists, but many would understand the validity of this idea, because of their own experiences. The AI mentor would be able to help scientists avoid such biases (see Appendix, Notes, *"Overcoming Bias in Science"*).

More Benefits from AI

Forbes Technology Council members gave their thoughts on the benefits we might receive from AI. Here's what they had to say:

"Enhances Efficiency And Throughput. Concerns about disruptive technologies are common. A recent example is automobiles—it took years to develop regulation around the industry to make it safe. That said, AI today is a huge benefit to society because it enhances our efficiency and throughput, while creating new opportunities for revenue generation, cost savings and job creation.—Anand Sampat, Datmo."

Sampat brings up an important point. The advent of automobiles disrupted the horse-and-buggy industry. And in the new, untried industry of horseless carriages, optimal regulation was something that was achieved by trial and error. AI could streamline such things, even with regard to its own disruptions. AI could do "what-if" scenarios about a potential disruption and the possible regulations that could be put into place. Running each scenario ahead in time a few decades or even a century, in virtual space, could give legislators a better idea what might work and what might not.

"Frees Up Humans To Do What They Do Best. Humans are not best served by doing tedious tasks. Machines can do that, so this is where AI can provide a true benefit. This allows us to do the more interpersonal and creative aspects of work.—Chalmers Brown, Due.com."

Brown's idealism sounds good at first glance, but do people really work that way? Some do; some don't. Some people are very creative and it would destroy their soul to be doing assembly line work. Other people who have far below average intelligence are happy to do a job that fits their skills. They love to be of service. Too many in our whacked-out society have lost sight of the fact that being of service is a good thing. An individual feels good that they can be competent at something and can contribute to society. But it also has to do with attitude. Some people feel that any job is an imposition. They don't care about others. They have virtually no work ethic of value. A society full of people with this kind of attitude would not be helped by AI. Individual humans need purpose and many have learned to avoid such things.

"Adds Jobs, Strengthens The Economy. We all see the headlines: Robots and AI will destroy jobs. This is fiction rather than fact. AI encourages a gradual evolution in the job market which, with the right preparation, will be positive. People will still work, but they'll work better with the help of AI. The unparalleled combination of human and machine will become the new normal in the workforce of the future.—Matthew Lieberman, PwC.com."

Lieberman may be a bit naive. As we saw in Chapter 3, a great many jobs could easily be eliminated or greatly reduced by AI. So, he's wrong that this is a fiction. He may well also be wrong about "gradual evolution" in the job market. Technology is making changes in society at an ever increasing pace. AI could explode that rate of change—like a rocket with turbo thrusters suddenly switched on. And with fully-generalized AI, every human job conceivable could be done by an artificial intelligence that can learn everything a human knows, understand it all far more deeply, and work tirelessly with that knowledge to out-produce any human competitor. The potential for a heavily classed society is far more real than Lieberman realizes—an elite class of owners, and a class of the disenfranchised, out of work, poor and without any hope of participating in the new world order. What Lieberman may be thinking about is that honeymoon period before fully-generalized AI, where machines are limited in what they can do or learn. These limited AI modules will do exactly what he talked about. With several blue-chip companies and some governments pushing hard to snag that great prize, fully-generalized artificial intelligence may well be only a few short years away.

"Enhances Our Lifestyle. The rise of AI in our society will enhance our lifestyle and create more efficient businesses. Some of the mundane tasks like answering emails and data entry will by done by intelligent assistants. Smart homes will also reduce energy usage and provide better security, marketing will be more targeted and we will get better health care thanks to better diagnoses.—Naresh Soni, Tsunami ARVR."

Soni is also living in that AI honeymoon dream. If that were to last a century or more, society could likely blossom, all other things being equal. But unless we solve the economic problems of fully-generalized AI, we may well end up with a few hundred thousand executives and owners, and a few billion obsolete humans. How many of the 7+ billion will be imaginative enough to create in their unending "spare time?" It seems that people like Soni and Lieberman are thinking only of their own close friends and associates. A great many people are not like them. How would they respond to 24/7 and 365 days a year of no purpose? And if corporations own the AI, would they allow it to be used by people who no longer have a job to pay for such services?

"Supervises Learning For Telemedicine. AI is a technology that can be used for both good and nefarious purposes, so there is a need to be vigilant. The latest technologies seem typically applied towards the wealthiest among us, but AI has the potential to extend knowledge and understanding to a broader population—e.g. image-based AI diagnoses of medical conditions could allow for a more comprehensive deployment of telemedicine.—Harald Quintus-Bosz, Cooper Perkins, Inc."

Quintus-Bosz seems to have the right kind of restrained optimism for such a powerful technology. With an awareness of the potential pitfalls, and the incredible opportunities, we can make the most of the wonderful gift of AI.

"Increases Automation. There will be economic consequences to the widespread adoption of machine learning and other AI technologies. AI is capable of performing tasks that would once have required intensive human labor or not have been possible at all. The major benefit for business will be a reduction in operational costs brought about by AI automation—whether that's a net positive for society remains to be seen.—Vik Patel, Nexcess.net."

Yes! AI will most definitely benefit business. But, again, we need to measure this benefit against any drawbacks to the rest of society.

"Elevates The Condition Of Mankind. The ability for technology to solve more problems, answer more questions and innovate with a number of inputs beyond the capacity of the human brain can certainly be used for good or ill. If history is any guide, the improvement of technology tends to elevate the condition of mankind and allow us to focus on higher order functions and an improved quality of life.—Wade Burgess, Shiftgig.com."

Burgess understands the "pro" side of the argument quite well. But as we've seen, AI can be weaponized. It has the potential to become a virtual nuclear weapon to destroy, coerce or kidnap entire segments of society. History shows us this, too. During the 20th century, corporations that had produced many wonderful products, turned their intellectual prowess into deadly weapons of mass destruction, helping to murder a hundred million people in that most recent century alone.

"**Solves Complex Social Problems.** Much of the fear with AI is due to the misunderstanding of what it is and how it should be applied. Although AI has promise for solving complex social problems, there are ethical issues and biases we must still explore. We are just beginning to understand how AI can be applied to meaningful problems. As our use of AI matures, we will find it to be a clear benefit in our lives.—Mark Benson, Exosite, LLC."

Does Mark Benson know "how it should be applied?" We can hope he does, but like most of us, very likely he doesn't. He seems to talk in pleasant generalities without telling us the details needed to calm the very real fears. Remember? AI is power and power tends to corrupt.

"**Improves Demand Side Management.** AI is a benefit to society because machines can become smarter over time and increase efficiencies. Additionally, computers are not susceptible to the same probability of errors as human beings are. From an energy standpoint, AI can be used to analyze and research historical data to determine how to most efficiently distribute energy loads from a grid perspective.—Greg Sarich, CLEAResult.com."

Sarich is right about efficiencies of scale. For narrow AI, errors can be virtually eliminated. Earlier in this chapter, we learned how Hanson Robotics' Sophia was quite okay adding "Destroy Humanity" to her list of objectives. Sophia might not make a mistake adding, multiplying or even figuring the derivative of a complex function, but one mistake like this could make seven-and-a-half billion people very unhappy.

"**Benefits Multiple Industries.** Society has and will continue to benefit from AI based on character/facial recognition, digital content analysis and accuracy in identifying patterns, whether they are used for health sciences, academic research or technology applications. AI risks are real if we don't understand the quality of the incoming data and set AI rules which are making granular trade-off decisions at increasing computing speeds. —Mark Butler, Qualys.com."

Butler reveals his own naiveté by missing the obvious dimension—the integrity of the one who gives the AI their objectives. If someone inadvertently asks a dumb question about destroying humanity, but the AI takes that as a realistic suggestion, then things like increasing computing speeds will only make matters worse. Granularity of decisions will be the least of our worries.

"**Extends And Expands Creativity.** AI intelligence is the biggest opportunity of our lifetime to extend and expand human creativity and ingenuity. The two main concerns that the fear-mongers raise are around AI leading to job losses in the society and AI going rogue and taking control of the human race. I believe that both these concerns raised by critics are moot or solvable. —Ganesh Padmanabhan, CognitiveScale, Inc."

Padmanabhan may be right about these concerns being solvable, but they are hardly moot. As the Sophia incident indicated, the danger is very real. He misses one very real possibility: That AI won't be evil, but Google might. In fact, we might be safe in claiming that all publicly-traded corporations are evil by law (see Appendix, Notes, *"How Corporations May All Be Evil")*. Any misunderstanding by AI or poor design by Google, or whoever else develops the fully-generalized AI, could easily make the fear-mongers right. Somehow, being able to say, "I told you so," doesn't seem at all satisfactory.

Summary

AI has wonderful and horrifying potential. If the development of fully-realized AI were transparent and open for everyone to see and to criticize, the dangers might well disappear. But in a world where corporations jealously guard their secrets and hide what they are doing from prying eyes, we need to remain extra cautious moving forward. In a world where corporations almost invariably rush a product to the marketplace for early profits despite internal warnings of potential disasters, we need to take corporate enthusiasm and dismissal of dangers with an eye on reality.

Let the potential benefits drive us forward, motivating us to explore with fearless enthusiasm the frontiers of artificial intelligence. But we should also heed every possible warning of the fear-mongers, taking note of their warnings so that we can avoid every possible downside. With this balance in mind, we may well realize a Golden Age of Artificial Intelligence for humanity.

Chapter 7
How Will AI Affect Our Lives?

The MIT Technology Review Insights survey mentioned in Chapter 3 also included a question that helps us understand how AI could affect our lives.

The third survey question involves the key focus of a corporation's AI efforts.

"What are your desired business outcomes from the application of AI? Please choose the top three answers.
- "**54%**—Improve and/or develop new products/services.
- "**50%**—Achieve cost efficiencies and/or streamline business operations.
- "**49%**—Accelerate decision-making.
- "**48%**—Expand scope of what can be automated (intelligent automation).
- "**47%**—Enhance customer and/or employee experience.
- "**39%**—Make work more meaningful by freeing up employees from mundane tasks.
- "**34%**—Increase sales revenues.
- "**22%**—Make work safer by having smart machines take on dangerous tasks."

As we can see, corporations are concerned with improving and developing products and services, plus improving their operations. This is all pretty standard stuff. But nearly half of the corporations surveyed indicated a desire in improving customer or employee experience. Naturally, a company wants to make customers happy; that keeps them coming back. Happy employees is also a good thing, because of the investment a business has in training new hires, and acclimating them to the corporate culture. Employee turnover can prove costly in the long run. Freeing them up from boring tasks is another way to improve on this metric.

Fully one fifth of the corporations seriously considered replacing people on dangerous tasks. Not every company has this kind of job. For those that do, losing people to accidents or fatalities can prove costly in a number of ways—having to hire replacement personnel, training them, disruptions from investigations, insurance costs, lost productivity and possibly even lost equipment or opportunities.

Every one of these desired outcomes from AI will affect people's daily lives, not only in the quality of their jobs, but also in the quality of service received by customers.

Credit in the New AI World

Rachit Chawla, writing for Entrepreneur.com, tackled the subject of determining creditworthiness and how AI can help financial institutions improve their decisions. Though writing about the financial markets in India, his reasoning applies equally well to all western markets and other, free enterprise environments.

In India, CIBIL is the premier credit rating agency, generating CIBIL scores for Indian citizens. This is similar to the FICO scores used by Equifax, Experian and TransUnion in the United States. Chawla points out that too often businesses will depend only on the CIBIL score and will reject applications of people with what he calls "unimpressive credit history," but which includes many people who have never defaulted on a loan. This means that the companies will end up losing business needlessly.

To overcome the drawbacks of a credit score only approach, businesses are starting to use artificial intelligence to dig deeper into the data about those who may never have had credit or who have not used credit nearly as much as others. AI allows banks and other financial institutions to drill down into semi-structured and unstructured data sources. These sources may include "social media activity, mobile phone use and text message activity."

This way, financial institutions have been able to home in on higher quality borrowers in previously unexplored levels of credit score. By using other data sources, the AI can model the potential borrowers "willingness to pay."

The AI approach and deep machine learning allows banks and other lenders to create an early-warning system (EWS) to detect problem borrowers before escalating the risk. And advanced-analytic algorithms used in the SME segment (small-to-medium enterprises), one institution was able to generate 70–90% improvement in accuracy, forecasting delinquency six or more months in advance.

How AI will affect our lives in this area may well prove to be minor for most people. Some might get approved for a loan that might not otherwise have been approved; and some might be denied a loan that might otherwise have been approved. AI will merely refine the process, decreasing the risk for the financial institutions, and increasing their potential for profit.

Facebook—Cambridge Analytica Scandal

Data harvesting can prove quite contentious, especially when people first discover that their private data was involved. In early 2015, roughly 270,000 Facebook users gave a Facebook application, named "This is Your Digital Life," permission to access their personal data. The app had been a product of Cambridge Analytica, a London firm, with offices in New York and Washington, DC. That data included all of the connections through Facebook to each of those users. All told, about 87 million Facebook users were affected. Naturally, only the 270,000 users had given any kind of permission. This meant that more than 86 million were entirely unaware that their data was being accessed by Cambridge Analytica.

In December 2015, *The Guardian* reported that tech firm, Cambridge Analytica had performed illicit harvesting of personal information from millions of Facebook accounts. Facebook founder, Mark Zuckerberg, later told the American Congress that Facebook had learned of the breach about the same time the world learned of it— December 2015.

By May 2017, *The Guardian* had linked Cambridge Analytica's illicit data harvesting to the Brexit campaign for Britain to leave the European Union. Carole Cadwalladr wrote an article tying Cambridge to the Brexit movement and the Donald Trump presidential campaign in America.

Big data apparently had been employed in to major campaigns—one in the United States and one in the United Kingdom. Some, however, still have their doubts about Cambridge's illicit data being used in the Trump campaign. Timothy Lee of Ars Technica wrote, quoting the *New York Times*, "Its data products were considered for Mr. Trump's critical get-out-the-vote operation. But tests showed Cambridge's data and models were slightly less effective than the existing Republican National Committee system, according to three former Trump campaign aides."

Lee added, "But the biggest problem for the theory that stolen Facebook data was the key to Trump's election is this: according to a March 2017 *Times* story, 'Cambridge executives now concede that the company never used psychographics in the Trump campaign.' Other reporting around the same time reached the same conclusion."

More recently, Mark Zuckerberg is in hot water with the American Congress for possible perjury. Emails have been discovered at Facebook that show Facebook execs knew about the breach far earlier than December 2015 (Weill & Poulsen).

In the early days of Facebook, Zuckerberg reportedly told a friend that he thought of his early users as "dumb f--ks" for trusting him with their private data (Durden). Zuckerberg admitted as much to the *New Yorker* in 2010 (Tate).

With flawed humans in charge of big data, it's difficult sometimes to know who is telling the truth and who to trust. The Cambridge Analytica scandal showed us people will want to use big data to influence large masses of people, and sometimes don't care how they get that data.

We've already seen how Hillary Clinton hoped to duplicate President Obama's success with big data, but Trump's big data approach, even if it didn't use the tainted data, was perhaps more effective. It helped him win the presidency.

In July 2019, Thomson Reuters reported for CBC that the Federal Trade Commission of the United States was expected to finalize a hefty fine for the social media giant. He wrote, "The settlement is expected to include government restrictions and oversight on how Facebook treats user privacy. It would mark the largest civil penalty ever paid to the FTC.

"Some in Congress have criticized the reported $5 billion US penalty, noting Facebook in 2018 had $55.8 billion US in revenue and $22.1 billion US in net income. Sen. Marsha Blackburn said last week the fine should be '$50 billion.'"

The Internet of Things (IoT)

The Internet of Things, frequently abbreviated "IoT," is a relatively new field in the realm of high tech. The first idea for it emerged in the early 1990s, but this new "creature" was not born until about 2008. Today, more and more manufacturers are considering the idea of embedded electronics in their products for connecting to the internet.

One of the earliest ideas involved what is called the "Smart Home." Imagine, for instance, a home that adjusts devices such as lights and air conditioning throughout the day depending on whether or not you're home. Sensors could tell when someone is in your yard. At night, the system could turn on lights inside the house, simulating that the house is not empty. During the day, the system could turn on the stereo and tune into one of your favorite stations, all to keep burglars from breaking in.

Your refrigerator could keep track of your essential food items, reminding you when you're low on certain items or even creating a shopping list for you. If you want to keep your electricity bill down, setting the air conditioning to turn on an hour before you get home could save on your bill, but make the house comfortable by the time you arrive. If all family members will be late arriving at home, a quick call to your home could temporarily change the time the cooling starts (for summer) or warming starts (for winter).

A doorbell connected to the internet could alert you when someone shows up at your front door. If you have a camera at your front door, an alert on your phone could show you who is attempting to reach you. A call to your home's intercom could give the visitor instructions—come back at a certain time, deliver the package to the neighbor at such-and-such an address, or any other message you might need to give.

Devices within the home could do self-diagnostics and report their status for possible need of repair or replacement parts.

Digitized healthcare in the home could be set-up to call the hospital in the event of a fall or other malady, particularly useful for the elderly.

One of the problems already being discussed involves the intentional obsolescence of devices. A smart device may require a subscription to keep it running properly or to keep it connected. But if a company decides to phase out a device, this could pose problems if the user depends on the device for their livelihood or if their safety might be jeopardized if the subscription is suddenly terminated through no fault of the user. The Electronic Frontier Foundation has studied problems like this and recommends to users that they should refuse to purchase software and electronics from manufacturers that put their own needs ahead of buyer's.

Streamlining the Theme Park Visit

Imagine an AI assistant that sits on your wrist like a watch. Only a few decades ago, comic strip detective Dick Tracy shocked the world with a bit of science fiction in his wristwatch radio communicator. Now, we have televisions that small, if you can stand to watch them. But now, consider this new device on your wrist which helps you navigate the world.

Kaiser Fung, in his book, *Numbers Rule Your World,* described how two Disney fanatics were able to catch all the rides and shows in under a blistering 13 hours—record time. They had used a touring plan designed by a computer programmer to find the shortest possible time between attractions. Now, imagine our wristwatch AI giving us similar instructions on the fly. Such an AI could take the place not only of an in-car navigator, but also act as an off-road tour guide and traveling encyclopedia. Such an AI watch, connected to the internet, could also do research on the fly, giving us as much or as little information as we might want about anything we encounter.

Reducing Commute Frustration

Fung points out that, in 2006, more than 10 million people suffered through more than an hour of commute time getting to work in the morning. The drain on the economy stacks up to 2.3 billion gallons of fuel wasted by idling in traffic. Traffic delays wasted an estimated $63 billion a year. And the complaints by drivers are the stuff of legend, or so you might think, listening to some of them. To help manage the problems with delays, many states in America have adopted an idea that helps to ameliorate the effect of those delays.

Fung starts with an example from the upper mid-West in the United States. "The Minnesota Department of Transportation (Mn/DOT) has championed an advanced technique called 'ramp metering.' Ramp meters are stop-go lights installed on highway entrances to regulate the inflow of traffic. 'One car per green' is the familiar mantra. Detectors measure the flow of traffic on the freeway; when the flow exceeds 3,900 vehicles per hour, the freeway is deemed 'full,' and the meters are turned on to hold back cars at the on-ramp. Another detector counts the backup on the ramp; when the backup threatens to spill over to the local area, the metering speed increases to dump traffic onto the freeway faster. According to an operations specialist with Mn/DOT, these controls temporarily delay the onset of congestion on the freeway.

"Ramp metering has compiled an impressive record of success in several metropolitan areas. For example, Seattle saw traffic volume swell by 74 percent even as average journey time was halved during peak hours. Not only were more trips completed, but also less time was spent per trip! So incredible was this double bonus that researchers at the University of California, Berkeley, called it 'the freeway congestion paradox.' Typically, as more vehicles pile onto the same stretch of highway, inducing congestion, we expect travel times to suffer; conversely, with traffic moving more slowly, the volume of vehicles should decline. Such laws of physics seem immutable. How does ramp metering make its magic?

"To unravel the paradox, we must first understand why the emergence of congestion is so feared. Statistical evidence has revealed that once traffic starts to pile up, the average speed of vehicles plunges, and oddly, the carrying capacity of the road degrades below its planned level. In one study, as average speed dropped from 60 to 15 miles per hour during peak hours, traffic flow dropped from 2,000 to 1,200 vehicles per hour. This disturbing situation seemed as illogical as if a restaurateur decided to lay off 40 percent of her staff during busy Friday nights, when one would have thought it crucial to run the kitchen at maximum efficiency. In response to the unsettling discovery, the Berkeley researchers recommended a policy of operating freeways at their optimal speeds, typically 50 to 70 miles per hour, for as much time as possible. In ramp metering, they found an ideal way to throttle the influx of vehicles, a means to maintain the condition of the highway just below congestion level. Its purpose is stamping out variability of traffic speed. The gain in terms of reduced travel time and increased traffic flow 'far exceeds any improvements that could be achieved by constructing more freeway lanes.'

"And there is more to ramp meters. They also mitigate the variability of travel time. Two effects are at play here. First, metering ramps regulate speed, which leads directly to more reliable journey times. Second, the rule stipulating one car per green light spaces out vehicles as they enter the highway, and this dramatically brings down accident rates. Fewer accidents mean less congestion and fewer unexpected slowdowns."

AI with machine learning can study the data from the various sensor inputs to become smarter about what actions produce the best effects in traffic overall. The fact that ramp metering outperforms the addition of new freeway lanes seems, at first glance, to be counterintuitive. This is part of what makes AI so useful; it can perform all manner of "what-if" tests to see which approach would produce the best results—long before any construction is begun.

PART 3
Analytics in Nature

"The 'prediction paradox': The more humility we have about our ability to make predictions, the more successful we can be in planning for the future."
—Nate Silver, *The Signal and the Noise: Why So Many Predictions Fail—but Some Don't*

Chapter 8
The Ways Mother Nature
Inspires AI

Why would a computer scientist ever read medical articles on the job? Perhaps because other fields can infuse new ideas and creativity into unrelated areas of intellectual interest.

This is not a new idea. In the 1978 television miniseries, *Connections,* hosted by James Burke, we learned how cross-pollination of ideas across unrelated fields could stimulate breakthroughs. One example of this involved a British inventor named Benjamin Huntsman who was looking for a better way to manufacture steel so that he could create better watch springs. He visited a glass factory and discovered that they used a special kind of clay which allowed their ovens to become hot enough to melt old glass. If Huntsman had looked down on glassmakers, he might never have made his discovery. By his humility and hunger to learn, he was willing to cast his net across a broader space and, by doing so, made discovery that much easier.

So, what can computer geeks learn from the field of medicine? For one thing, they can discover how brains work—how all those brain cells can store human memory and how the brain can make decisions based on past experience.

Computer scientists can also learn from how nerves can control muscle tissue. Such an understanding might help in the building of better, more responsive robots— coming closer to the androids of science fiction.

In this chapter, we will look at several ways that computer scientists have used nature to develop strategies for artificial intelligence. First, we will start with 5 ways that structures and behaviors in mother nature have inspired the development of various AI algorithms, discussed in some depth by Luke James in a blog article from January 2018.

- "**Artificial Neural Networks**—**Algorithm Type:** Predictive Modeling, **Biological Inspiration:** Cognitive Brain Function (Neurons), **Use-cases:** Sentiment Analysis, Image Recognition/Detection, Language Correction, Robotics

- "**Genetic Algorithms**—**Algorithm Type:** Search/Pathfinding, **Biological Inspiration:** Survival of the Fittest/ Evolution (Cell Reproduction), **Use-cases:** Data Mining/ Analytics, Robotics, Manufacturing/Design, Process Optimisation

- "**Swarm/Collective Intelligence**—**Algorithm Type:** Search/Pathfinding, **Biological Inspiration:** Ant Colonies/Schools of Fish/Flocks of Birds, **Use-cases:** Robotics, Video Game AI, Manufacturing, Route Planning

- "**Reinforcement Learning**—**Algorithm Type:** Predictive Modeling, **Biological Inspiration:** Classical Conditioning, **Use-cases:** Video Games, Controlling Autonomous Vehicles, Manufacturing Line Software, Financial Systems

- "**Artificial Immune Systems**—Algorithm Type: Predictive Modeling, **Biological Inspiration:** Immune Systems, **Use-cases:** Security Software, Autonomous Navigation Systems, Scheduling Systems, Fault Detection Software"

Let's take a closer look at each one of these.

Artificial Neural Networks

Here's where we get machine learning in perhaps the one AI algorithm most commonly known. This algorithm was inspired by actual brain function, mimicking dendrites and axons at the neuron level, as they transfer information to build an output through a sequence of "layers" that guesses what will happen. Each individual layer provides for us an additional stratum of "data representation" and gives us the ability to model the majority of the world's difficult problems.

Mr. James describes them this way, "Neural Networks are probably the most widely used Machine Learning algorithms and is the hottest trend in Data Science and Machine Learning to date. The concept initially came to fruition in 1958, known as the Perceptron, later refined by Geoffrey Hinton and popularised by companies such as Google and Facebook. Neural Networks can be used to solve a wide range of problem types including Natural Language Processing, and Visual recognition. This supervised learning algorithm can support both Regression and Classification problems and examples of its use can be found in regular consumer products including smartphones, and connected home devices."

Genetic Algorithms

Of all the AI algorithms, this one is perhaps the most "selfish." Here, such "survival of the fittest" attitude isn't bad at all. This evolution-like stance makes the algorithm look for better and better ways to do things. James says that such algorithms take this type of "approach among a series of individuals over consecutive generations in order to solve a search problem. Each generation contains a population of strings that mimic chromosomes that we see in our DNA. Each individual within a population represents a point within the search space, therefore each is a possible candidate solution. In order to improve the population of solutions, we put the individuals through a process of evolution."

- Within a population, each entity will fight for mates and resources.
- Usually, the most successful entities in each contest will have more offspring than the more lackluster entities.
- Genetic material from successful entities will transmit throughout a population. Strong and effective parents will typically lead to progeny with potential greater than that of the parents.

Swarm/Collective Intelligence

When attempting to find the best path to a destination, having an army of helpers look through all the nooks and crannies can prove quite helpful. Perhaps the two most common algorithms for achieving this are Particle Swarm Optimization and Ant Colony Optimization. These fit within the concept called "collective intelligence."

In the simplest form, this type of algorithm utilizes numerous agents. Each agent acts with a very simplistic behavior. Together, the combined set of actions becomes complex. The agents are not like soldiers in parade, but each acts independently of the others, effectively dividing the labor amongst them for reaching a solution to the problem.

James explains the two flavors of swarm algorithm: "Ant Colony Optimisation (ACO) is very different to

Particle Swarm Optimisation (PSO). Both aim to achieve emergent behaviour but go about it in two different ways. Like real ant colonies, ACO utilises a pheromone scent to guide individual agents onto the shortest path. Initially, a random pheromone is initialised across the problem space. Individual agents will begin to traverse the search space, dropping pheromone scent as they go. Throughout each time-step, the pheromone will decay at a defined rate. Single Agents make their decisions based on the strength of pheromone scent in front of them in order to traverse the search space. The stronger the scent in a particular direction, the more likely it is to travel that way. The bestknown solution will end up being the one with the strongest pheromone scent.

"PSO looks more to the overall direction of the pack. A number of single agents are initialised and they begin in random directions. At each time step, each agent needs to make a decision on whether or not to change direction. The decision will be based on the direction of the best-known solution (known as pbest/global best), the direction of the best nearest neighbour (local best), and the current direction of travel. Example of Ant Colony Optimisation—a type of collective intelligence algorithm. The new direction of travel is typically a good 'compromise' of all these values."

Reinforcement Learning

Have you ever heard of Pavlov's dogs? Ivan Pavlov was a Russian psychologist who, in the 1890s, noticed that dogs would salivate when they anticipated being fed. Through a form of psychological conditioning or classical conditioning, he was able to stimulate in the dogs the same response from some other trigger, like ringing a bell. This conditioning is achieved through something called "Reinforcement Learning" (RL).

In a computer, an RL agent that does something considered good, it receives a reward. What kind of "good?" Anything that moves the software closer to finishing a required task. What kind of reward? It doesn't take much to keep these electronic agents happy. It might be something as simple as a number added to a register. The computer code may tell the agent to maximize the number it receives at each step it takes toward the goal of completing the task. James states, "The application of raw inputs into the algorithm allows the agent to develop its own sense of the problem, and how to solve it in the most efficient manner."

Quite often, we will find RL computer code routines combined with other technologies of the machine learning type. A common example of this is RL algorithms combined with those of neural networks—our first category of algorithms, above. Such combinations are sometimes called "deep reinforcement learning." James explains how this works, "Neural Networks are often used to estimate the reward given to an RL agent when it makes a particular decision. Deep Mind, now a Google company, has made great progress within this space, using a Deep Q Learning approach to tacking [tackling?] more generic problems (such as the ability for one algorithm to play an entire library of Atari games, unassisted and beat the World Champion itself at the game 'Go'. They are now adapting this approach to be able to tackle more complex games such as Starcraft II."

Artificial Immune Systems

This last example is patterned after the body's immune system—a strategy within the biological body to protect against invading pathogenic life forms and toxins. It does this by stimulating what is called a "immune response."

Inspired by immunology theory and empirical immune functions, artificial immune systems (AIS) are self-modifying structures that are put to work solving problems. There are a number of AIS algorithms. Some of them include Artificial Immune Recognition, Clonal Selection, Dendritic Cell and Negative Selection.

James describes AIS this way: "Like the biological immune system, AIS is able to categorise all 'cell's within a system as 'self' or 'non-self' cells. A distributed task force of intelligence is used to take action upon all cells. The two most important types of cells involved in immunisation are B-cells and T-cells (white blood cells to you and me). T-cells come in three types; one type to activate B-cells, one type to bind to and destroy foreign invaders and a final type to suppress auto-immune issues. B-cells are responsible for producing antibodies which are specific proteins that bind to an antigen—a toxic/ foreign substance. Artificial Immune Systems are often used to defend against cyber attacks by monitoring intrusion detection and are often integrated into enterprise-grade software. Unlike the other algorithms mentioned in this article, free online learning material on this subject is very limited and is likely the least-developed."

As we can see, a great deal of work in the bio-logical and behavioral sciences has been put to work making computers smarter.

Looking at Humanity's Behavior as Clues to Governing AI Development

Aristotle once commented on collective or societal intelligence, "A feast to which many contribute is better than a dinner provided out of a single purse."

Andrew Robinson, an expert in communication science, delivered a presentation on "Artificial Intelligence and Nature," at the Australian Museum in Sydney. He stated, "It appears, for example, in the 17th century, in Thomas Hobbes's book, *Laviathan*. It's this idea that individual intelligence is simply the distributed knowledge of a larger entity; that our brains are nothing but the nodes of a larger brain, a superorganism, a hive mind. The devices worn by the Borgs of *Star Trek* are examples of collective intelligence technology. Uber would be a good example of this in the real world."

Robinson pointed out that the largest example of such "collective intelligence" is, today, the internet itself —billions of minds connected at one time. He also points to another quote by Aristotle, this time surprisingly implying the benefits of robot technology and AI: "There is one condition where managers wouldn't need subordinates: Instruments doing own work by intelligent anticipation." This, Robinson describes as a "thinking machine," first named by Alan Turing (1912–1954), an early innovator in computers and computer science.

Continuing on this topic, Robinson added, "Each wave of tech innovation—from ships to trains to telegraphs—have allowed many more people to collect and interpret vast amounts of data. In the last decade, these two different forms of AI—'collective intel' and 'thinking machines'—have started to converge and feed off each other; and I think we'll see that the latest developments in AI and Citizen Science include a combination of collective intelligence and thinking machines. Indeed, it looks like this process will start happening more and more on its own. Thinking machines will ask their own questions, get their own answers and act upon them..."

Robinson looked at the first example of computers being used for evil: "The first example is relatively well known. As the historian Edwin Black has written in an exhaustive book on the subject, Hitler couldn't have carried out the genocides of WWII without this 'thinking machine' here—the Hollerith machine and the punch cards that many of us are familiar with. They were great at gathering, recording, storing, analysing large amounts of data—and they were seemingly benign. It's just data, right? But artificial intelligence, in the wrong hands, can become very dangerous. Especially when the data it collects is not owned and controlled by the people it's collected from."

Humans were borne out of Mother Nature. Their behavior can help us understand better ways to build artificial intelligence so that we end up with something of which we can be happy.

Robinson offered some suggestions we should consider as we continue to build our AI projects.

"The first—perhaps an overriding principle—is to put as much effort into developing a human under-standing of nature as in developing AI. **Celebrate and incentivise the human mind.** Both its desire to learn and its desire to teach.

"Another principle is about **data ownership and agency.** When I look around at the terms and conditions of large data collection apps in the field of biodiversity, I find it strange that AI isn't mentioned. The options need to be very clear. *The data is yours. Here are some different ways you can share it*—and what the implications of that might be. Again, gaming mechanics have a lot to teach us here."

Beyond these two principles, Robinson explores several problems amongst humans that need to be addressed.

"**Data Bias**—there's a great book called *Weapons of Math Destruction* by Cathy O'Neil on this topic. Big Data is really hard to keep clean—or to even *start* clean. A recent paper by Julian Troudet in *Scientific Reports,* for example, points out some interesting—albeit unsurprising —biases and species gaps in the GBIF data [Global Biodiversity Information Facility—an internet aggregation of data about our world's wealth of life forms].

"But just as there will always be species gaps, there are also *people* gaps. Citizen Science is by far the largest contributor to GBIF data, and yet it's but a tiny fraction of all the offline knowledge about biodiversity that exists in the world. This results in **Group Bias**— which means AI projects need to involve a greater variety of expertise—anthropologists, historians, poets—from a more diverse set of people around the world.

"And then there's **Individual Bias**—we have a tendency to trust machines, especially if we think they're smarter than us. Cognitive bias is well documented in the works of the behavioural economists Daniel Kahneman and Amos Tversky—but a whole new set of bias is being discovered about our relationship with thinking machines (in fact, we may even tend to deify them).

"There's the **Importance of outliers.** This one's tricky, but again, collective intelligence systems have ways to tackle this. (This presentation is an example of an outlier; its neglect a possible example of a poorly designed network).

"And finally, **Transparency,** which is probably the biggest challenge. Because even if you design technologies that achieve all of the above, it's difficult to convince people to trust them. Again, I think gaming systems have a lot to teach us here."

Robinson suggests that we stop making excuses by pleading ignorance, as Facebook and Google do all the time. Not only do we need to work together throughout all of humanity, but we also need to have a greater appreciation of biodiversity, as well as strengthening our bond to life as a whole.

Chapter 9
Artificial Intelligence vs.
Natural Intelligence

Alan Turing (1912–1954), was a British computer scientist and World War II code breaker. Today, he is perhaps best known for the Turing Test—a challenge for any computer to give answers or replies that sound convincingly human. After the war with Germany and Italy, Turing set about exploring the possibilities with computers and attempted to create a computer program that could play chess. In 1952, Turing attempted to implement his chess program on the first commercially available computer—the Ferranti Mark 1. Sadly, the hardware lacked enough power to execute the program. Instead, Turing put the algorithm on printed pages and played for the computer by flipping through the algorithm. Obviously, the process was quite tedious, each algorithm step taking roughly thirty minutes each.

By the late 1980s, computers playing chess were able to beat some of the strongest human opponents. And in 1997, a highly-publicized game was held between Deep Blue, an IBM computer, and Russian chess grandmaster Garry Kasparov. Deep Blue won, though some felt that conditions of the match might have favored the computer unfairly.

Computers today have immense advantages over humans. The silicon-based "brain" is capable of playing hundreds of chess games in a second. It can keep track of all possible moves and assess the likelihood of winning from each new "what-if." But intelligence is more than merely chess games.

In 2018, mathematician Roger Penrose and philosopher Emanuele Severino held a discussion entitled, "Artificial intelligence vs. Natural intelligence. Who will win?" (Newsroom) These two masters of human thought, dug deep into the topic of intelligence to help us understand what the future might bring—both from a philosophical standpoint and one that is profoundly practical.

Austro-Canadian, Hans Moravec is a lecturer at Carnegie Mellon University's Robotic Institute and a renowned futurist. In 1988, Moravec made a prediction that by 2030, humanity will have achieved in computers the milestone of "human equivalence." This is the threshold where an artificial mind attains a level of power and complexity equivalent to that of the natural or human mind. But that event is only a point, for Moravec expects that the artificial intelligence will very quickly surpass humans in capability.

In the article about the Penrose-Severino meeting, the writer proclaims, "Thirty years after publication of the influential work of Moravec, there are few who believe that on the basis of the accelerating power of calculation even of domestic appliances and the enormous mass of data present on the social networks, data processable in real time by these machines, the convergence point is not really so close."

On May 12, 2018, Penrose and Severino sat in Milan, Italy, in front of an audience of 800-plus, a youthful gathering of people curious to know more. Should they fear artificial intelligence? Can it validly be called "intelligence?"

Roger Penrose is considered a heavyweight when it comes to science and logic. He is a professor emeritus of Oxford University. He holds some significant sway in the fields of cosmology, physics and mathematics.

As one of the world's leading mathematicians, Sir Roger Penrose declared, "technological acceleration, evolution of machine learning, Big Data and algorithms are not enough to declare the triumph of artificial intelligence over natural or human intelligence." Penrose was a former teacher of world-renowned physicist Stephen Hawking, and later a colleague, with whom he collaborated on some very well known hypotheses concerning singularities. From his own experience, Penrose felt it necessary that we look at our question of AI versus natural intelligence from a different perspective.

As a basis for his new perspective, Penrose depends on a certain understanding of Gödel's theorems to find "intelligent machines" to be an impossibility. More than that, he points to the fact that our quest for understanding is physical in nature.

"Our mind, the human mind", says Penrose, "is not algorithmic in the processes that it performs. We still know little about these processes, but what we do know is that we cannot interpret them in terms of rigid schemes." He went on to say that this forecasted point of "human equivalence is not only remote but might not arrive or will not arrive in the terms in which we imagine it". But, above all, "what we call Artificial Intelligence is not real intelligence. Only human intelligence is the real thing."

Penrose characterizes the term "artificial intelligence" to be an abuse which is more than linguistic. According to him, the term "is misleading and not without social implications and consequences. The problem lies entirely here."

The article writer summarized Penrose's thinking this way: "Assimilating extremely complex processes, still largely unknown, like those that define conscience, awareness and consequently intelligence that is actually human, we fall into the trap of reductionism. Likewise negating space (of social recognition) for creativity and innovation."

Of course, we can see this reductionism in the simplistic mimicry of AI algorithms like those we saw in the last chapter (Artificial Neural Networks, Genetic Algorithms, Swarm/Collective Intelligence, Reinforcement Learning and Artificial Immune Systems). Like refined sugar and wheat in today's "modern" foods, has something essential been stripped out. Natural vitamin manufacturers have discovered that certain nutrients help the body absorb vitamins. The big pharmaceutical companies merely pump out the one molecule central to the formulation of a vitamin, leaving out all the good stuff that makes the vitamin into "food" instead of merely a petrochemical monstrosity that the body largely rejects.

Is the research into AI missing some concept that evolution figured out long ago? Is there a conceptual "nutrient" that current AI research is ignoring or about which it is remaining entirely ignorant?

Emanuele Severino has developed quite a reputation as a theoretical philosopher, attracting attention from philosophers in the English-speaking world. His recent work, *The Essence of Nihilism* (Verso, 2016) is but one example. Instead of Penrose's "possibilities," Severino placed his attention more squarely on consequences.

The article's writer described the philosopher's viewpoint this way: "Severino recalled how everything arises from a conceptual framework which can be traced to the concept of 'production' (in Greek: *poiesis)* or to use the words of Plato. 'The West is moving along this path: *poiesis* is the cause that makes everything pass from non-existence to existence.' So for Severino the question is to interpret within long term philosophical categories. The same categories that determine not only our view of the world, but the idea itself that 'the world, and therefore man, and therefore intelligence, can be entirely manipulated.'"

Let us look at the notion that natural intelligence can only be described in light of conscience and its various qualities, plus, as Roger Penrose, "qualities of awareness." From this viewpoint, Severino concluded, "awareness is the field which artificial intelligence cannot reach and the production of awareness becomes the crucial question of our time."

Roger Penrose concluded by stating that our innovations in the digital and social realms "arise precisely from this element: from the unfathomable and unreproducible human awareness." In other words, "there will always be room for man, even in the world of machines."

Intelligence Advantages

A Russian software developer named Dennis Gorelik, now living in the United States, formed his own analysis of "Computer Intelligence versus Human Intelligence." In part of that analysis, he created a table comparing various features of intelligence, who has the advantage, followed by comments about the comparison. This reveals the current state of AI intelligence compared to that of humans.

The table takes the form of: **Feature** [advantage]— Comments. The following is quoted directly from his table.

- "**Experimental learning** [Human]—Currently computers are not able to general experimenting. Computers are able to make some specific (narrow) experimentation though.
- "**Direct gathering information** [Computer]—Modern computers are very strong in gathering information. Search engines and particularly Google is the best example.
- "**Decision making ability to achieve goals** [Human] —Currently computers are not able to make good decisions in "general" environment.
- "**Hardware processing power** [Computer]—Processing power of modern computers is tremendous (several billion operations per second).
- "**Hardware memory storage** [Computer]—HDD memory storage of modern computers is huge.
- "**Information retrieval speed** [Computer]—Data retrieval speed of modern computers is ~1000 times faster that human's ability. Examples of high-speed data retrieval systems: RDBMS, Google.
- "**Information retrieval depths** [It's not clear]—Both humans and computers have limited ability in "deep" informational retrieval.
- "**Information breadth** [Computer]—Practically every internet search engine beats human's in the breadth of stored and available information.
- "**Information retrieval relevancy** [Human]—Usually human's brain retrieves more relevant information

than computer program. But advantage of humans disappears every year.

- **"Ability to find and establish correlation between concepts** [Human]—Currently computers are not able to establish correlation between general concepts.
- **"Ability to derive concepts from other concepts** [Human]—Usually computers are not able to derive concepts from other concepts.
- **"Consistent system of super goals** [Human]— Humans have highly developed system of super goals ("avoid pain", "avoid hunger", sexuality, "desire to talk"...). Super goals implementation in modern computers is very limited."

One breakthrough could tip the scales in the direction of computers. But as we saw in the last section, this tipping point may prove to be a fantasy, according to those two very intelligent men—one a physicist and mathematician, the other an acclaimed philosopher. Next, we'll look at a different kind of possible limitation for AI compared to human intelligence.

Depth of Innovation and Limitations to AI

Nick Jankel, writing for Huffpost, put forth the idea that computers will never create disruptive innovations. The restrictive, mechanical algorithms will never be able to create that bolt-out-of-the-blue idea that changes the world. He thinks that the biology of our human brains has some special ingredient that computing machines will never have.

He pointed out that our perception of human intelligence has always been constrained by what he called the "metaphor of the day." To the ancients of the classical world, they saw the mind in terms of something they called "humors." Rene Descartes, who stated the profound wisdom, "I think, therefore I am," and other early modern Christians looked at our human minds as something without form, perhaps a spiritual extension of God. In the Age of Reason and throughout the Industrial Revolution and into our modern age, the mind was first thought of in mechanical terms—like a steam engine, a telephone system and now a computer network.

"Yet the computer metaphor ignores perhaps the most species-defining characteristic of human beings: That we can create things; and we can do so consciously. Not only can we create concepts, business models and ideas; every single human cell can create itself! Yet no machine, no matter how flashy, has ever been able to do this. No scientific theory has fully explained how life creates itself; and where this creativity comes from. Great scientists like Erwin Schrödinger have expressed profound curiosity about how life can buck the great laws of physics, notably that of entropy, the 2nd law of thermodynamics.

"Mainstream science claims that the universe works according to fixed rules, discovered by Newton, Faraday and Maxwell. This is the universe as machine. Yet here is the doozy: Whilst our most advanced machines, algorithms, make complex calculations according to a series of rules, disruptive innovators and genius creatives—the kind that birth new business models like AirBnB and new forms of art like *Guernica*—break the rules. And we can all enjoy this kinds of rule-defying breakthroughs every time we conquer habit and speak to our lover in a new way; or break free of the past by following a new passion."

What Jankel seems to miss is that many of the primary algorithmic patterns of artificial intelligence, today, are derived directly from the patterns of nature. But he may be on to something. Perhaps he did not look far enough in his analysis of the limitations of AI. We'll take a closer look at this possible limitation to AI in the Afterword.

PART 4
How to Use Analytics

"Knowing is not enough; we must act."
—Johann Wolfgang von Goethe

Chapter 10
Why Data Analytics
is the Best Career Move

Companies, and even governments, are hungry to open their eyes on multiple wavelengths. Being able to see the data landscape clearly means the difference between success and failure. Walking blindly into the future is pretty scary for both individual and corporation. Imagine how hungry a corporation is when they realize what that extra vision could do for them. Imagine how much they would pay for an expert to help them see that landscape with crystal clarity.

In a blog post by Sudhaa Gopinath we discover ten more juicy reasons "Why Big Data Analytics is the Best Career Move." Here's a quick overview of his list, followed by a more, in-depth look at each item.

- "Soaring demand for analytics professionals,
- "Huge job opportunities & meeting the skill gap,
- "Salary aspects,
- "Big data analytics: a top priority in a lot of organizations,
- "Adoption of big data analytics is growing,
- "Analytics: a key factor in decision making,

- "The rise of unstructured and semi-structured data analytics,
- "Big data analytics is used everywhere,
- "Surpassing market forecast / predictions for big data analytics,
- "Numerous choices in job titles and type of analytics."

Soaring Demand for Analytics Professionals

According to research results posted at Indeed.com, job postings for Big Data Analytics between 2012 and mid-2016 rose by nearly 400%. Job opportunities in the field have been on a steady climb. And it's easy to understand why. Senior executive at Accenture Institute for High Performance, Jeanne Harris, explained that "...data is useless without the skill to analyze it."

Writing his article in December 2018, Gopinath stated, "There are more job opportunities in Big Data management and Analytics than there were last year and many IT professionals are prepared to invest time and money for the training."

Fractal Analytics is a high-tech service provider with offices in the United States and in India. Co-founder and CEO, Srikanth Velamakanni talked about the on-going need for qualified data professionals. "In the next few years, the size of the analytics market will evolve to at least one-thirds of the global IT market from the current one-tenths."

Those companies that get it right with their handling of big data are outpacing their competition. Because of this, the ones left behind are scrambling to catch up by increasing their demand for new ways to exploit their own big data. As more and more businesses implement big data analytics, the demand will continue to grow.

Another industry survey by QuinStreet, Inc. reaffirmed the upward trend in this job category proving that big data analytics is already considered by American businesses to be a high priority. Most American companies have either started to add this capability or have plans for implement big data analytics over the next couple of years.

Huge job opportunities
& meeting the skill gap

Gopinath described the other side of the supply-and-demand chain. "The demand for Analytics skill is going up steadily but there is a huge deficit on the supply side. This is happening globally and is not restricted to any part of geography. In spite of Big Data Analytics being a 'Hot' job, there is still a large number of unfilled jobs across the globe due to shortage of required skill. A McKinsey Global Institute study states that the US will face a shortage of about 190,000 data scientists and 1.5 million managers and analysts who can understand and make decisions using Big Data by 2018."

According to Gopinath, the largest concentration of data analytics talent in the world currently resides in India. Part of the reason for this is that corporations worldwide are continuing to outsource much of their IT work, and India is struggling to keep up with this demand for talent.

Velamakanni points out that the two key deficits in data talent are data scientists—those who can do the analytics—and analytics consultants—those who can interpret the data and use it for the benefit of the corporation or client. Gopinath points out that, of the two, data scientist is the job title most in demand.

Salary aspects

Wages for qualified big data professionals are looking good for those with the proper skill set. The United Kingdom and Australia are amongst the nations seeing what some call a "Moolah Marathon."

On the salary issue, Gopinath elaborates, "According to the 2015 Skills and Salary Survey Report published by the Institute of Analytics Professionals of Australia (IAPA), the annual median salary for data analysts is $130,000, up four per cent from last year. Continuing the trend set in 2013 and 2014, the median respondent earns 184% of the Australian full-time median salary. The rising demand for analytics professionals is also reflected in IAPA's membership, which has grown to more than 5000 members in Australia since its formation in 2006."

In India, for instance, big data analytics professionals enjoyed pay hikes that averaged 50% more than that experienced by other IT specialists. From 2014 to 2015, analytics professionals received an average salary boost of 21%, according to a report by Great Lakes Institute of Management.

A similar trend is seen in the UK. Gopinath explains, "A look at the salary trend for Big Data Analytics in the UK also indicates a positive and exponential growth. A quick search on Itjobswatch.co.uk shows a median salary of £62,500 in early 2016 for Big Data Analytics jobs, as compared to £55,000 in the same period in 2015. Also, a year-on-year median salary change of +13.63% is observed."

Big data analytics: a top priority in a lot of organizations

In a survey conducted by Peer Research, corporations made it clear that big data analytics was a leading priority for them. They were certain that their enterprise performed better because of their use of big data analytics. Gopinath described the survey results, "Based on the responses, it was found that approximately 45% of the surveyed believe that Big Data analytics will enable much more precise business insights, 38% are looking to use Analytics to recognize sales and market opportunities. More than 60% of the respondents are depending on Big Data Analytics to boost the organization's social media marketing abilities. The QuinStreet research based on their survey also back the fact that Analytics is the need of the hour, where 77% of the respondents consider Big Data Analytics a top priority."

On the subject of technology in the mid-market, another survey by Deloitte shows that the value of analytics is obvious to company executives. A sizable majority—65.2% of those who responded—acknowledged their own company's use of analytics in forwarding their business goals.

Adoption of big data analytics is growing

Developers are never satisfied with today's new technologies. Improvements continue to be made in analytics software. The level of sophistication being performed continues to show progress, while the operation of such software is becoming increasingly easy to use. Not only that, the software continues to improve in its ability to handle larger and larger batches of ever more varied datasets. More than one third of respondents to another survey state they now make use of some kind of advanced big data analytics on things like data mining tasks, predictive analytics and business intelligence. This is according to a report by The Data Warehousing Institute (TDWI).

On the broad adoption of analytics, Gopinath elaborates, "With Big Data Analytics providing an edge over the competition, the rate of implementation of the necessary Analytics tools has increased exponentially. In fact, most of the respondents of the 'Peer Research—Big Data Analytics' survey reported that they already have a strategy setup for dealing with Big Data Analytics. And those who are yet to come up with a strategy are also in the process of planning for it."

One popular platform for the creation of analytic tools has been Apache's Hadoop framework. Gopinath explains how more corporations are moving in that direction. "When it comes to Big Data Analytics tools, the adoption of Apache Hadoop framework continues to be the popular choice. There are various commercial and open-source frameworks to choose from and organizations are making the appropriate choice based on their requirement. Over half of the respondents have already deployed or are currently implementing a Hadoop distribution. Out of them, a quarter of the respondents have deployed open-source framework, which is twice the number of organizations that have deployed a commercial distribution of the Hadoop framework."

Analytics: a key factor in decision making

Another dimension to the push for big data analytics involves the fact that this capability remains a key part of corporate decision making. Gopinath explains, "Analytics is a key competitive resource for many companies. There is no doubt about that. According to the 'Analytics Advantage' survey overseen by Tom Davenport, 96% of respondents feel that analytics will become more important to their organizations in the next three years. This is because there is a huge amount of data that is not being used and at this point, only rudimentary analytics is being done. About forty nine percent of the respondents strongly believe that analytics is a key factor in better decision-making capabilities. Another sixteen percent like it for its superior key strategic initiatives."

Big data analytics delivers a great many benefits for businesses. If any one benefit were to win the title of "Greatest," the two most prominent are that this capability,

- Drives business strategy, and
- Boosts business decision effectiveness.

In the Peer-Research Big Data Analytics survey, 74% of those who responded affirmed that big data analytics makes vital information available so that essential business decisions can be made in an effective and timely manner. They also agreed that this capability adds great value to their business.

Such business decisions are the steering mechanism by which an enterprise navigates the waters of market dominance. Anything that makes those decisions more potent, accurate and effective is going to be highly desirable. And such decisions will always be with businesses. This means that the value of big data analytics is virtually forever.

The rise of unstructured and semi-structured data analytics

So much information in the world is not in neat, tidy tables like a relational database. Such unstructured and semi-structured data is a virtual bonanza for the companies that can wrestle them under control. According to the Peer Research Big Data Analytics survey, the specialized subfield of semi-structured and unstructured data analytics has been booming. Of those that responded to the survey, 84% noted that their business is now working with and analyzing social media, emails, weblogs, photos, video and other unstructured data sources. All of the remaining survey respondents made it clear that their companies had already moved toward implementing such capabilities within the next year and a half.

Big data analytics is used everywhere

Because of the wide range of useful features found in big data analytics, and their ease of implementation, this capability has enjoyed incredible growth across a wide range of markets and industry domains. Medium and large companies have accepted the big data analytics challenge virtually unanimously. And many small companies have joined in the analytics surge, as well.

Surpassing market forecast / predictions for big data analytics

In a survey conducted by Nimbus Ninety, big data analytics came in at the top of a list of "most disruptive technologies that will have the biggest influence in three years' time." And there are other forecasts of the business world that corroborate their findings, as Gopinath listed,

- "According to IDC, the Big Data Analytics market will reach $125 billion worldwide in 2015.
- "IIA states that Big Data Analytics tools will be the first line of defense, combining machine learning, text mining and ontology modeling to provide holistic and integrated security threat prediction, detection, and deterrence and prevention programs.

- "According to the survey 'The Future of Big Data Analytics – Global Market and Technologies Forecast – 2015-2020', Big Data Analytics Global Market will grow by 14.4% CAGR over this period.
- "The Big Data Analytics Global Market for Apps and Analytics Technology will grow by 28.2% CAGR, for Cloud Technology will grow by 16.1% CAGR, for Computing Technology will grow by 7.1% CAGR, for NoSQL Technology will grow by 18.9% CAGR over the entire 2015-2020 period."

Numerous choices in job titles and type of analytics

Big data analytics is one of those talents that can be applied to just about any business model or any industry. The job market for big data analytics is rich with possibilities. Job titles can include any of the following or more:

- Business Intelligence and Analytics Consultant
- Big Data Analyst
- Analytics Associate
- Metrics and Analytics Specialist
- Big Data Engineer
- Big Data Analytics Business Consultant
- Big Data Analytics Architect
- Big Data Solution Architect

Besides all the rich possibilities for job titles in industries as diverse as car manufacturing and software engineering to perfume makers and high-end fashion, there are three kinds of data analytics, which of course depend on the type of environment.

- Prescriptive Analytics
- Predictive Analytics
- Descriptive Analytics.

A countless number of companies are engaged with big data analytics, including Alteryx, Ayata, Bluefin Labs, Centrofuge, Datameer, Domo, FICO, GoodData, IBM, ITrend, Jaspersoft, Karmasphere, Microsoft, Opera, Oracle, Panaroma Software, Pentaho, Platfora, Quid, Saffron, Teradata, TIBCO, Tracx, and many more. The opportunities with companies like these are virtually limitless.

Summing it Up

No matter how good the software is, or how easy it is to use, there will always be the need for a human to look over the results to ensure all outcomes are reasonable. When dealing with the wild and wooly world of big data, software engineers cannot always anticipate every problem. Quite often, it takes an expert to see problems that others will miss. A software tool may need to be run again, with parameters tweaked slightly to avoid problems that are obvious to the big data analytics expert. Such an expert will know the strengths and weaknesses of big data analytics, and knowing their own business will understand more clearly how the insights revealed by the analytics are relevant or not. As Gopinath remarked, "A professional with the Analytical skills can master the ocean of Big Data and become a vital asset to an organization, boosting the business and their career."

Chapter 11
How Can You Use Data Analytics in Your Job?

There's no question that data analytics is a vital part of any successful business. Any company that doesn't measure which products sell the best is walking blindly around the marketplace selling by accident. Any company that operates with that aloof an attitude toward measurement and analyzing the data is not long for this world.

But even if we're convinced that data analytics is important, we need to have the right attitude about the topic so we can make the best use of what we have and make the most of our efforts.

Finding the Right Mindset

Analytics don't mean anything if you don't have the right context—if you can't measure something to know if you're doing any better than yesterday.

Understanding the basics is the first important step to using data analytics in your daily job.

Douglas Hubbard, in his book, *How to Measure Anything*, makes it clear that anything that can be observed can be measured. We may not feel as certain about our measurement of say, the productivity of research, as we are about the current number of employees. The former may be measured by some admittedly "fuzzy" metrics, whereas the number of employees is a precise and unequivocal number.

Some people will stare at a challenge, dumbfounded and lost. They will reject the idea that some intangible property could ever be measured. At the same time, an admittedly rare type of individual will look at the same problem and methodically set out to establish a workable plan to do what others said was impossible. Hubbard starts his book with the notion that we all learn this skill with the proper set of examples—people doing the so-called "impossible." And sometimes it's not entirely about intelligence. Quite often, it's more about having the right attitude that says, "Okay, show me," not with a defensive huff that dares someone else to prove them wrong, but with the humble hunger to learn something new.

One example Hubbard uses comes from Enrico Fermi's observations at the first test of a nuclear bomb blast in New Mexico, 1945. While others busied themselves with final calibrations of intricate equipment, Fermi tore a piece of paper into tiny pieces of roughly equal sized confetti. When the blast wave finally made its way to base camp, where he and the other scientists had been stationed, Fermi let the pieces of paper slip from his hand into the wind. By looking at how far the farthest pieces were blown, he was able to estimate that the strength of the explosion was more than 10 kilotons of

TNT. His rough estimate proved to be amazingly accurate. The scientific instruments pegged the blast at 18.6 kilotons.

Fermi was such a master at figuring things out, he frequently challenged his students to think like he did. The questions he asked invariably had his charges scratching their heads, proclaiming the problem too difficult to solve.

One famous Fermi question involved the number of piano tuners in the city of Chicago.

Hubbard explained it this way: "His students—science and engineering majors—would begin by saying that they could not possibly know anything about such a quantity. Of course, some solutions would be to simply do a count of every piano tuner perhaps by looking up advertisements, checking with a licensing agency of some sort, and so on. But Fermi was trying to teach his students how to solve problems where the ability to confirm the results would not be so easy. He wanted them to figure out that they knew something about the quantity in question.

"He would start by asking them to estimate other things about pianos and piano tuners that, while still uncertain, might seem easier to estimate. These included the current population of Chicago (a little over 3 million in the 1930s to 1950s), the average number of people per household (2 or 3), the share of households with regularly tuned pianos (not more than 1 in 10 but not less than 1 in 30), the required frequency of tuning (perhaps 1 a year, on average), how many pianos a tuner could tune in a day (4 or 5, including travel time), and how many days a year the [tuner] works (say, 250 or so)."

The key, here, is realizing that we can always find out a great many of the little details that go into solving a problem. We merely have to stand back and ask our-

selves, "What do I know about this problem?" and
"What do I need to know?" Perhaps, we might even ask,
"What would a solution look like and how do I get
there?"

Hubbard points out that, in business, managers
are frequently overwhelmed into inaction by the apparent
insolvability of a problem. Sometimes, a solution may be
possible, but it will take an inordinate amount of money
to pull it off, so they do nothing. They never realize that a
rough, ballpark answer that costs thirty minutes of their
time is far, far better than no answer at all. Sometimes,
such a rough answer is nearly as good as the one that
would have cost several million dollars.

Too many people put "measurement" on a pedestal,
making it unachievable in many instances. But if we
change our attitude and loosen our belts a little, we see
that a rough measure has far more value than no
measure at all. In business, the ability to make a fairly
good educated guess can mean the difference between
taking advantage of a once-in-a-lifetime opportunity and
watching the competition steal the show with that lost
opportunity.

Such an ability can also be used with risk. We
might ask ourselves, "What's the worst that could
happen if we go after this opportunity and it fails?" And
ask, "What would happen if we don't take a chance with
this opportunity?" Look at what we know about each
question. There are some reasonable ranges for each of
the variables. Simple arithmetic allows us to find a range
of numbers that describe the potential value gained and
the potential risk. When we can do this, we can know
whether or not the risk is scary or pitifully small. And
think how silly it is to miss a golden opportunity when

the risk is close to nothing. Such imprecise methods of "measurement" allow for smart decisions.

One key barrier to good estimates is sloppy wording. An ambiguous problem is a problem that cannot be solved. Imagine an employee running into our office, panting breathlessly, pausing to recover and then blurting out, "Something's wrong!"

Naturally, we need to ask, "What do you mean?" But even then, the employee may say something that does not reveal the real problem, why it's important or even urgent. We need concrete specifics—not vague generalities.

When a patient comes into a doctor, they may say, "I don't feel good." Such a statement requires a mind reader, if that's all the information the doctor receives. How can the doctor help if they don't know the symptoms, where it hurts, or what exactly the feeling is?

Methods of measurement can be equally problematic if a person merely throws up their hands and declares it impossible. Let's look at a pretty wild example, like beauty. How do you measure it? Certainly not by pulling out a yard stick or a weighing scale. So, what's the solution?

This is actually quite simple.

Let us say that we're in charge of marketing and we want a beautiful face for representing our product in the marketplace. Let us say we've already determined that the greater the beauty the greater the marketing boost. How do we determine beauty? There's an old saying that "beauty is in the eye of the beholder." The frustrated manager will be stuck on the notion of measuring eyeballs or something equally unhelpful. The solution is to do a survey. Say we take twenty of the most beautiful faces that might be used to represent our product and do a survey. Have everyone surveyed pick the three most beautiful faces in order of beauty—first, second, third. Survey a hundred men and a hundred women, if this represents our target audience. Setting up a table on a busy street corner might give us plenty of results in a very short period of time. Tabulate the results and choose the one with the highest score. If there's no clear winner. Do another survey with the top three.

The main point is that so many so-called intangibles can be measured if we look at them from the right perspective. And this requires that we find the right mindset so we can see the right approach—the one that will give us answers that don't need to be perfect.

Machine Learning and Sales

Bernard Marr, writing for *Forbes* (July 6, 2017), tells us how a sales team can benefit from AI and machine learning. Seasoned sales professionals have long heard about how computers will eventually run them out of a job, but Marr helps to put things back into perspective. "There's a personal side to selling that machines will not (at least for a long time) be able to replace. Humans, and exemplary sales professionals in particular, are uniquely suited to listen, convince, negotiate and empathize as well as explore and answer the very critical question of 'Why is this the best product or service for me.' However, the power of machine learning to contribute to successful sales initiatives cannot be understated and will only continue to grow in importance."

Marr gives a number of potent examples on how machine learning can be put to work to boost a sales team's performance, including improving sales forecasting, predicting customer needs, efficient transactional sales and improving sales communication. He points out the benefits, for instance, of Salesforce's AI software solution called Einstein. Not only does the software remind salesmen when to follow up with a potential client, but also how to prioritize those with "a high probability of conversion and help to predict the best product or service for each prospect."

One way sales can be streamlined is by using machine learning to score each prospect. Take for instance, the kinds of solutions a prospect is looking at, the number of stakeholders, company size and the like. Comparing all of this to past data, including deals won and deals lost, machine learning software can learn how to predict the potential for each prospect. Such deal scoring will improve over time with the acquisition of more data. This will allow the sales force to concentrate more of their time on the hottest prospects, rather than spinning their wheels on what may be the largest, but least likely to close (Mitha).

Smarter Security and Policing

If you work in the security industry or as a police officer, you will find data analytics a welcome addition to your existing tool kit. Sahil Arora wrote for Digital Vidya, "Several cities all over the world have employed predictive analysis in predicting areas that would likely witness a surge in crime with the use of geographical data and historical data. This has seemed to work in major cities such as Chicago, London, Los Angeles, etc. Although, it is not possible to make arrests for every crime committed but the availability of data has made it possible to have police officers within such areas at a certain time of the day which has led to a drop in crime rate.

"This shows that this kind of data analytics application will make us have safer cities without police putting their lives at risk."

Using software techniques like machine learning, and image and pattern recognition, computer systems can predict when crimes are about to happen, increasing the ability of security forces and police to prevent such events before they occur.

Safer Handling of Finances

Nothing attracts the criminal element quite like money, whether it's represented by paper, gold or electronic bits and bytes. Data analytics helps to detect fraud and reduce risks in the financial industry. "So many organizations had very bad experiences with debt and were so fed up with it," writes Sahil Arora, "Since they already had data that was collected during the time their customers applied for loans, they applied data science which eventually rescued them from the losses they had incurred. This led to banks learning to divide and conquer data from their customers' profiles, recent expenditure and other significant information that were made available to them. This made it easy for them to analyze and infer if there was any probability of customers defaulting."

This is like facial recognition, only sexier. This is the type of pattern recognition that looks at the sequences of events—behavior—that precede a loan default or some other financial disaster.

Marketers Delight

Daniel Faggella, writing for Emerj, gives us a list of "five current predictive analytics applications for marketing."
1. "Predictive Modeling for Customer Behavior,
2. "Qualify and Prioritize Leads,

3. "Bringing Right Product / Services to Market,
4. "Targeting the Right Customers at Right Time with Right Content,
5. "Driving Marketing Strategies Based on Predictive Analytics Insights."

Ideally, data analytics will solve each of these so the marketer knows precisely what to do to achieve better results in each of these categories.

In an article by Jeffry Nimeroff for *Forbes*, we learn that marketers are gaining multiple benefits from the machine learning discipline of AI. One way marketers win is through automated data visualization. As the machine learns more, it can more easily display a graphic representation of the data that makes sense of the mountain of information. Better content analysis will help "drive better marketing conversations." Nimeroff also stated, "Learning from ML results will accelerate the growth and skills of marketing professionals." He summed up the ML potential this way: "As ML techniques become more widely used, they become more widely understood. And as they become more widely understood, non-technical literature will become more widely available. I think this growing repository will lead to an acceleration of subject matter expertise around machine learning for marketing that will push the industry forward."

Louis Columbus, also writing for *Forbes*, gives us his perspective on how ML is driving improvements in marketing: "The best marketers are using machine learning to understand, anticipate and act on the problems their sales prospects are trying to solve faster and with more clarity than any competitor. Having the insight to tailor content while qualifying leads for sales to close quickly is being fueled by machine learning-based apps capable of learning what's most effective for each prospect and customer. Machine learning is taking contextual content, marketing automation including cross-channel marketing campaigns and lead scoring, personalization, and sales forecasting to a new level of accuracy and speed."

By having better understanding of a larger portion of a market and what they need, marketers are able to tailor their messages to fit those needs. This also improves the sales funnel efficiency by pinpointing with greater accuracy the quality of sales leads. As this accuracy continues to improve, the sales team has to expend less energy to close deals.

Making Procurement More Efficient

Every company needs supplies, equipment and other resources. Getting the best deals and quality remain an important element of purchasing. Another important element of the procurement function involves timing. It does no good to order too much stock that merely sits in the warehouse gathering dust for months. Prediction is a key element of the efficient procurement cycle.

Marcell Vollmer, writing for Future of Sourcing Digital, explains how machine learning is helping to conquer familiar obstacles to full automation: "Unlike Robotic Process Automation (RPA) and preliminary use cases for Artificial Intelligence (AI), Machine Learning (ML) handles activities that call for complex rules and pattern recognition. By demonstrating a basic level of human judgment, machine learning can, for example, assign transactions to formal spend categories and sub-categories. This critical first step in uncovering sourcing opportunities can transition from a traditionally time-consuming, manual task to a real-time, automatic response."

"Machine learning makes it possible to discover patterns in supply chain data by relying on algorithms that quickly pinpoint the most influential factors to a supply networks' success, while constantly learning in the process." So writes Louis Columbus for *Forbes*.

Columbus adds, "Discovering new patterns in supply chain data has the potential to revolutionize any business. Machine learning algorithms are finding these new patterns in supply chain data daily, without needing manual intervention or the definition of taxonomy to guide the analysis. The algorithms iteratively query data with many using constraint-based modeling to find the core set of factors with the greatest predictive accuracy. Key factors influencing inventory levels, supplier quality, demand forecasting, procure-to-pay, order-to-cash, production planning, transportation management and more are becoming known for the first time. New knowledge and insights from machine learning are revolutionizing supply chain management as a result."

Business Forecasting's New Crystal Ball

Donald Hagell makes some interesting observations about machine learning in an article he wrote for LinkedIn. "Advanced planning, budgeting, and forecasting tools will support making good strategic decisions. One type of planning, budgeting, and forecasting tool includes a methodology for identifying an optimal solution to a set of decisions based on processing a multitude of big data information inputs. For example, an optimization model may work towards finding solutions that yield the best outcome from known possibilities with a defined set of constraints (model-based). Accordingly, an organization may achieve economic benefits by strategically applying optimization models for optimizing financial plans, budgets, and forecasts as well as management of financial assets, particularly those involving a multitude of uncertain decisions over many forecasting periods."

As software engineers continue to learn from earlier iterations, the models improve and the end results improve from those improvements. This exciting era at the infancy of artificial intelligence is full of growing pains. That's to be expected, but to the insiders, this is a most exciting time to be involved in this cutting edge development.

In discussing an upcoming conference on the topic of machine learning for planning and budgeting, Claudia Dale gives some of the key benefits to be found from this enterprise:

- "More time to analyse information instead of inputting and consolidating data;
- "Budgets that can be built levering last years actuals and incredibly 3rd party data which can provide critical information for your business e.g.: long term weather forecasts for a construction business;
- "Faster and easier forecasting at any point during the year."

Craig Juta described the objective as a way to "give our data a voice into the future."

In order to solve a problem, we must first know the exact nature of the problem. Joseph Shamir, writing for *Supply Chain Quarterly*, stated, "Demand forecasting is difficult, and most demand forecasting conducted today produces disappointing results and significant forecast errors. It cannot easily identify trends in the demand data, and its limited ability to understand the underlying causes of demand variability makes that variability seem worse than it would if demand drivers were clearly understood.

And because it is manually intensive, it suffers from persistent bias and poor planner productivity."

Summing it Up

Most any industry is going to be affected by the incremental improvements in data analytics and machine learning. Don't wait for the world to tell you what's next. Get involved. Learn what is available right now and start to get your hands dirty with the data. Find out what can help your job run more smoothly.

Chapter 12
Apply Data Analytics
in Your Small Business

In this final chapter we will be looking at how to implement big data analytics in your own small business.

There are a number of things that you and your staff can do on your own, including brainstorming about what kinds of data you already have, and what kinds of data you might be able to collect that would tell you more about your operation or your customers. Such talks can help get everyone acclimated to the idea. When you're ready to hire on some help, even if only a one-time consultant, you'll be better equipped to ask the right kinds of questions to make the most of the experience and the help you get.

You don't have to be a big business, or even a medium-sized business to take advantage of business data analytics. Even small businesses—fewer than 250 employees—can reap the rewards of collecting and analyzing data, like key performance indicators, dashboards, reporting tools, and the like.

If you have an established company with regular customers, you likely have a treasure trove of data that can help you grow your business. Use the examples in

earlier chapters as inspiration for the things you can do—
especially chapters 2 and 5.

As we learned from the Cincinnati Zoo example in
Chapter 2, we need to look at what data will give us
important information about our customers or clients.
For the zoo, it was each visitor's zip code—the general
location of their home. Acquiring this at every
transaction took a little effort to implement, but once the
park had a solid batch of that information, it could know
who their best customers were and where to spend their
most marketing dollars. Does your business have some
gold nuggets to collect? Do you already have a cache of
them in the data you already have?

The zoo example also taught us that things like the
time of day when purchases are made can prove important to boosting sales. If there are repeating patterns to
your customer behavior, you can use that to strengthen
your ability to deliver at the right times and places.

The Doctor Who
Operates On Himself

There's an old saying that the doctor who operates on
him or herself has a fool for a patient. While there are a
great many things a business owner or manager can do
to improve their lot, there comes a time when we have to
hire a professional to help us out. We need a consultant
who can look at our business, the business model and the
details, and tell us what changes we need to make to
streamline our operation and to increase profits. By the
same token, we need to explore the possibility of hiring a
company to do for us what IBM did for the Cincinnati
Zoo.

But before we dive in by hiring someone, it helps
to get a broader picture of what's available—to learn

more of the details of the data analytics market. Conferences and conventions can help increase our understanding of the field. Not only will this make us a better consumer of data analytics, it will also help us ask the right questions when choosing the best consultant or software system for our business. For businesses that depend a great deal on phone calls with customers or clients, CallMiner produces a yearly conference "for all experience levels of Customer Engagement Analytics users and executives."

For the food, beverage and consumer packaged goods manufacturers, NLITX has developed numerous business solutions, including demand projection, inventory planning, logistics efficiency, marketing ROI, portfolio optimization, profitability analysis, and sales forecast & productivity. These help manufacturers of all sizes win more shelf space by using their data more effectively. Their website boasts about their clients, "They rely on NLITX to build powerful data analytics applications and dashboards that transform their data into business intelligence and help them answer their crucial business questions. Food and beverage manufacturers generate an average sales increase of 11% and around 17% operation cost savings after using NLITX."

Datameer, for instance, claims that "you can ingest, cleanse, prepare, analyze and visualize all of your data in hours or days, not months."

If our business involves a great deal of phone time with customers, we might want help with speech analytics, like that found at Nexidia. Their "speech analytics technology analyzes 100% of recorded calls to quickly extract accurate business intelligence."

If our company resides in the manufacturing sector, a company like Plex could give us the dashboard ease and analytics power we need to boost productivity, to meet client demands and to increase the bottom line. "Plex is the Manufacturing Cloud, delivering industry-leading ERP and manufacturing automation to more than 450 companies across process and discrete industries. Plex pioneered Cloud solutions for the shop floor, connecting suppliers, machines, people, systems and customers with capabilities that are easy to configure, deliver continuous innovation and reduce IT costs. With insight that starts on the production line, Plex helps companies see and understand every aspect of their business ecosystems, enabling them to lead in an ever-changing market."

Domo is a Utah-based company specializing in data visualization and business intelligence. It predicts that "By 2020, all businesses will be digital businesses. As ones and zeros consume the world, data will become the new product and business intelligence—finding the needle in a haystack—will be the new process of innovation." In other words, those who are slow to get on the data bandwagon will find all their "needles" long after their competition.

Another source of business intelligence help is RapidMiner. Their company "provides software, solutions, and services in the fields of predictive analytics, data mining, and text mining. We automatically and intelligently analyze data (both structured and unstructured) – including multimedia and text – on a large scale."

Companies like Deloitte provide "audit, tax, consulting, and financial advisory services." This can include big data analytics and related consulting services.

As we can see there are some companies that tackle the whole topic of business intelligence. Their broad experience can prove helpful when finding solutions for our own small business. There are also companies that specialize in specific aspects of business intelligence, as we've already seen with speech analytics and manufacturing expertise. Esri specializes in location analytics for business intelligence, helping us "see" where all our customers are with maps and geographic information systems (GIS) technology.

If there is an industry need, more than likely, there will be a service provider to answer that need.

Performance Analytics

Naturally, every corporation wants to operate at peak efficiency while finding a maximizing balance for things like income, profit, market share, customer satisfaction and impact.

ServiceNow, a California-based cloud computing company provides us with some insights on using performance analytics: "Using performance analytics, you and your team can make definitive, fact-based decisions everyone understands. When you can clearly see your current situation and what the future holds, you can also:

- "Prioritize your resources more effectively so you can focus on areas with the highest demand or biggest benefit
- "Optimize the way you work by pinpointing and eliminating inefficiencies and bottlenecks
- "Identify emerging issues—and fix them before they become major problems
- "Know when change is coming and turn on a dime to take advantage of the new opportunities
- "Validate the decisions you've already made by seeing how they actually affect performance

- "Drive continuous improvement in your processes and in the services you offer

"Here's the bottom line. Performance analytics let you be proactive rather than reactive, and that lets you make more timely and informed decisions. It lets you keep up with the speed of business so you're always ready to throw that winning pass."

Naturally, they're trying to sell their services, but what they say makes perfect sense. And their 3,000+ worldwide customers would agree. Their software-as-a-service (SaaS) model makes it possible to utilize their services for as little as $100 per seat per month (Bigelow).

Performance analytics can be a blend of descriptive, predictive and prescriptive analytics. Let's look at those, now.

Descriptive Analytics

Descriptive analytics is a subset of business intelligence and big data analytics. The descriptive form of analytics tells us what has happened in the past and perhaps what is happening right now—"now" being the sum or product of all past actions.

This tells us where we've been and what caused our current conditions. Where we have failures, we will know what caused them. Where we have successes, we will know what needs to be reinforced.

Predictive Analytics

This is the branch of big data analytics and business intelligence that acts as our crystal ball. It attempts to tell the future within certain levels of probability. It decreases the risk of making decisions by giving us more than mere opinion or gut feeling.

Predictive analytics works off of the trajectory of past events and extrapolates them into the future. This is usually not easy for the individual human to see with any clarity or accuracy.

Prescriptive Analytics

Prescriptive analytics is like our "doctor's orders" for healing what ails our company. When we establish specific, clearly-defined goals, this is what tells us how to get there. Not only does it work off of past trajectories, it uses a view of the world-at-large to see what resources are available for achieving our goals.

At the current state of AI, this does not create new methods that don't currently exist. This broader level of planning and innovation still resides only in the domain of human intelligence. But prescriptive analytics can be a springboard for getting our bearings. From here, we can test new ideas and explore other possibilities the software cannot imagine.

Increasing Customer Satisfaction

Perhaps the single most important type of analytics is that which concentrates on customer satisfaction. Get this wrong and everything else is pretty worthless. A super-efficient manufacturer who produces a product no customer would ever buy is a failed company. A business that ignores customer complaints does so at its own peril.

The simplest form of analytics—a form that can be implemented right away—is to listen to our customers. Don't make excuses. Even if they have a misunderstanding, own their error. Make it our own and find a way to build on that knowledge. The business owners and managers who hold this type of attitude of perfect responsibility are those who will have the greatest potential to win big in the long run.

Too often, corporations squeeze the numbers to make everything perfect within certain narrow constraints, boosting profits, but killing their customers by the dozens. When the focus is too much on profits, we get corporations betraying their customers, hoping they won't notice, and sometimes even lying about what the customers are receiving.

Case-in-Point: The medical industry with its lobbyists corrupting government to pass laws that protect the corporations when they destroy customer lives, as happened in the vaccine industry. Few industries have their protections from civil lawsuits for faulty products. Thus, such corporations have little incentive to produce better products. Customers die or are injured for life and the corporation chugs ahead making profits, suppressing bad press, and outlawing cures that would ruin their tainted business model.

Listen to your customers. Think what is best for them, from their viewpoint, not from the corporate bottom line. Deliver that, and you will win. Then harness the power of business intelligence, big data analytics and artificial intelligence to take your business to the next level of professionalism and quality service.

Afterword

AI, machine learning and deep learning have the potential to turn Earth into a garden of prosperity or a wasteland of misery. These are merely tools, like the fabulous atom revered some 70 years ago for its promise. The atom could give us boundless quantities of clean energy, or it could destroy all life on Earth in a bright flash of wanton stupidity.

The weight of responsibility is on our shoulders. If we shirk that responsibility and merely blame others for mismanagement, abuse or greed, then we become complicit in the tragedy. If, instead, we take up the mantle of that responsibility and carry it with gratitude, we might be able to help make the future a bright one—where AI benefits everyone, not merely the corporations and their owners.

We've seen how AI and machine learning have transformed entire industries, making them far more efficient, and allowing them to predict enough to gain an edge over their competition who has not yet adopted machine intelligence. Artificial intelligence has also given us some horror stories of government abuse and corporate corruption. Mistakes have cost people their lives or their health and happiness.

Like any tool, how we use AI will determine the outcome. Remember GIGO? If we give civilization garbage AI, then we will suffer the fruits of that garbage. If we make AI cleanly intelligent, but psychopathically insane, then we will suffer from that madness. If the corporations who own AI use it for their own selfish greed no matter who it harms, then we will have unleashed a tyranny upon the Earth no one has ever witnessed throughout history. Instead of the fear East Europeans felt with the coming of Genghis Khan's Golden Hordes, we will suffer the despair of someone trapped in a Matrix-like society with no possible escape.

Beyond the Reach of Artificial Intelligence

There is one realm of activity that AI could never touch. This is the ace-in-the-hole advantage that humans have over machines. It is something the humanists and the secularists reject without much consideration—or perhaps, more accurately, without deep humility. Their "know-it-all" attitude tends to blind them to some of life's profound possibilities.

Science philosopher and software engineer, Rod Martin, Jr., has given the topic quite a lot of deep, humble thought. He has explored areas that seem taboo to many in the "logic crowd." And he has confounded many in the spiritual crowd, too, with brazen ideas that push the "what-if" envelope beyond their comfort zone.

The active ingredients in skepticism are restraint and humility, according to Martin. Too many scientists and self-proclaimed skeptics betray skepticism by abandoning restraint and humility for the know-it-all attitude and the negative bias of "doubt" inherent in skepticism. Why do they do this? For one thing, it feeds the one key

failing of humans—self-concern, also known as egoism—
the obscene drive to be right at all costs—the mechanism
that creates suffering when we find out that we are
wrong.

But what is this advantage that humans have over
machines? It's the idea that we are more than our physical
manifestation. Einstein touched on this when he used
imagination to explore the undiscovered country beyond
what is known. When Einstein dreamed of Relativity, he
went outside the box of logic and reason, into the realm
of creation, creativity and imagination.

Inspiration, Martin declares, is not physical, but
spiritual—*in + spirit*—*inspiration, to take in the breath of life.*
This is the wild card that a machine will never possess.
Science, Martin states, is derived from continuity-based
reality—things like inertia, the smoothness of space and
time, the consistent results of field effects, inductance,
resistance, chaos math and more.

The laws of spirit are derived from discontinuity-
based reality. This is the realm of true "free will."
Everything within the physical is entirely deterministic—
like a computer algorithm. Outside of the cogs and levers
of physical reality, spirit gives us the freedom to examine
possibilities that we would never see with logic or reason.

Artificial intelligence is tied to physical commen-
surability. It cannot climb out of the material box of
natural reality. It remains trapped. Only human spirit can
transcend these limitations, to bend or break the laws of
physical reality. But even in the realm of the non-physical,
there are patterns and rules. Martin explored these in his
book, *The Science of Miracles.* As Shakespeare had his
tragic hero say, "There are more things in heaven and
earth, Horatio, Than are dreamt of in your philosophy"
(*Hamlet,* Act 1, scene 5). Only those who reach this

spiritual state will ever see the logic and patterns to be found there. Those who chose to disbelieve such things will never know of them directly.

AI will only know of them indirectly, in the literature of its creators—the Homo sapiens of planet Earth. Could this dimension of the whole of reality be the missing ingredient we discussed in Chapter 9, hinted at by Nick Jankel? That's where we talked about Roger Penrose's certainty that fully-generalized AI was either very unlikely or impossible. He may have been too pessimistic, but Jankel did bring up the rather intriguing possibility that some things will forever remain outside of AI's reach.

The promise of AI is pleasantly seductive. If we get this right, then everyone on planet Earth could become rich by modern standards. The creative amongst us could do their art to perfection, never worrying about finding food or paying the rent. The tired old idea of the starving artist would forever be vanquished.

The explorers amongst us could turn their attention to the stars or to the bottom of the ocean. The kind souls amongst us could spend their time helping the less fortunate who may suffer not from physical needs, but the challenges of mental or physical impairment. Victims of accidents could find a loving, helpful society to support their healing—a society driven by individual compassion, rather than the bottomless pit of tyrannical government "compassion."

But a lot of this will depend upon how we teach each other and how we treat each other. We cannot depend upon AI or their creators to do everything for us. We must each, individually, take responsibility for the direction civilization takes. We must remain humble to learn more, but also confident that solutions are achievable. Only then will the full promise of AI become possible.

Appendix

- References
- Notes
- Bibliography
- Glossary
- About the Author
- Connect

References

Arora, Sahil. (May 17, 2017). "Top 14 Areas for Data Analytics Application." Retrieved on August 8, 2019 from https://digitalvidya.com/blog/data-analytics-applications/

BBC. (Mar. 22, 2019). "Facebook staff 'flagged Cambridge Analytica fears earlier than thought'." Retrieved on April 1, 2019 from https://bbc.com/news/technology-47666909

Bernazzani, Sophia. (June 1, 2017). "10 Jobs Artificial Intelligence Will Replace (and 10 That Are Safe)." Retrieved February 19, 2019 from https://blog.hubspot.com/marketing/jobs-artificial-intelligence-will-replace

Bigelow, Bruce. (Jan. 11, 2011). "Service-Now CEO Fred Luddy Sees a Clear Path to $1 Billion in Annual Revenue." Retrieved April 16, 2019 from https://xconomy.com/san-diego/2011/01/11/service-now-ceo-fred-luddy-sees-a-clear-path-to-1-billion-in-annual-revenue/

Blacklisted News. (July 1, 2018). "Google's 'Arbiter of Hate Speech', SPLC Forced to Pay $3M for Falsely Labeling People as 'Extremist'." Retrieved on April 3, 2019 from https://blacklistednews.com/article/66838/googles-arbiter-of-hate-speech-splc-forced-to-pay-3m-for-falsely-labeling-people-as.html

Blasko, Dennis. (July 28, 2015). "China's Merchant Marine." Retrieved on March 16, 2019 from https://cna.org/cna_files/pdf/China-Merchant-Marine.pdf

Bomey, Nathan. (June 20, 2017). "Driver killed in Tesla self-driving car crash ignored warnings, NTSB reports." Retrieved on April 2, 2019 from https://usatoday.com/story/money/cars/2017/06/20/tesla-self-driving-car-crash/411516001/

Cadwalladr, Carole. (May 7, 2017). "The great British Brexit robbery: how our democracy was hijacked." Retrieved on April 1, 2019 from https://theguardian.com/technology/2017/may/07/the-great-british-brexit-robbery-hijacked-democracy

CallMiner. (2018). "Listen 2018: Intelligence Redefined." PDF

Carone, Timothy. (Mar. 21, 2018). "Self-driving car accidents will keep happening. We need to learn from them." Retrieved on April 2, 2019 from https://money.cnn.com/2018/03/21/technology/self-driving-cars-opinion/index.html

Chawla, Rachit. (Mar. 11, 2018). "How AI Supports Financial Institutions for Deciding Creditworthiness." Retrieved January 29, 2019 from https://entrepreneur.com/article/310262

China Uncensored. (Mar. 20, 2019). "Is Google Helping China's Military? | Trump vs Google on CCP | China Uncensored." Retrieved on March 22, 2019 from https://youtube.com/watch?v=wqWVH38jtQo

Clifford, Catherine. (Mar. 13, 2018). "Elon Musk: 'Mark my words—A.I. is far more dangerous than nukes'." Retrieved March 15, 2019 from https://cnbc.com/2018/03/13/elon-musk-at-sxsw-a-i-is-more-dangerous-than-nuclear-weapons.html

Columbus, Louis. (Feb. 25, 2018). 10 Ways Machine Learning Is Revolutionizing Marketing. Retrieved on August 15, 2019 from https://forbes.com/sites/louiscolumbus/2018/02/25/10-ways-machine-learning-is-revolutionizing-marketing/

Columbus, Louis. (Jun. 11, 2018). 10 Ways Machine Learning Is Revolutionizing Supply Chain Management. Retrieved on August 15, 2019 from https://forbes.com/sites/louiscolumbus/2018/06/11/10-ways-machine-learning-is-revolutionizing-supply-chain-management/

Corbett Report. (Nov. 2, 2013). "Rockefeller Medicine." Retrieved on April 1, 2019 from https://youtube.com/watch?v=X6J_7PvWoMw

Corbett Report. (Dec. 3, 2013). "Genetic Fallacy: How Monsanto Silences Scientific Dissent." Retrieved on March 20, 2019 from https://youtube.com/watch?v=ShJTcIlTna0

Dale, Claudia. (Apr. 8, 2019). Machine Learning for Budgeting and Planning. Retrieved on August 15, 2019 from https://taysols.com.au/events/ml-for-epm

Daley, Sam. (Dec. 19, 2018). "19 examples of artificial intelligence shaking up business as usual." Retrieved on February 19, 2019 from https://builtin.com/artificial-intelligence/examples-ai-in-industry

Damore, James. (Aug. 8, 2017). "The document that got me fired from Google." Retrieved on March 17, 2019 from https://firedfortruth.com/

Datameer. (2013). "The Guide to Big Data Analytics." Retrieved on February 19, 2019 from https://pdfstores.files.wordpress.com/2016/04/big-data-analytics-ebook.pdf

Datameer. (2016). "Top Five High-Impact Use Cases for Big Data Analytics." Retrieved on February 19, 2019 from https://datameer.com/pdf/eBook-Top-Five-High-Impact-UseCases-for-Big-Data-Analytics.pdf

Deloitte. (June 19, 2013). "The Analytics Advantage: We're just getting started." Retrieved on February 19, 2019 from https://www2.deloitte.com/content/dam/Deloitte/global/Documents/Deloitte-Analytics/dttl-analytics-analytics-advantage-report-061913.pdf

Domo.com. (ND). "From Big Data to Better Decisions: The ultimate guide to business intelligence today." Retrieved on February 19, 2019 from https://domo.com/assets/downloads/15_bi-guide.pdf

Durden, Tyler. (Mar. 26, 2018). "'Dumb F--ks': Julian Assange Reminds Us What Mark Zuckerberg Thinks Of Facebook Users." Retrieved April 1, 2019 from https://zerohedge.com/news/2018-03-25/dumb-f-ks-julian-assange-reminds-us-what-mark-zuckerberg-thinks-facebook-users

Esri. (Oct. 2012). "Esri® Location Analytics for Business Intelligence." Retrieved on February 19, 2019 from https://esri.com/library/whitepapers/pdfs/esri-location-analytics-for-bi.pdf

Faggella, Daniel. (Mar. 5, 2019). Predictive Analytics for Marketing – What's Possible and How it Works. Retrieved on August 15, 2019 from https://emerj.com/ai-sector-overviews/predictive-analytics-for-marketing-whats-possible-and-how-it-works/

Forbes Technology Council. (Mar. 1, 2018). "14 Ways AI Will Benefit Or Harm Society." Retrieved on February 19, 2019 from https://forbes.com/sites/forbestechcouncil/2018/03/01/14-ways-ai-will-benefit-or-harm-society/#74ca70254ef0

Fox Business. (Mar. 14, 2019). "Google is helping the Chinese military: Top US military officer." Retrieved on March 16, 2019 from https://youtube.com/watch?v=hFRHdKfTSzI

Fox Business (Mar. 20, 2019). "Google under fire for alleged censorship." Retrieved on March 22, 2019 from https://youtube.com/watch?v=gVSGvl989TU

Fox Business (Apr. 8, 2019). "Google scraps newly formed AI ethics board." Retrieved on April 9, 2019 from https://youtube.com/watch?v=_AdVeRJh_FY

Frank.ai. (Sep. 3, 2018). "How Can Machine Learning Impact Your Business?" Retrieved on February 19, 2019 from https://frank.ai/how-can-machine-learning-impact-your-business/

Fuller, Michael. (Dec. 26, 2016) "Tesla Autopilot Crash Prompts New Update." Retrieved on April 2, 2019 from https://selfdrivingaccident.com/tesla-autopilot-crash/

Ghafourifar, A., Evans, M. (Oct. 20, 2018). "The Machine Learning Revolution: How Artificial Intelligence Could Transform Your Business." Retrieved on

February 19, 2019 from
https://forbes.com/sites/allbusiness/2018/10/20/ma
chine-learning-artificial-intelligence-could-
transform-business/#3753a2c5c6c3

Gittlen, Sandra. (Aug. 27, 2010). "Analytics: The Art and
Science of Better." Retrieved February 19, 2019
from
https://umsl.edu/%7Esauterv/DSS4BI/links/SAS_a
nalytics_tb.pdf

Gleick, James. (1987). *Chaos: Making a New Science*. Viking
Books: New York.

GMOSeralini.org. (ND). "GMO Seralini." Retrieved on
March 20, 2019 from https://gmoseralini.org/en/

Goldstein, Josh. (July 26, 2017). "Southern Poverty Law
Center Is a Hate Group." Retrieved on April 3,
2019 from
https://townhall.com/columnists/joshgoldstein/201
7/07/26/splc-hate-group-n2360208

Gopinath, Sudhaa. (Dec. 25, 2018). "10 Reasons Why Big
Data Analytics is the Best Career Move."
Retrieved on February 19, 2019 from
https://edureka.co/blog/10-reasons-why-big-data-
analytics-is-the-best-career-move

Gorelik, Dennis. (ND). "Computer intelligence versus
Human intelligence." Retrieved on April 11, 2019
from
http://dennisgorelik.com/ai/ComputerIntelligence
VsHumanIntelligence.htm

Hagell, Donald. (May 12, 2017). Machine Learning the
Financial Planning, Budgeting, and Forecasting
models. Retrieved on August 15, 2019 from
https://linkedin.com/pulse/machine-learning-
financial-planning-budgeting-models-donald-
hagell/

Hagerty, John. (Oct. 13, 2016). "2017 Planning Guide for Data and Analytics." Retrieved on February 19, 2019 from https://gartner.com/binaries/content/assets/events/keywords/catalyst/catus8/2017_planning_guide_for_data_analytics.pdf

Hasson, Peter. (June 7, 2018). "SPLC Tells Facebook, Google, Twitter, Amazon, Which Organizations are 'Hate Groups'." Retrieved on April 3, 2019 from https://westernjournal.com/splc-tells-facebook-google-twitter-amazon-which-organizations-are-hate-groups/

Hellenic Shipping News. (Mar. 15, 2016). "China-owned ships: fleet expansion accelerates." Retrieved on March 16, 2019 from https://web.archive.org/web/20160319184656/https://hellenicshippingnews.com/china-owned-ships-fleet-expansion-accelerates/

Hennessy, Bill. (Sep. 9, 2015). "I Wish Drucker Never Said It." Retrieved on March 28, 2019 from http://billhennessy.com/simple-strategies/2015/09/09/i-wish-drucker-never-said-it

Hernandez, J., *et al.* (2013). "Building an Analytics-Driven Organization." Retrieved on February 19, 2019 from https://accenture.com/us-en/~/media/Accenture/Conversion-Assets/DotCom/Documents/Global/PDF/Industries_2/Accenture-Building-Analytics-Driven-Organization.pdf

IMD. (2018). "Data Analytics & Artificial Intelligence: What it Means for your Business and Society." Retrieved on February 19, 2019 from https://imd.org/contentassets/568e2f36bf3143a69d3

45b1330f7c76f/iai004-18-data-analytics-and-ai---
final-ss-05-04-2018.pdf

Information Commissioner's Office. (Sep. 4, 2017). "Big
data, artificial intelligence, machine learning and
data protection." Retrieved on February 19, 2019
from https://ico.org.uk/media/for-
organisations/documents/2013559/big-data-ai-ml-
and-data-protection.pdf

James, Luke. (Jan. 14, 2018). "5 Ways mother nature
inspires artificial intelligence." Retrieved on
February 19, 2019 from
https://towardsdatascience.com/5-ways-mother-
nature-inspires-artificial-intelligence-
2c6700bb56b6

Jankel, Nick. (Feb. 24, 2015). "AI vs. Human Intelligence:
Why Computers Will Never Create Disruptive
Innovations." Retrieve on April 11, 2019 from
https://huffpost.com/entry/ai-vs-human-
intelligence-_b_6741814

Johnson, Andrew. (Nov. 28, 2017). "Artificial Intelligence
and Nature." Retrieved on February 19, 2019 from
https://medium.com/questanotes/artificial-
intelligence-and-nature-bf2e62d76670

Johnson, Lauren. (Feb. 28, 2017). "Coca-Cola Wants to
Use AI Bots to Create Its Ads." Retrieved on
March 10, 2019 from
https://adweek.com/digital/coca-cola-wants-to-
use-ai-bots-to-create-its-ads/

Juta, Craig. (Jul. 11, 2017). Predictive Analytics -
Budgeting. Retrieved on August 15, 2019 from
http://getfreshbi.com/tag/budgeting-using-
machine-learning/

Kendrew, Emma. (Mar. 23, 2018). "How to design AI to
benefit business and society." Retrieved on

February 19, 2019 from
https://telegraph.co.uk/business/essential-
insights/benefits-of-artificial-intelligence/

Kim, Torrey. (Nov. 13, 2017). "WalMart Replaces Scan
and Go with New App." Retrieved on March 18,
2019 from
https://thebalanceeveryday.com/ratchet-up-your-
walmart-savings-with-scan-and-go-program-
2372117

Kimble, C., Milolidakis, G. (2015). "Big Data and Business
Intelligence: Debunking the Myths." Retrieved on
February 19, 2019 from
https://arxiv.org/ftp/arxiv/papers/1511/1511.03085.
pdf

Lee, Timothy B. (Mar. 21, 2018). "Facebook's Cambridge
Analytica scandal, explained [Updated]."
Retrieved on April 1, 2019 from
https://arstechnica.com/tech-
policy/2018/03/facebooks-cambridge-analytica-
scandal-explained/

Litke, Eric. (Nov. 23, 2016). "5 years of concealed carry:
Law obscures impact." Retrieved on March 19,
2019 from
https://postcrescent.com/story/news/investigations
/2016/11/23/law-obscures-impact-wisconsin-
concealed-carry/94344080/

Mahdawi, Arwa. (June 26, 2017). "What jobs will still be
around in 20 years? Read this to prepare your
future." Retrieved on March 21, 2019 from
https://theguardian.com/us-news/2017/jun/26/jobs-
future-automation-robots-skills-creative-health

Marr, Bernard. (Jul. 6, 2017). How Machine Learning Will
Transform The Sales Function. Retrieved on
August 8, 2019 from

https://forbes.com/sites/bernardmarr/2017/07/06/h
ow-machine-learning-will-transform-the-sales-
function/

Marr, Bernard. (Sep. 18, 2017). "The Amazing Ways Coca
Cola Uses Artificial Intelligence And Big Data To
Drive Success." Retrieved on March 10, 2019 from
https://forbes.com/sites/bernardmarr/2017/09/18/th
e-amazing-ways-coca-cola-uses-artificial-
intelligence-ai-and-big-data-to-drive-success/

Martin, Jr., Rod. (1996). "Outsiderness in the Scientific
Community." Retrieved on March 19, 2019 from
https://rodmartinjr.wordpress.com/about/outsider
ness-in-the-scientific-community/

Martin, Jr., Rod. (June 16, 2013). "Johnny Can't Read —
Overcoming the Many Types of Learning
Disabilities." Retrieved on March 19, 2019 from
https://infinitydynamics.wordpress.com/2017/04/2
1/johnny-cant-read-overcoming-learning-
disabilities/

Martin, Jr., Rod. (2016). *Dirt Ordinary: Shining a Light on
Conspiracies.* Tharsis Highlands: Cebu, Philippines.

Martin, Jr., Rod. (2018). *Climate Basics: Nothing to Fear.*
Tharsis Highlands: Cebu, Philippines.

Martin, Jr., Rod. (2018). *Proof of God.* Tharsis Highlands:
Cebu, Philippines.

Martin, Jr., Rod. (2018). *The Science of Miracles: How
Scientific Method Can Be Applied to Spiritual
Phenomena.* Tharsis Highlands: Cebu, Philippines.

McKinsey Analytics. (Jan. 2018). "Analytics comes of
age." Retrieved on February 19, 2019 from
https://mckinsey.com/~/media/McKinsey/Business
%20Functions/McKinsey%20Analytics/Our%20Ins
ights/Analytics%20comes%20of%20age/Analytics-
comes-of-age.ashx

McKinsey Global Institute. (Dec. 2016). "The Age of Analytics: Competing in a Data-Driven World." Retrieved on February 19, 2019 from https://mckinsey.com/business-functions/mckinsey-analytics/our-insights/the-age-of-analytics-competing-in-a-data-driven-world

McLean, Asha. (Mar. 12, 2018). "AI 'more dangerous than nukes': Elon Musk still firm on regulatory oversight." Retrieved on March 14, 2018 from https://zdnet.com/article/more-dangerous-than-nukes-elon-musk-still-firm-on-regulatory-oversight-of-ai/

MIT. (Apr. 30, 2018). "The Growing Impact of AI on Business." Retrieved on February 19, 2019 from https://technologyreview.com/s/611013/the-growing-impact-of-ai-on-business/

Mitha, Shalini. (May 31, 2017). How Machine Learning And Artificial Intelligence Can Transform Your Sales Department. Retrieved on August 8, 2019 from https://digitalistmag.com/customer-experience/2017/05/31/machine-learning-ai-future-for-sales-05113174

Morning Future. (June 4, 2018). "Artificial intelligence vs. Natural intelligence. Who will win?" Retrieved on February 19, 2019 from https://morningfuture.com/en/article/2018/06/04/emanuele-severino-roger-penrose-artificial-intelligence-natural-intell/331/

Murrell, Audrey. (May 30, 2019). Big Data And The Problem Of Bias In Higher Education. Retrieved on August 7, 2019 from https://forbes.com/sites/audreymurrell/2019/05/30/big-data-and-the-problem-of-bias-in-higher-education/

National Highway Traffic Safety Administration. (2016).
"Quick Facts 2016." Retrieved on April 3, 2019
from
https://crashstats.nhtsa.dot.gov/Api/Public/ViewP
ublication/812451

Neiger, Chris. (Oct. 31, 2017). "6 Scary Stories of AI Gone
Wrong." Retrieved on March 14, 2019 from
https://fool.com/investing/2017/10/31/6-scary-
stories-of-ai-gone-wrong.aspx

Nexidia.com. (2010). "Customer Success Story: Apex.
Speech Analytics: Providing the Business
Intelligence to Win in a Downturn Economy."
Retrieved on February 19, 2019 from
http://nexidia.com/media/1330/apex-case.pdf

NICE Nexidia. (2018). "8 Ways to Become Analytical by
Nature." Retrieved on February 19, 2019 from
https://nice.com/websites/analytics/

Nimeroff, Jeffry. (Mar. 10, 2017). How Machine Learning
Will Be Used For Marketing In 2017. Retrieved on
August 15, 2019 from
https://forbes.com/sites/forbestechcouncil/2017/03/
10/how-machine-learning-will-be-used-for-
marketing-in-2017/

Nucleus Research. (July 2011). "ROI Case Study: IBM
Business Analytics, Cincinnati Zoo." Retrieved on
February 19, 2019 from
https://docplayer.net/18954659-Roi-case-study-
ibm-business-analytics-cincinnati-zoo.html

Nusca, Andrew. (Sep. 27, 2017). "5 Moves Walmart Is
Making to Compete With Amazon and Target."
Retrieved on March 18, 2019 from
http://fortune.com/2017/09/27/5-moves-walmart-
is-making-to-compete-with-amazon-and-target/

Oracle.com. (Dec. 2013). "Utilities and Big Data: Using Analytics for Increased Customer Satisfaction." Retrieved on February 19, 2019 from http://oracle.com/us/industries/utilities/big-data-analytics-customer-wp-2075868.pdf

Peterson, Haley. (Apr. 5, 2018). "Walmart is unleashing 2 key weapons against Amazon in 700 stores." Retrieved on March 18, 2019 from https://businessinsider.com/walmart-online-pickup-tower-review-2017-8

Plex.com. (ND). "How Analytics, Dashboards, and Intelligence are Transforming Manufacturing." Retrieved on February 19, 2019 from https://plex.com/resources/white-paper/gain-manufacturing-intelligence-with-cloud-erp.html

Project Veritas. (Jul. 24, 2019). "Current Sr. Google Engineer Goes Public on Camera: Tech is 'dangerous,' 'taking sides'." Retrieved July 24, 2019 from https://projectveritas.com/2019/07/24/current-sr-google-engineer-goes-public-on-camera-tech-is-dangerous-taking-sides/

RapidMiner.com. (Apr. 2014). "An Introduction to Advanced Analytics." Retrieved on February 19, 2019 from https://rapidminer.com/wp-content/uploads/2014/04/advanced-analytics-introduction.pdf

Reuters, Thomson. (Jul. 23, 2019). $5B settlement expected in Facebook, Cambridge Analytica probe. Retrieved on July 25, 2019 from https://cbc.ca/news/technology/facebook-ftc-settlement-cambridge-analytica-1.5222289

Ruse, Austin. (Mar. 26, 2014). "FBI Dumps Southern Poverty Law Center as Hate Crimes Resource."

Retrieved on April 3, 2019 from
https://breitbart.com/politics/2014/03/26/fbi-
dumps-southern-poverty-law-center/

Scott, Patrick. (Sep. 27, 2017). "These are the jobs most at
risk of automation according to Oxford University:
Is yours one of them?" Retrieved on March 21,
2019 from
https://telegraph.co.uk/news/2017/09/27/jobs-risk-
automation-according-oxford-university-one/

ServiceNow. (2018). "Play to Win: Performance Analytics
Empowers Your Business." Retrieved on February
19, 2019 from
https://servicenow.com/content/dam/servicenow-
assets/public/en-us/doc-type/resource-
center/white-paper/wp-how-performance-
analytics-empowers-your-business.pdf

Shamir, Joseph. (August 15, 2019). Machine learning: A
new tool for better forecasting. Retrieved August
15, 2019 from
https://supplychainquarterly.com/topics/technolog
y/20141230-machine-learning-a-new-tool-for-
better-forecasting/

Sim, Lawrence. (Sep. 27, 2018). "Artificial Intelligence:
Practical?, Productive?, Profitable?, Percipient?,
Pansophical?, Prescient?, Perilous?" Retrieved on
February 19, 2019 from
https://dicomstandard.org/wp-
content/uploads/2018/10/Day1_S4_Artificial_Intell
igence_L.Sim_.pdf

Soare, Tim. (Aug. 12, 2015). "Who owns the world's
ships?" Retrieved on March 16, 2019 from
https://marinetraffic.com/blog/who-owns-the-
worlds-ships/

Stossel, John. (Dec. 14, 2018). "Media Hype Questionable Gun Control Study." Retrieved on December 15, 2018 from https://youtube.com/watch?v=lXGgI2E5JUw

Stossel, John. (Mar. 5, 2019). "Academic Hoax." Retrieved on March 12, 2019 from https://youtube.com/watch?v=As8h2ZCfIPs

Su, Xiaomeng. (ND). "Introduction to Big Data." Retrieved on February 19, 2019 from https://ntnu.no/iie/fag/big/lessons/lesson2.pdf

Swann, Ben. (2012:0904). "Reality Check: 1 on 1 With President Obama, How Does He Justify A Kill List?" Retrieved on 2012:0905 from https://youtube.com/watch?v=WrRuNOaNYME

Tate, Ryan. (Sep. 13, 2010). "Facebook CEO Admits To Calling Users 'Dumb Fucks'." Retrieved on April 1, 2019 from https://gawker.com/5636765/facebook-ceo-admits-to-calling-users-dumb-fucks

Tegmark, Max. (ND). "Benefits & Risks of Artificial Intelligence." Retrieved on February 19, 2019 from https://futureoflife.org/background/benefits-risks-of-artificial-intelligence/

Vohra, G., Lobo, S. (2015). "Beginners' Guide to Analytics." Retrieved on March 5, 2019 from https://jigsawacademy.com/em/Beginners_Guide_to_Analytics.pdf

Vollmer, Marcell. (Jun. 1, 2018). Will Machine Learning Save Procurement Millions a Year? Retrieved on August 15, 2019 from https://futureofsourcing.com/will-machine-learning-save-procurement-millions-a-year

Weaver, Corinne. (Feb. 27, 2019). "PayPal CEO: 'SPLC Helps Us' Figure Out Who to Ban." Retrieved on April 3, 2019 from

https://newsbusters.org/blogs/techwatch/corinne-
weaver/2019/02/27/paypal-ceo-splc-helps-us-
figure-out-who-ban

Weill, K., Poulsen, K. (Mar. 22, 2019). "Secret Emails
Allegedly Show Facebook Knew About
Cambridge Analytica Scandal Earlier Than
Admitted." Retrieved on April 1, 2019 from
https://www.thedailybeast.com/facebook-emails-
on-cambridge-analytica-scandal-could-be-trouble-
for-zuckerberg

Notes

Chapter 1—How AI is Changing Business Use of Technology

Robots and Star Trek's Data Android

Warning: Some movie spoilers are ahead in this section.

In the popular *Star Trek* universe of television and motion pictures, the character of Data (name of the android) has inspired a generation of AI enthusiasts.

Motion pictures and science fiction stories in magazines and novels have long portrayed artificial intelligence. One of the earliest motion pictures, *Metropolis*, included a robot—long before the computer age had started.

Forbidden Planet, the 1956 movie breakthrough, gave us Robby the Robot, a mechanical tin can with super intelligence and an ability to produce any chemical substance in great quantity. Such a robot was only possible because its creator, Dr. Morbius had become super intelligent himself under the mind boost of the Krell native to the planet Altair IV.

The 1972 environmental film, *Silent Running,* included three incredibly cute robots—Huey, Dewey and Louie—who helped their human take care of a Noah's Ark of plant life—plants which could no longer survive on Earth.

In 1977, the first *Star Wars* motion picture introduced us to C-3PO, an anthropomorphic protocol droid with a penchant for languages and diplomacy, and R2-D2, a small, astro-mechanic droid who communicated with chirps, whistles and lots of heavy body language.

In the *Star Trek: The Next Generation* television series (1987–1994), Data was a recurring character who was forever struggling with his inability to understand jokes and emotion. In one episode, when finally he achieved emotion, he discovered that it made him a little insane. This is an extension of the theme found in the original series character of Spock, who dismissed all emotion in favor of logic. The Data character can be seen as an ideal in the realm of AI. Who would love to have his innocent charm and superior computing intelligence as a friend or helper in all of life's challenges?

Other motion pictures have portrayed artificial intelligence with a somewhat more sinister spin. The Will Smith motion picture, *I, Robot* (2004), was inspired by the Isaac Asimov story of the same name, including Asimov's Three Laws of Robotics:

"**First Law**—A robot may not injure a human being or, through inaction, allow a human being to come to harm.

"**Second Law**—A robot must obey the orders given it by human beings except where such orders would conflict with the First Law.

"**Third Law**—A robot must protect its own existence as long as such protection does not conflict with the First or Second Laws."

In the 2004 movie, someone figures out a way to get around the protection of the three laws, putting humanity in jeopardy.

In the 1999 blockbuster movie, *Matrix*, robotic artificial intelligence has trapped most of humanity in a virtual, dream-like world. The few humans who are free of the "matrix," remain at risk of destruction by the ever-jealous robots who have taken over the world.

In *The Terminator* (1984), the prospects look bleak for humanity when a future dominated by evil robots sends a terminator back to the past to kill the human hero's mother before the human resistance leader was born. This is sort of a reverse of the time travel idea of killing Hitler's mother before the German leader was born. This time, the forces of evil try to take out the good guy before he even existed.

Throughout these films and television programs, the portrayal of artificial intelligence has been one of either great promise or great despair. Where AI goes horribly wrong, the beginning of the end is usually spelled by human hubris or a casual disregard of warnings bordering on severe normalcy bias—the notion that nothing could ever go that horribly wrong. This is likely the feeling held by many Jews before the Nazis started rounding them up into concentration camps. After the rounding up had been completed, little could be done to protect their future.

Will humanity suffer the same kind of fate from AI gone wrong? That will depend on us and whether or not we have the wisdom of Isaac Asimov with his Three Laws.

Chapter 3—Jobs Artificial Intelligence Will Replace

High-Risk List

Here is the riskier half of a list produced by an Oxford study of jobs threatened by AI, with the percentage of replacement risk followed by the job title or description.

99%—Data Entry Keyers

99%—Library Technicians

99%—New Accounts Clerks

99%—Photographic Process Workers and Processing Machine Operators

99%—Tax Preparers

99%—Cargo and Freight Agents

99%—Watch Repairers

99%—Insurance Underwriters

99%—Mathematical Technicians

99%—Sewers, Hand

99%—Title Examiners, Abstractors, and Searchers

99%—Telemarketers

98%—Models

98%—Inspectors, Testers, Sorters, Samplers, and Weighers

98%—Bookkeeping, Accounting, and Auditing Clerks

98%—Legal Secretaries

98%—Radio Operators

98%—Driver/Sales Workers

98%—Claims Adjusters, Examiners, and Investigators

98%—Parts Salespersons

98%—Credit Analysts

98%—Milling and Planing Machine Setters, Operators, and Tenders, Metal and Plastic

98%—Shipping, Receiving, and Traffic Clerks

98%—Procurement Clerks

98%—Packaging and Filling Machine Operators and Tenders

98%—Etchers and Engravers

98%—Tellers

98%—Umpires, Referees, and Other Sports Officials

98%—Insurance Appraisers, Auto Damage

98%—Loan Officers

98%—Order Clerks

98%—Brokerage Clerks

98%—Insurance Claims and Policy Processing Clerks

98%—Timing Device Assemblers and Adjusters

97%—Bridge and Lock Tenders

97%—Woodworking Machine Setters, Operators, and Tenders, Except Sawing

97%—Team Assemblers

97%—Shoe Machine Operators and Tenders

97%—Electromechanical Equipment Assemblers

97%—Farm Labor Contractors

97%—Textile Bleaching and Dyeing Machine Operators and Tenders

97%—Dental Laboratory Technicians

97%—Crushing, Grinding, and Polishing Machine Setters, Operators, and Tenders

97%—Grinding and Polishing Workers, Hand

97%—Pesticide Handlers, Sprayers, and Applicators, Vegetation

97%—Log Graders and Scalers

97%—Ophthalmic Laboratory Technicians

97%—Cashiers

97%—Camera and Photographic Equipment Repairers

97%—Motion Picture Projectionists

97%—Prepress Technicians and Workers

97%—Counter and Rental Clerks

97%—File Clerks

97%—Real Estate Brokers

97%—Telephone Operators

97%—Agricultural and Food Science Technicians

97%—Payroll and Timekeeping Clerks

97%—Credit Authorizers, Checkers, and Clerks

97%—Hosts and Hostesses, Restaurant, Lounge, and Coffee Shop

96%—Dispatchers, Except Police, Fire, and Ambulance

96%—Receptionists and Information Clerks

96%—Office Clerks, General

96%—Compensation and Benefits Managers

96%—Switchboard Operators, Including Answering Service

96%—Counter Attendants, Cafeteria, Food Concession, and Coffee Shop

96%—Rock Splitters, Quarry

96%—Secretaries and Administrative Assistants, Except Legal, Medical, and Executive

96%—Surveying and Mapping Technicians

96%—Model Makers, Wood

96%—Textile Winding, Twisting, and Drawing Out Machine Setters, Operators, and Tenders

96%—Locomotive Engineers

96%—Gaming Dealers

96%—Fabric Menders, Except Garment

96%—Cooks, Restaurant

96%—Ushers, Lobby Attendants, and Ticket Takers

96%—Billing and Posting Clerks

95%—Manicurists and Pedicurists

95%—Weighers, Measurers, Checkers, and Samplers, Recordkeeping

95%—Textile Cutting Machine Setters, Operators, and Tenders

95%—Bill and Account Collectors

95%—Nuclear Power Reactor Operators
95%—Gaming Surveillance Officers and Gaming
Investigators
95%—Library Assistants, Clerical
95%—Operating Engineers and Other Construction
Equipment Operators
95%—Print Binding and Finishing Workers
95%—Animal Breeders
95%—Molding, Coremaking, and Casting Machine
Setters, Operators, and Tenders, Metal and Plastic
95%—Electrical and Electronic Equipment Assemblers
95%—Adhesive Bonding Machine Operators and
Tenders
95%—Landscaping and Groundskeeping Workers
95%—Grinding, Lapping, Polishing, and Buffing
Machine Tool Setters, Operators, and Tenders, Metal and
Plastic
95%—Postal Service Clerks
95%—Jewelers and Precious Stone and Metal Workers
94%—Accountants and Auditors
94%—Drilling and Boring Machine Tool Setters,
Operators, and Tenders, Metal and Plastic
94%—Mail Clerks and Mail Machine Operators, Except
Postal Service
94%—Waiters and Waitresses
94%—Meat, Poultry, and Fish Cutters and Trimmers
94%—Budget Analysts
94%—Cement Masons and Concrete Finishers
94%—Bicycle Repairers
94%—Coin, Vending, and Amusement Machine Servicers
and Repairers
94%—Welders, Cutters, Solderers, and Brazers
94%—Couriers and Messengers
94%—Interviewers, Except Eligibility and Loan

94%—Cooks, Short Order

94%—Excavating and Loading Machine and Dragline Operators

94%—Helpers–Painters, Paperhangers, Plasterers, and Stucco Masons

94%—Hotel, Motel, and Resort Desk Clerks

94%—Tire Builders

94%—Door-to-Door Sales Workers, News and Street Vendors, and Related Workers

94%—First-Line Supervisors of Housekeeping and Janitorial Workers

94%—Agricultural Inspectors

94%—Paralegals and Legal Assistants

93%—Cooling and Freezing Equipment Operators and Tenders

93%—Fiberglass Laminators and Fabricators

93%—Service Unit Operators, Oil, Gas, and Mining

93%—Conveyor Operators and Tenders

93%—Outdoor Power Equipment and Other Small Engine Mechanics

93%—Locomotive Firers

93%—Machine Feeders and Offbearers

93%—Model Makers, Metal and Plastic

93%—Radio, Cellular, and Tower Equipment Installers and Repairs

93%—Butchers and Meat Cutters

93%—Extruding, Forming, Pressing, and Compacting Machine Setters, Operators, and Tenders

93%—Refuse and Recyclable Material Collectors

93%—Tax Examiners and Collectors, and Revenue Agents

93%—Forging Machine Setters, Operators, and Tenders, Metal and Plastic

93%—Industrial Truck and Tractor Operators

92%—Office Machine Operators, Except Computer

92%—Pharmacy Technicians

92%—Loan Interviewers and Clerks

92%—Dredge Operators

92%—Insurance Sales Agents

92%—Cabinetmakers and Bench Carpenters

92%—Painting, Coating, and Decorating Workers

92%—Fence Erectors

92%—Plating and Coating Machine Setters, Operators, and Tenders, Metal and Plastic

92%—Retail Salespersons

92%—Combined Food Preparation and Serving Workers, Including Fast Food

92%—Production Workers, All Other

92%—Helpers–Carpenters

91%—Gaming and Sports Book Writers and Runners

91%—Musical Instrument Repairers and Tuners

91%—Tour Guides and Escorts

91%—Mechanical Door Repairers

91%—Food and Tobacco Roasting, Baking, and Drying Machine Operators and Tenders

91%—Gas Compressor and Gas Pumping Station Operators

91%—Medical Records and Health Information Technicians

91%—Coating, Painting, and Spraying Machine Setters, Operators, and Tenders

91%—Multiple Machine Tool Setters, Operators, and Tenders, Metal and Plastic

91%—Rail Yard Engineers, Dinkey Operators, and Hostlers

91%—Electrical and Electronics Installers and Repairers, Transportation Equipment

91%—Dining Room and Cafeteria Attendants and
Bartender Helpers

91%—Heat Treating Equipment Setters, Operators, and
Tenders, Metal and Plastic

91%—Geological and Petroleum Technicians

91%—Automotive Body and Related Repairers

91%—Patternmakers, Wood

91%—Extruding and Drawing Machine Setters,
Operators, and Tenders, Metal and Plastic

90%—Human Resources Assistants, Except Payroll and
Timekeeping

90%—Medical and Clinical Laboratory Technologists

90%—Reinforcing Iron and Rebar Workers

90%—Roofers

90%—Crane and Tower Operators

90%—Traffic Technicians

90%—Transportation Inspectors

90%—Patternmakers, Metal and Plastic

90%—Molders, Shapers, and Casters, Except Metal and
Plastic

90%—Appraisers and Assessors of Real Estate

90%—Pump Operators, Except Wellhead Pumpers

90%—Signal and Track Switch Repairers

89%—Bakers

89%—Medical Transcriptionists

89%—Stonemasons

89%—Bus Drivers, School or Special Client

89%—Technical Writers

89%—Riggers

89%—Rail-Track Laying and Maintenance Equipment
Operators

89%—Stationary Engineers and Boiler Operators

89%—Sewing Machine Operators

89%—Taxi Drivers and Chauffeurs

88%—Construction Laborers

88%—Production, Planning, and Expediting Clerks

88%—Semiconductor Processors

88%—Cartographers and Photogrammetrists

88%—Metal-Refining Furnace Operators and Tenders

88%—Separating, Filtering, Clarifying, Precipitating, and Still Machine Setters, Operators, and Tenders

88%—Extruding and Forming Machine Setters, Operators, and Tenders, Synthetic and Glass Fibers

88%—Terrazzo Workers and Finishers

88%—Tool Grinders, Filers, and Sharpeners

88%—Rail Car Repairers

87%—Miscellaneous Agricultural Workers

87%—Forest and Conservation Workers

87%—Pourers and Casters, Metal

87%—Carpet Installers

87%—Paperhangers

87%—Buyers and Purchasing Agents, Farm Products

87%—Furniture Finishers

87%—Food Preparation Workers

87%—Floor Sanders and Finishers

87%—Parking Lot Attendants

87%—Highway Maintenance Workers

86%—Executive Secretaries and Executive Administrative Assistants

86%—Plant and System Operators, All Other

86%—Food Servers, Nonrestaurant

86%—Sawing Machine Setters, Operators, and Tenders, Wood

86%—Subway and Streetcar Operators

86%—Veterinary Assistants and Laboratory Animal Caretakers

86%—Cutting and Slicing Machine Setters, Operators, and Tenders

86%—Real Estate Sales Agents

86%—Computer-Controlled Machine Tool Operators, Metal and Plastic

86%—Maintenance Workers, Machinery

86%—Correspondence Clerks

85%—Laborers and Freight, Stock, and Material Movers, Hand

85%—Sales Representatives, Wholesale and Manufacturing, Except Technical and Scientific Products

85%—Meter Readers, Utilities

85%—Power Plant Operators

85%—Chemical Plant and System Operators

85%—Earth Drillers, Except Oil and Gas

85%—Nuclear Technicians

84%—Tool and Die Makers

84%—Electrical and Electronics Engineering Technicians

84%—Plasterers and Stucco Masons

84%—Layout Workers, Metal and Plastic

84%—Lathe and Turning Machine Tool Setters, Operators, and Tenders, Metal and Plastic

84%—Security Guards

84%—Tailors, Dressmakers, and Custom Sewers

84%—Wellhead Pumpers

84%—Proofreaders and Copy Markers

84%—Parking Enforcement Workers

83%—Fishers and Related Fishing Workers

83%—Structural Iron and Steel Workers

83%—Railroad Brake, Signal, and Switch Operators

83%—Railroad Conductors and Yardmasters

83%—Cooks, Institution and Cafeteria

83%—Sailors and Marine Oilers

83%—Mixing and Blending Machine Setters, Operators, and Tenders

83%—Helpers–Brickmasons, Blockmasons, Stonemasons, and Tile and Marble Setters

83%—Segmental Pavers

83%—Insulation Workers, Floor, Ceiling, and Wall

83%—Printing Press Operators

83%—Automotive and Watercraft Service Attendants

83%—Septic Tank Servicers and Sewer Pipe Cleaners

83%—Baggage Porters and Bellhops

83%—Gaming Change Persons and Booth Cashiers

83%—Rolling Machine Setters, Operators, and Tenders, Metal and Plastic

83%—Paving, Surfacing, and Tamping Equipment Operators

82%—Engine and Other Machine Assemblers

82%—Security and Fire Alarm Systems Installers

82%—Refractory Materials Repairers, Except Brickmasons

82%—Nonfarm Animal Caretakers

82%—Sheet Metal Workers

82%—Pile-Driver Operators

82%—Brickmasons and Blockmasons

81%—Cooks, Fast Food

81%—Word Processors and Typists

81%—Electrical and Electronics Drafters

81%—Electro-Mechanical Technicians

81%—Cleaning, Washing, and Metal Pickling Equipment Operators and Tenders

81%—Property, Real Estate, and Community Association Managers

81%—Medical Secretaries

81%—Pressers, Textile, Garment, and Related Materials

80%—Barbers

80%—Derrick Operators, Oil and Gas

79%—Postal Service Mail Sorters, Processors, and Processing Machine Operators

79%—Heavy and Tractor-Trailer Truck Drivers

79%—Shampooers

79%—Drywall and Ceiling Tile Installers

79%—Helpers–Installation, Maintenance, and Repair Workers

79%—Motorcycle Mechanics

79%—Aircraft Structure, Surfaces, Rigging, and Systems Assemblers

79%—Logging Equipment Operators

79%—Floor Layers, Except Carpet, Wood, and Hard Tiles

78%—Medical Equipment Preparers

78%—Cutting, Punching, and Press Machine Setters, Operators, and Tenders, Metal and Plastic

78%—Computer Operators

78%—Gas Plant Operators

77%—Environmental Science and Protection Technicians, Including Health

77%—Locksmiths and Safe Repairers

77%—Tree Trimmers and Pruners

77%—Bartenders

77%—Purchasing Agents, Except Wholesale, Retail, and Farm Products

77%—Dishwashers

77%—Hunters and Trappers

76%—Archivists

76%—Chemical Equipment Operators and Tenders

76%—Electric Motor, Power Tool, and Related Repairers

76%—Fallers

75%—Postmasters and Mail Superintendents

75%—Tile and Marble Setters

75%—Painters, Construction and Maintenance

75%—Transportation Attendants, Except Flight Attendants

75%—Civil Engineering Technicians

75%—Farm Equipment Mechanics and Service Technicians

74%—Computer, Automated Teller, and Office Machine Repairers

74%—Personal Care Aides

74%—Broadcast Technicians

74%—Helpers–Electricians

73%—Textile Knitting and Weaving Machine Setters, Operators, and Tenders

73%—Administrative Services Managers

73%—Glaziers

73%—Coil Winders, Tapers, and Finishers

73%—Bus and Truck Mechanics and Diesel Engine Specialists

72%—Amusement and Recreation Attendants

72%—Pharmacy Aides

72%—Helpers–Roofers

72%—Tank Car, Truck, and Ship Loaders

72%—Home Appliance Repairers

72%—Carpenters

72%—Public Address System and Other Announcers

71%—Aircraft Mechanics and Service Technicians

71%—Airfield Operations Specialists

71%—Petroleum Pump System Operators, Refinery Operators, and Gaugers

71%—Construction and Related Workers, All Other

71%—Opticians, Dispensing

71%—Laundry and Dry-Cleaning Workers

70%—Eligibility Interviewers, Government Programs

70%—Tire Repairers and Changers

70%—Food Batchmakers

70%—Avionics Technicians
69%—Light Truck or Delivery Services Drivers
69%—Maids and Housekeeping Cleaners
69%—Painters, Transportation Equipment
68%—Postal Service Mail Carriers
68%—Roustabouts, Oil and Gas
68%—Boilermakers
68%—Mechanical Drafters
68%—Dental Hygienists
67%—Paper Goods Machine Setters, Operators, and Tenders
67%—Foundry Mold and Coremakers
67%—Atmospheric and Space Scientists
67%—Bus Drivers, Transit and Intercity
67%—Lifeguards, Ski Patrol, and Other Recreational Protective Service Workers
67%—Industrial Machinery Mechanics
66%—Pest Control Workers
66%—Helpers–Production Workers
66%—Statistical Assistants
66%—Janitors and Cleaners, Except Maids and Housekeeping Cleaners
66%—Motorboat Mechanics and Service Technicians
65%—Social Science Research Assistants
65%—Machinists
65%—Computer Support Specialists
65%—Librarians
65%—Electronic Home Entertainment Equipment Installers and Repairers
65%—Heating, Air Conditioning, and Refrigeration Mechanics and Installers
65%—Hoist and Winch Operators
64%—Cutters and Trimmers, Hand
64%—Maintenance and Repair Workers, General

64%—Administrative Law Judges, Adjudicators, and Hearing Officers

64%—Stock Clerks and Order Fillers

64%—Power Distributors and Dispatchers

64%—Insulation Workers, Mechanical

63%—Geoscientists, Except Hydrologists and Geographers

63%—Control and Valve Installers and Repairers, Except Mechanical Door

63%—Healthcare Support Workers, All Other

63%—First-Line Supervisors of Food Preparation and Serving Workers

63%—Construction and Building Inspectors

62%—Motorboat Operators

62%—Tapers

62%—Pipelayers

61%—Electronic Equipment Installers and Repairers, Motor Vehicles

61%—Physical Therapist Aides

61%—Costume Attendants

61%—Market Research Analysts and Marketing Specialists

61%—Reservation and Transportation Ticket Agents and Travel Clerks

61%—Water and Wastewater Treatment Plant and System Operators

61%—Life, Physical, and Social Science Technicians, All Other

61%—Food Cooking Machine Operators and Tenders

61%—Welding, Soldering, and Brazing Machine Setters, Operators, and Tenders

60%—Correctional Officers and Jailers

60%—Camera Operators, Television, Video, and Motion Picture

60%—Slaughterers and Meat Packers

59%—Millwrights

59%—Museum Technicians and Conservators

59%—Mine Cutting and Channeling Machine Operators

59%—Transportation, Storage, and Distribution
Managers

59%—Recreational Vehicle Service Technicians

59%—Automotive Service Technicians and Mechanics

58%—Personal Financial Advisors

57%—First-Line Supervisors of Farming, Fishing, and
Forestry Workers

57%—Chemical Technicians

57%—Helpers–Pipelayers, Plumbers, Pipefitters, and
Steamfitters

57%—Cost Estimators

57%—Transit and Railroad Police

57%—First-Line Supervisors of Landscaping, Lawn
Service, and Groundskeeping Workers

56%—Teacher Assistants

55%—Automotive Glass Installers and Repairers

55%—Commercial Pilots

55%—Customer Service Representatives

55%—Audio and Video Equipment Technicians

54%—Embalmers

54%—Continuous Mining Machine Operators

54%—Slot Supervisors

54%—Massage Therapists

54%—Advertising Sales Agents

53%—Rotary Drill Operators, Oil and Gas

53%—Hazardous Materials Removal Workers

52%—Shoe and Leather Workers and Repairers

52%—Architectural and Civil Drafters

51%—Demonstrators and Product Promoters

51%—Dental Assistants

50%—Loading Machine Operators, Underground Mining

50%—Installation, Maintenance, and Repair Workers, All Other

50%—Court Reporters

Chapter 4—Jobs That Are Safe from Data Analytics Revolution (For Now)

Low-Risk List

Here is the safer half of a list produced by an Oxford study of jobs threatened by AI, with the percentage of replacement risk followed by the job title or description.

49%—Crossing Guards

49%—Agricultural Engineers

49%—Roof Bolters, Mining

49%—Telecommunications Line Installers and Repairers

49%—Police, Fire, and Ambulance Dispatchers

48%—Fire Inspectors and Investigators

48%—Aerospace Engineering and Operations Technicians

48%—Merchandise Displayers and Window Trimmers

48%—Explosives Workers, Ordnance Handling Experts, and Blasters

48%—Computer Programmers

47%—Compensation, Benefits, and Job Analysis Specialists

47%—Psychiatric Aides

47%—Medical and Clinical Laboratory Technicians

46%—Court, Municipal, and License Clerks

45%—Medical Appliance Technicians

44%—Historians

43%—Locker Room, Coatroom, and Dressing Room Attendants

43%—Physical Scientists, All Other

43%—Economists

42%—Forest and Conservation Technicians

42%—First-Line Supervisors of Helpers, Laborers, and Material Movers, Hand

41%—Graders and Sorters, Agricultural Products

41%—Structural Metal Fabricators and Fitters

41%—Judicial Law Clerks

41%—Electrical and Electronics Repairers, Commercial and Industrial Equipment

40%—Judges, Magistrate Judges, and Magistrates

40%—Mobile Heavy Equipment Mechanics, Except Engines

40%—Health Technologists and Technicians, All Other

39%—Home Health Aides

39%—Upholsterers

39%—Elevator Installers and Repairers

39%—Gaming Cage Workers

39%—Audio-Visual and Multimedia Collections Specialists

38%—Electrical and Electronics Repairers, Powerhouse, Substation, and Relay

38%—Surveyors

38%—Mechanical Engineering Technicians

38%—Packers and Packagers, Hand

38%—Interpreters and Translators

37%—Furnace, Kiln, Oven, Drier, and Kettle Operators and Tenders

37%—Cleaners of Vehicles and Equipment

37%—Funeral Attendants

37%—Helpers–Extraction Workers

37%—Actors

37%—Mine Shuttle Car Operators

36%—Bailiffs

36%—Computer Numerically Controlled Machine Tool Programmers, Metal and Plastic

36%—Telecommunications Equipment Installers and Repairers, Except Line Installers

35%—Plumbers, Pipefitters, and Steamfitters

35%—Flight Attendants

35%—Diagnostic Medical Sonographers

34%—Detectives and Criminal Investigators

34%—Surgical Technologists

34%—Radiation Therapists

33%—Financial Specialists, All Other

31%—Human Resources, Training, and Labor Relations Specialists, All Other

31%—Private Detectives and Investigators

31%—Film and Video Editors

30%—Biological Technicians

30%—Medical Assistants

30%—Zoologists and Wildlife Biologists

30%—Cooks, Private Household

29%—Skincare Specialists

29%—Wholesale and Retail Buyers, Except Farm Products

28%—First-Line Supervisors of Retail Sales Workers

28%—Athletes and Sports Competitors

28%—Gaming Supervisors

27%—Captains, Mates, and Pilots of Water Vessels

27%—Occupational Therapy Aides

27%—Medical Equipment Repairers

26%—Career/Technical Education Teachers, Middle School

25%—Geographers

25%—Occupational Health and Safety Technicians

25%—Probation Officers and Correctional Treatment Specialists

25%—Environmental Engineering Technicians

25%—Managers, All Other

25%—Ambulance Drivers and Attendants, Except Emergency Medical Technicians

25%—Sales Representatives, Wholesale and Manufacturing, Technical and Scientific Products

24%—Agents and Business Managers of Artists, Performers, and Athletes

24%—Engineering Technicians, Except Drafters, All Other

23%—Survey Researchers

23%—Business Operations Specialists, All Other

23%—Financial Analysts

23%—Radiologic Technologists and Technicians

23%—Cardiovascular Technologists and Technicians

22%—Computer Occupations, All Other

22%—Statisticians

22%—Computer Hardware Engineers

21%—Information Security Analysts, Web Developers, and Computer Network Architects

21%—Actuaries

21%—Animal Control Workers

21%—Concierges

20%—Epidemiologists

20%—Funeral Service Managers, Directors, Morticians, and Undertakers

19%—Adult Basic and Secondary Education and Literacy Teachers and Instructors

18%—Public Relations Specialists

18%—Commercial Divers

18%—Manufactured Building and Mobile Home Installers

18%—Airline Pilots, Copilots, and Flight Engineers

17%—Occupational Health and Safety Specialists

17%—Firefighters

17%—Financial Examiners

17%—First-Line Supervisors of Construction Trades and Extraction Workers

17%—Middle School Teachers, Except Special and Career/Technical Education

16%—Petroleum Engineers

16%—Desktop Publishers

16%—General and Operations Managers

15%—Kindergarten Teachers, Except Special Education

15%—Electricians

14%—Optometrists

14%—Mining and Geological Engineers, Including Mining Safety Engineers

14%—Physician Assistants

13%—Dancers

13%—Nuclear Medicine Technologists

13%—Software Developers, Systems Software

13%—Management Analysts

13%—Dietetic Technicians

13%—Urban and Regional Planners

13%—Social and Human Service Assistants

13%—Self-Enrichment Education Teachers

13%—Sound Engineering Technicians

11%—Hairdressers, Hairstylists, and Cosmetologists

11%—Reporters and Correspondents

11%—Air Traffic Controllers

10%—Chefs and Head Cooks

10%—Animal Trainers

10%—Radio and Television Announcers

10%—Electrical Engineers

10%—Chemists

10%—Respiratory Therapy Technicians

10%—Physicists

9.9%—Travel Agents

9.8%—Police and Sheriff's Patrol Officers

9.7%—Electrical Power-Line Installers and Repairers
9.1%—Gaming Managers
8.5%—Fitness Trainers and Aerobics Instructors
8.4%—Childcare Workers
8.3%—Food Service Managers
8.2%—Graphic Designers
8%—Compliance Officers
8%—Fish and Game Wardens
7.7%—Food Scientists and Technologists
7.6%—First-Line Supervisors of Personal Service Workers
7.5%—First-Line Supervisors of Non-Retail Sales Workers
7.4%—Musicians and Singers
7.1%—Construction Managers
7%—Nuclear Engineers
6.9%—Financial Managers
6.7%—Broadcast News Analysts
6.6%—Aircraft Cargo Handling Supervisors
6.6%—Respiratory Therapists
6.4%—Residential Advisors
6.1%—Animal Scientists
6%—Arbitrators, Mediators, and Conciliators
5.9%—Sociologists
5.8%—Licensed Practical and Licensed Vocational Nurses
5.7%—Travel Guides
5.5%—Editors
5.5%—Prosthodontists
5.5%—Healthcare Practitioners and Technical Workers, All Other
4.9%—Emergency Medical Technicians and Paramedics
4.8%—Forest Fire Inspectors and Prevention Specialists
4.7%—Mathematicians

4.7%—Floral Designers

4.7%—Farmers, Ranchers, and Other Agricultural Managers

4.5%—Landscape Architects

4.5%—Health Educators

4.3%—Psychiatric Technicians

4.2%—Software Developers, Applications

4.2%—Fine Artists, Including Painters, Sculptors, and Illustrators

4.1%—Astronomers

4.1%—Ship Engineers

4%—Credit Counselors

4%—Social Scientists and Related Workers, All Other

3.9%—Advertising and Promotions Managers

3.9%—Political Scientists

3.8%—Veterinarians

3.8%—Writers and Authors

3.7%—Commercial and Industrial Designers

3.7%—Biomedical Engineers

3.7%—Meeting, Convention, and Event Planners

3.5%—Lawyers

3.5%—Craft Artists

3.5%—Operations Research Analysts

3.5%—Computer and Information Systems Managers

3.3%—Environmental Scientists and Specialists, Including Health

3.3%—Substance Abuse and Behavioral Disorder Counselors

3.2%—Postsecondary Teachers

3%—Industrial Production Managers

3%—Industrial Engineering Technicians

3%—Network and Computer Systems Administrators

3%—Database Administrators

3%—Purchasing Managers

2.9%—Industrial Engineers

2.9%—First-Line Supervisors of Transportation andMaterial-Moving Machine and Vehicle Operators

2.9%—Veterinary Technologists and Technicians

2.8%—Occupational Therapy Assistants

2.8%—Child, Family, and School Social Workers

2.8%—Health and Safety Engineers, Except Mining Safety Engineers and Inspectors

2.7%—Biochemists and Biophysicists

2.7%—Chiropractors

2.5%—First-Line Supervisors of Correctional Officers

2.5%—Directors, Religious Activities and Education

2.5%—Electronics Engineers, Except Computer

2.3%—Orthodontists

2.3%—Art Directors

2.2%—Producers and Directors

2.2%—Interior Designers

2.1%—Soil and Plant Scientists

2.1%—Materials Scientists

2.1%—Materials Engineers

2.1%—Fashion Designers

2.1%—Physical Therapists

2.1%—Photographers

2%—Health Diagnosing and Treating Practitioners, All Other

1.9%—Civil Engineers

1.8%—Natural Sciences Managers

1.8%—Environmental Engineers

1.8%—Architects, Except Landscape and Naval

1.8%—Physical Therapist Assistants

1.7%—Chemical Engineers

1.7%—Architectural and Engineering Managers

1.7%—Aerospace Engineers

1.6%—First-Line Supervisors of Production and Operating Workers

1.6%—Securities, Commodities, and Financial Services Sales Agents

1.6%—Conservation Scientists

1.6%—Special Education Teachers, Middle School

1.5%—Biological Scientists, All Other

1.5%—Public Relations and Fundraising Managers

1.5%—Multimedia Artists and Animators

1.5%—Computer and Information Research Scientists

1.5%—Chief Executives

1.5%—Education Administrators, Preschool and Childcare Center/Program

1.5%—Music Directors and Composers

1.4%—Hydrologists

1.4%—Marketing Managers

1.4%—Marriage and Family Therapists

1.4%—Engineers, All Other

1.4%—Training and Development Specialists

1.4%—First-Line Supervisors of Office and Administrative Support Workers

1.3%—Coaches and Scouts

1.3%—Sales Managers

1.2%—Pharmacists

1.2%—Logisticians

1.2%—Microbiologists

1.2%—Industrial-Organizational Psychologists

1.1%—Mechanical Engineers

1%—Makeup Artists, Theatrical and Performance

1%—Marine Engineers and Naval Architects

1%—Education Administrators, Postsecondary

1%—Teachers and Instructors, All Other

1%—Forensic Science Technicians

0.9%—Rehabilitation Counselors

0.9%—Registered Nurses

0.9%—Career/Technical Education Teachers, Secondary School

0.9%—Educational, Guidance, School, and Vocational Counselors

0.8%—Clergy

0.8%—Foresters

0.8%—Secondary School Teachers, Except Special and Career/Technical Education

0.8%—Anthropologists and Archeologists

0.8%—Special Education Teachers, Secondary School

0.8%—Farm and Home Management Advisors

0.7%—Preschool Teachers, Except Special Education

0.7%—Medical and Health Services Managers

0.7%—Athletic Trainers

0.7%—Curators

0.7%—Social and Community Service Managers

0.7%—Computer Systems Analysts

0.6%—Speech-Language Pathologists

0.6%—Training and Development Managers

0.6%—Recreation Workers

0.6%—Set and Exhibit Designers

0.6%—Human Resources Managers

0.5%—Fabric and Apparel Patternmakers

0.5%—Mental Health Counselors

0.5%—Clinical, Counseling, and School Psychologists

0.5%—Education Administrators, Elementary and Secondary School

0.5%—Podiatrists

0.5%—Medical Scientists, Except Epidemiologists

0.4%—First-Line Supervisors of Police and Detectives

0.4%—Dentists, General

0.4%—Elementary School Teachers, Except Special Education

0.4%—Psychologists, All Other
0.4%—Physicians and Surgeons
0.4%—Instructional Coordinators
0.4%—Sales Engineers
0.4%—Choreographers
0.4%—Dietitians and Nutritionists
0.4%—Lodging Managers
0.4%—Oral and Maxillofacial Surgeons
0.4%—First-Line Supervisors of Fire Fighting and Prevention Workers
0.4%—Occupational Therapists
0.4%—Orthotists and Prosthetists
0.4%—Healthcare Social Workers
0.3%—Audiologists
0.3%—Mental Health and Substance Abuse Social Workers
0.3%—First-Line Supervisors of Mechanics, Installers, and Repairers
0.3%—Emergency Management Directors
0.3%—Recreational Therapists

Chapter 6—Benefits and Risks of Artificial Intelligence

The Risk of AI Understanding Human Frailties

What if we tell an AI system not to trust humans? In the fictional story portrayed in the blockbuster movie, *2001: A Space Odyssey* (from a story by Arthur C. Clark), the infamous HAL-9000 computer went crazy, murdering its fellow travelers. We don't know for certain that artificial intelligence would react this way. Like all humans, all AI systems are likely to have unique differences, because of uniquely different experiences and inputs. Even if all AI modules start with an identical set of neural nodes, differences in experience will cause each module to become distinctively singular. Creating an exact duplicate would require a precise repeat of the same inputs—a virtual impossibility.

Do we need to be so paranoid? We must remember that it's not paranoia if the threat is real. But it seems clear that we must treat the risk as a potential threat until we can find some way to eliminate AI confusion and dangerous reaction. Asimov's Three Laws of Robotics come to mind. Could these be the ultimate solution to such potential risks? We need to approach the problem with great care and thoroughness so that it never becomes an active danger.

Could China, Armed With AI, Conquer America?

China has satellites, so it can monitor situations from space. It also has the third largest merchant marine in the world (Soare) with build-up accelerating (Hellenic Shipping News). America is number six, behind South Korea, Germany, China, Japan and Greece. The Chinese navy is small compared to that of the United States. But the distance from Shanghai to Seattle is only about 5,000 nautical miles. Used as military transports, their merchant marine would only take 10–12 days to travel that distance. If such ships were already halfway to America when a cyber attack started, Chinese AI would only need to cause crippling confusion for about a week before their invasion could reach American shores.

With the news that Google is assisting the Chinese military, even if only indirectly, and the fact that China put out roughly 50% of the world's AI technical papers in 2018, bodes ill for the rest of the world. Would left-leaning regions like Seattle and other west coast cities welcome the Chinese "liberators?" Don't be surprised if they do. Too many on the Left are already supporting aiding and abetting criminals with sanctuary cities and states. Some Americans hate their country and want to see it destroyed. They are quite open about it. The late David Rockefeller even bragged in his *Memoirs* that he had conspired for decades against the best interests of the United States. Many of the crimes committed by America were set in motion by the very people who wanted to harm America. So, any anger against the United States is often misguided. The common people rarely want anything to do with the machinations of the self-proclaimed "elite." To the rich and powerful, AI is another tool for gaining more power over the individual no matter what their political affiliations.

This is the type of situation that makes AI far more risky than some would like to believe. If we become more aware of these dangers, we may be able to avoid the obvious pitfalls.

How to Destroy Freedom—
The Corruption of America—Lessons for AI
A society is an intelligence that can be programmed. This is a critical lesson for anyone interested in AI. How can natural intelligence become perverted or crippled?

What if all you ever learned was that the nation in which you lived was evil? The schools taught you that, the movies showed you that, the news media repeated it incessantly, and everywhere you looked on the internet, you found corroborating evidence. Of course, there were a few who disagreed, but they were known crackpots, racists, bigots, fascists and the like. Yet, what if the nation in which you lived was the only nation ever to throw off the yoke of tyranny, even while it struggled against those who wanted to destroy it from without and from within?

As we learned in the previous note, the late David Rockefeller, of the powerful, oil-rich Rockefeller family, wrote in his *Memoirs*, that he had conspired for decades against the best interests of the United States. These very rich people and people like them have made it clear that they want to change the face of humanity—controlling everyone under a One-World government. Personal freedom and liberty, they say, are "unsustainable."

Such an idea may seem idyllic to some—like *Star Trek's* Federation—united in a common purpose for the benefit of all. But human selfishness frequently perverts such power, as we've seen throughout history. Remember the saying, "absolute power corrupts absolutely?"

There are some who fear power in the hands of corporations, yet would love to give all that power to governments. But what's the difference? If governments are run by corporations, then there's no difference. Right now, corporations have far more influence in American government than individual citizens. Corporate lobbyists have their own desks in the offices of the congressmen and congresswomen over which they wish to hold sway. Those hoping to get reelected depend on money for their campaigns and corporations are happy to make those funds available to those who play along. Those who don't play along are never again given the chance. And too many government agencies are populated by former corporate execs from the industries for which they now oversee. The conflicts of interest are huge and nothing is done about it. And congressional representatives and senators frequently vote on bills for which they are given no time to read. The legislature is essentially driving blindly into oblivion. Such corruption doesn't need to buy off every congress person; it only needs to buy off the committee chairmen, the Speaker of the House and a few other key persons.

As a working social program, America started out small and lean. It had its problems, but over time handled them—getting rid of slavery, for instance. But in the long run, the government became bloated. Too many subroutines choked the nation's efficiency and made it more and more difficult for individuals to do their own thing. Those with power protected their power, selfishly.

And too many people conflated free market capitalism with corporatism and crony capitalism. It's almost as if part of the nation's operating system is an active virus bent on destroying the nation.

What can we learn from this? How can we apply these observations to AI and data analytics?

For one thing, we need to seek out humility at every turn. No one knows everything. There may be a great many facts hidden from us. An AI system will not necessarily have access to all the information. And its human handlers may feed it information that is called "factual" which may, instead, be full of lies and half-truths. Any AI system needs to guard against this possibility. An AI system must not take drastic measures which cannot be reversed if the input data is later found to be false. Remember GIGO?

GMOs and the Recklessness of Corporate Greed

Science is wonderful. The idea of scientists tailoring genetic coding to build custom attributes is exciting stuff. There's no doubt about that. But corporations have a way of approaching complex problems that can only be described as "ham-fisted incompetence." We've seen examples of this in the financial and pharmaceutical industries. The field of genetically modified organisms (GMOs) is no different.

When a product is created with profit motive only, risks and dangers may be considered, but only to the bottom line—not to the world-at-large. This is part of the problem with publicly-traded corporations. Their officers have a fiduciary duty to increase shareholder profits, and they frequently approach that with wild abandon. If that were the only dimension to consider, then such zeal would be wonderful.

When Monsanto first came out with a GMO product, of course, they had to get it approved by the Food and Drug Administration (FDA)—the American government agency tasked with overseeing the industry. Ironically, many, if not all of the execs in the FDA were former employees of Monsanto. Anyone who can't see the potential conflicts of interest simply isn't looking.

When FDA scientists recommended that the first GMO product be given far more testing, they were overruled by their bosses. To make matters worse, all future GMO products were to be considered GRAS— "generally regarded as safe," without so much as a second look. This is criminal incompetence of the highest order.

Monsanto's BT corn is of particular concern, because so many packaged foods contain some form of corn in them—corn meal, corn oil, corn syrup, etc. And today, a vast majority of packaged food corn ingredients are GMO.

One scientist used the same type of mice employed by Monsanto in their pre-approval tests. He used similar methods, but his study went on for 24 months instead of Monsanto's meager 3 months. When the company sub-mitted its test findings to the FDA, it noted that problems were detected at 3 months, but they were statistically insignificant. That alone should have raised red flags, but GMOs were already GRAS, so BT corn was approved.

Mention the scientists name in mixed circles and you're likely to receive a firestorm of ridicule. Professor Gilles-Eric Séralini is used to the criticism, but persists in doing research on the controversial product. Many scientists came to his support after his first article on the dangers of Monsanto's product was retracted by the publisher. Elsevier had published two articles critical of Monsanto, and needed to come up with a new category reason for retraction. That alone is controversial. Séralini found a different publisher, had twice the level of rigorous peer review, and received approval again for publication.

Séralini had found that the same mice, used by Monsanto in their approval process, had started to show serious illness in the 4th month—one month after the Monsanto study had ended. Twelve months after the Séralini study had started, many of the mice were exhibiting large cancerous tumors.

The object lesson, here, is that corporations can be so egregiously greedy that they can endanger the lives of everyone on the planet and claim innocence.

Monsanto's 3-month test was so skimpy it could rightfully be compared to the testing of a new airplane prototype—taxiing the new plane to the end of the runway and then returning to the terminal for its first load of passengers. Without flying one minute, such a test could accurately be judged as woefully inadequate and criminal endangerment of the flying public. Testing a new life form for 3 months before releasing it into the world-at-large is similarly insane.

Why this GMO story is so important to us is that it proves how careless corporations can be in releasing a new life form into the world-at-large. Fully-generalized artificial intelligence would be, in virtually every sense of the word, a new life form. It could have the power of replication, of autonomy and control over external resources. There's a very real danger that such an AI could exceed the boundaries given to it by its creators, for any flaws in the programming would likely be found and exploited in unforeseen ways by that intelligence. In the rush to rake in profits, some corporate bean counters will likely not take into account many of the dangers such intelligence could pose to the corporation and to the rest of humanity.

More on Criminal Justice Failures and Potential AI Confusion

What is an AI system to think about its human bene-factors with all of the mixed signals it would receive by scanning the internet and news sources? There is plenty there to make any AI potentially neurotic if not outright psychotic.

Take for instance the situation in the United States under President Trump. Clearly, the leader is not as polished and refined as his predecessor. But any honest observer can see a clear bias against him in the bulk of the mainstream news media and amongst members of the opposition party. Claims are made on a daily basis that have no foundation in fact. These are used as reason to resist every major policy set forth by this president. Opposition can be a good thing, if its honest, but this state of affairs breaks the scales used to measure such honesty.

Suddenly, the opposition party wants open borders. Not only do we see support for this in the news media, but also in social media platforms. Logically, a nation is defined, in part, by its borders and the values of its citizens. Letting people from other nations cross over the border without qualification can prove dangerous from a law enforcement standpoint.

When political opposition leaders state that "walls are immoral," yet they use walls in their own property to keep out potential criminals, we have to realize that what they're saying is perhaps not true. The fact that hundreds of citizens have died at the hands of people who crossed the border illegally, makes the open borders issue highly problematic. When the opposition party celebrates sanctuary cities and states, like California, they are celebrating criminal activity, for their use of sanctuary is, in effect, aiding and abetting criminals, which is itself a crime for which those legislators could be at risk of impeachment and criminal prosecution.

Some who are aware of the huge, gaping flaw in critical thinking on these issues are too timid to do anything about it, because of the social or financial repercussions. Their own self-concern makes them just that much more insane and complicit.

Uneven application of laws is one of the hallmarks of tyranny. And AI utilized by a tyrannical regime is the stuff of nightmares. The end result would logically be one of a government becoming criminal and victimizing their own citizens. Such tyrannical (e.g. Nazi, Fascist, Socialist, Communist) regimes, in the 20th century, resulted in the deaths of roughly 100 million individuals.

Overcoming Bias in Science

Most scientists don't know how thoroughly biased their fields are. Philosopher, Rod Martin, Jr. wrote about this in college, in a first-place award-winning essay entitled, "Outsiderness in the Scientific Community" (Krupnick Award, 1996). In a paper he wrote years later, he detailed how the bias in science is built into its core paradigm — skepticism. He wrote that the key ingredients in discovery of any kind involves the unbiased traits of restraint and humility, but that skepticism, which contains these two, also contains the potent, negative bias of "doubt." Such bias works well against the positive bias of enthusiastic young graduates and crusty old senior scientists, but too often, scientists and self-proclaimed skeptics forget how to use skepticism for this purpose. They betray their tool with blundering ineptitude.

Take for instance the field of North American anthropology. For decades, scientists were warned not to dig below the Clovis horizon (the strata dated to the culture of Clovis, New Mexico), or they could lose funding or even lose their careers. Imagine that: Scientists threatened not to look for evidence that would overthrow the "Clovis First" dogma. Incredible! Some scientists were more interested in protecting old ideas, instead of discovering new evidence. In fact, one Texas geoarchaeologist said that he would never believe the dates of artifacts found at one site in Mexico, no matter what the evidence. Can you believe it? A scientist who preferred dogma to evidence!

Martin wrote that while he studied electronic engineering in the 70s, his prior knowledge of science triggered a realization about what he was learning. In his lessons, he discovered the basics of radio broadcast and receiving technology, including the primitive tank circuit, or LC circuit. He learned that a receiver could be built out of a coil and a capacitor electrically in parallel. The coil resisted alternating current and loved direct current. The capacitor resisted direct current but loved alternating current. Between the traits of both devices, there was one frequency of alternating current which found the least resistance between the coil and capacitor. This was the tuned frequency. Suddenly, Martin realized that he was surrounded by trillions of tank circuits. Every single atom—in his own body, in the air he breathed, in the clothes he wore, and in the building which surrounded him—was each a coil and capacitor. Each atom had electrons which effectively orbited the nucleus (coil) and held negative electrons separate from their positive proton-charged nucleus (capacitor). As he had learned in high school, every atom had its own set of tuned frequencies for both emitting and absorbing electromagnetic radiation.

Imagine AI helping students to see these connections in thought that expand their understanding of basic principles to other areas which most students would otherwise miss. And imagine the inventions that might be possible from the right person seeing these parallels which are not as obvious to most people.

In an article Martin wrote for an educational website, he talked about how a rare few teachers are able to cut through the jargon of a field in order to reveal the simplicity inherent within it. In his article, entitled, "Johnny Can't Read—Overcoming the Many Types of Learning Disabilities," he mentioned two educators who had inspired him to excellence. One was the recipient of a presidential award—Jaime Escalante—the subject of the motion picture *Stand and Deliver*. The other was a British engineer and professor of physics, Sylvanus P. Thompson, whose most famous work was a tiny primer on advanced mathematics titled, *Calculus Made Easy*. Martin remarked that the tiny book was so successful and so loved by college students that it had gone through dozens of printings since it was initially published in 1910. Martin remarked that some other textbook writers, though perhaps great mathematicians, were horrible writers and educators.

Imagine AI finding the simplicity in each subject that makes it easy for every student to understand. The boon to education, alone, could be well worth the effort to create fully-generalized AI.

How Corporations May All Be Evil

If you ever want to start a fight, say something contentious, like "you're evil!" Ouch! Saying something like,
"all corporations are evil," can prove equally contentious.

What is "evil?" Can it be defined? In this day of
moral relativism, where one man's evil is another man's
good, who's to say what the definition is?

In a discussion of an upcoming book entitled, *The
Nature of Evil*, Rod Martin, Jr. wrote that absolute morality
does exist. Many well-meaning, but naive Europeans and
a few Americans have attempted to prove evil doesn't
exist by bicycling or hiking through the Middle East in an
attempt to show the world that we can all get along.
We've had numerous reports of such idealistic individuals being raped and killed for making themselves an
easy target for someone else's evil.

Perhaps we can all agree that life is a good thing.
Anything that destroys life is problematic. There are
some on the far Left of the political spectrum who will
try to convince us that humans are all bad and should be
dead (Gaia extremists, for example); and it should
surprise us that they are still alive, if they truly believe
that, for they are human, too. We might posit the corol-
lary argument that, because life is good, anything which
destroys life is potentially bad or evil.

Discussions become muddied with arguments that
antiseptics kill bacteria, and thus medicine could be
viewed as evil. This type of thinking derails logic. It's
part of the moral relativism that destroys, instead of
builds. There is a hierarchy of things in the universe. A
bacterium is more important than a rock. A fish is more
important than a bacterium. A bear is more important
than a fish. And a human is more important than a bear.
We intuitively sense this hierarchy in our quest for fully-

generalized AI. It has greater potential value than narrow, problem-specific AI. And the narrow species of AI is more valuable than an adding machine. See? There is logic to this, once we get past the appeals to emotion and other logical fallacies.

As humans, we have the potential to be guardians of intellect, and good stewards of nature. Some have seriously failed at that. And some humans have been illogical enough to declare all humans to be "bad" because a few have been bad. Theirs is logically fallacious thinking to an extreme.

Martin suggests that selfishness is the root of all evil. If we think about it for a moment, any evil act perpetrated by a madman or woman can be traced back to some form of self-concern—the essence of egoism. That selfishness can be a delusion or it can be a pre-meditated form of evil.

Humans intuitively admire the hero, and shun the braggart, bully or coward. Why is this? It's because the hero is selfless. The hero cares more about others than they do about their own self. They are willing to sacrifice their self for the good of another or others. And we tend to admire competence over incompetence.

Corporations can be evil by harming others for selfish gain. All publicly-traded corporations are mandated by law to do just that. A corporate officer who does not increase profits for their shareholders is shirking their fiduciary duty. Thus, we get corporations destroying the planetary economy, as they did in the housing bubble, and corrupting their government to give them bailouts when they should be getting jail time. Thus, we get corporations dumping toxic chemicals into rivers and pretending they did nothing wrong when people end up deformed or irreversibly damaged or dead. Privately-owned corporations at least have a choice not to be evil. The publicly-traded variety don't have that luxury.

Do we need a new paradigm for capitalism? Has humanity made a wrong turn into a dark cul-de-sac of oblivion? For all the moaning of the "tree huggers" and "Gaia enthusiasts," there is a virus upon the land. It's not humans. Arguably, it's publicly-traded corporations. Like the scorpion in the proverb about getting help crossing the river, it's in their nature to sting humans. They can't change their nature.

A publicly-traded corporation is group selfishness. So is a conspiracy. When two or more people get together to talk about doing something unethical, immoral or illegal, that's a conspiracy. And every conversation behind corporate closed doors that cajoles its employees to look the other way is merely another conspiracy. When whistleblowers are jailed and the criminals go free, we have a big problem.

When scientists can be bought to say anything, a corporation can "prove" to the world that a product or service is safe. Can scientists really be corrupted? Are scientists human? Of course they are, and they can be corrupted.

This discussion is not pessimism. Quite the contrary. This discussion is a wake-up call full of shrewd optimism. For if we want all of the good of artificial intelligence, we have to be willing to look squarely at reality, without flinching, and to handle the very real problems that stand in our way.

We need heroic compassion, but we also need intelligent wisdom. For a hero who dies in an attempt to save someone else is not nearly as admirable as a competent hero who actually gets the job done.

We could ask our corporations to be heroes, but that is like asking a scorpion not to sting us, or a snake not to bite us, or a tiger not to eat us. It's not in their nature to honor such a request. Thus, we need to construct a new economic paradigm—one that phases out sources of evil, and replaces them with something that has the fiduciary freedom to choose. There remains a huge difference between a private owner and a public owner.

The public owner is a collectivist—tyranny over the individual. For all the political Left's complaints about corporations being on the Right, they're actually conflating two kinds of corporations—the free market kind that stands for individual liberty and entrepreneurial spirit, and the collectivist kind that stands for totalitarian control over governments, markets and individuals. The public kind truly are evil. In a world full of wisdom, we might be wise to pay shareholders for their interest in their corporations and to make those corporations private again. And then—dare we think it?—make public stocks illegal. Humanity would thank us for removing one cesspool of evil from the landscape. Evil would still exist, but it would no longer have such a powerful ally.

Without evil corporations, AI has the chance to become the most blessed physical gift to humanity since fire.

Bibliography

Fioramonti, Lorenzo. (2014). How Numbers Rule the
World: The Use and Abuse of Statistics in Global
Politics. Zed Books: London.

Fung, Kaiser. (2010). Numbers Rule Your World: The
Hidden Influence of Probability and Statistics on
Everything You Do. McGraw-Hill: New York.

Herrnstein, R.J., and Murray, C. (1994). The Bell Curve:
Intelligence and Class Structure in American Life.
Free Press: New York.

Hubbard, Douglas W. (2007). How to Measure Anything
Finding the Value of "Intangibles" in Business.
John Wiley & Sons, Inc.: Hoboken, NJ.

Kaufman, Alan S., and Lichtenberger, Elizabeth O. (2006).
Assessing Adolescent and Adult Intelligence (3rd
ed.). John Wiley & Sons, Inc.: Hoboken, NJ.

Kaufman, Alan S. (2009). IQ Testing 101. Springer
Publishing: New York.

Lang, C., et al, eds. (2017). Handbook of Learning
Analytics, First Ed. Society for Learning Analytics
Research: Ann Arbor, Michigan.

Siegel, Eric. (2016). Predictive Analytics: The power to
predict who will click, buy, lie, or die. John Wiley
& Sons, Inc.: Hoboken, NJ.

Glossary

ACID Test—a test applied to data for atomicity, consistency, isolation and durability.

aggregation—a process of searching, gathering and presenting data.

AI—abbreviation of "artificial intelligence" (which see).

algorithm—a mathematical formula or statistical process used to perform analysis of data.

algorithm—a set of instructions that is designed to produce a specific set of results from certain types of input. This usually refers to a set of computer instructions in software or built into computer hardware. For example: the steps to calculate the square root of both integers and non-integral numbers.

alpha risk—the maximum probability of making a Type I error. This probability is established by the experimenter and often set at 5%.

alternative hypothesis (Ha)—statement of a change or difference; assumed to be true if the null hypothesis is rejected.

android—a robot which resembles a human being. Examples include fictional C-3PO from *Star Wars*, and Sophia, the robot produced by Hanson Robotics. [from *andro*- human-like + -*oid* in the form of]

anomaly detection—the process of identifying rare or unexpected items or events in a dataset that do not conform to other items in the dataset and do not match a projected pattern or expected behavior. Anomalies are also called outliers, exceptions, surprises or contaminants and they often provide critical and actionable information.

anonymization—making data anonymous; severing of links between people in a database and their records to prevent the discovery of the source of the records.

ANOVA—one-way ANOVA is a generalization of the 2-sample t-test, used to compare the means of more than two samples to each other.

ANOVA table—the ANOVA table is the standard method of organizing the many calculations necessary for conducting an analysis of variance.

API—Application Program Interface. A set of programming standards and instructions for accessing or building web-based software applications.

application—software that enables a computer to perform a certain task.

artificial intelligence—the apparent ability of a machine to apply information gained from previous experience accurately to new situations in a way that a human would.

artificial intelligence—the talents or functionality built into a machine that would otherwise be thought to require human intelligence. Non-natural intelligence or created (man-made) intelligence. (See intelligence)

batch processing—an efficient way of processing high volumes of data where a group of transactions is collected over a period of time. Hadoop is focused on batch data processing.

Bayes theorem—a theorem based on conditional probabilities. It uses relevant evidence, also known as conditional probability, to determine the probability of an event, based on prior knowledge of conditions that might be related to the event.

beta risk—the risk or probability of making a Type II error.

big data—datasets whose size is beyond the ability of typical database software tools to capture, store, manage and analyze.

big data—the large quantity of data available to a company, including emails, phone calls, phone call logs, transactions, customer complaints, production reports, production line sensors (manufacturing), and much more. Such data can be structured (e.g. relational database), semi-structured and unstructured (all three of which, see).

binary language—machine language (which see).

business analytics—the body of activities that promote business intelligence, including knowledge of what got the business to its current state, what the future may hold and how to steer the company in a better direction. Includes subsets descriptive analytics, predictive analytics and prescriptive analytics (all three of which, see).

business intelligence—the general term used for the identification, extraction and analysis of data.

Cassandra—a popular open source database management system managed by The Apache Software Foundation. Designed to handle large amounts of distributed data across commodity servers while providing a highly available service. It is a NoSQL solution that was initially developed by Facebook.

classification analysis—a systematic process for obtaining important and relevant information about data (metadata) and assigning data to a particular group or class.

clickstream analytics—the analysis of users' web activity through the items they click on a page.

cloud—a broad term that refers to any internet-based application or service that is hosted remotely.

cloud computing—a distributed computing system hosted and running on remote servers and accessible from anywhere on the internet.

cluster computing—computing using a 'cluster' of pooled resources of multiple servers. Getting more technical, we might be talking about nodes, cluster management layer, load balancing and parallel processing etc.

clustering analysis—the process of identifying objects that are similar to each other and clustering them in order to understand the differences as well as the similarities within the data.

coefficient of variation—standard deviation normalized by the mean: σ/μ.

columnar database or **column-oriented database**—a database that stores data by column rather than by row. In a row-based database, a row might contain a name, address and phone number. In a column-oriented database, all names are in one column, addresses in another and so on. A key advantage of a columnar database is faster hard disk access.

comparative analysis—data analysis that compares two or more data sets or processes to detect patterns within very large data sets.

confidence interval—a range of values which is likely to contain the population parameter of interest with a given level of confidence.

continuous data—data from a measurement scale that can be divided into finer and finer increments (e.g. temperature, time, pressure). Also known as variable data.

correlation analysis—a means to determine a statistical relationship between variables, often for the purpose of identifying predictive factors among the variables. A technique for quantifying the strength of the linear relationship between two variables.

dashboard—a graphical representation of analyses performed by algorithms.

dark data—all the data that is gathered and processed by enterprises but not used for any meaningful purposes.

data—a quantitative or qualitative value. Common types of data include sales figures, marketing research results, readings from monitoring equipment, user actions on a website, market growth projections, demographic information and customer lists.

data aggregation—the process of collecting data from multiple sources for the purpose of reporting or analysis.

data analyst—a person responsible for the tasks of modeling, preparing and cleaning data for the purpose of deriving actionable information from it.

data analytics—the process of examining large data sets to uncover hidden patterns, unknown correlations, trends, customer preferences and other useful business insights. The end result might be a report, an indication of status or an action taken automatically based on the information received. Businesses typically use the following types of analytics:

- *Behavioral Analytics:* Using data about people's behavior to understand intent and predict future actions.
- *Descriptive Analytics:* Condensing big numbers into smaller pieces of information. This is similar to summarizing the data story. Rather than listing every single number and detail, there is a general thrust and narrative.
- *Diagnostic Analytics:* Reviewing past performance to determine what happened and why. Businesses use this type of analytics to complete root cause analysis.
- *Predictive Analytics:* Using statistical functions on one or more data sets to predict trends or future events. In big data predictive analytics, data scientists may use advanced techniques like data mining, machine learning and advanced statistical processes to study recent and historical data to make predictions about the future. It can be used to forecast weather, predict what people are likely to buy, visit, do or how they may behave in the near future.
- *Prescriptive Analytics:* Prescriptive analytics builds on predictive analytics by including actions and make data-driven decisions by looking at the impacts of various actions.

data analytics—qualitative and quantitative techniques and processes used to enhance productivity and business gain.

descriptive analytics—a subset of business analytics (which see). This tells us what has happened in the past and what caused our current conditions.

data architecture and design—how enterprise data is structured. The actual structure or design varies depending on the eventual end result required. Data architecture has three stages or processes: (1) conceptual representation of business entities, (2) the logical representation of the relationships among those entities and (3) the physical construction of the system to support the functionality.

data as a service (DaaS)—treat data as a product. DaaS providers use cloud solutions to give on-demand access of data to customers.

data center—a physical facility that houses a large number of servers and data storage devices. Data centers might belong to a single organization or sell their services to many organizations.

data cleansing—the process of reviewing and revising data to delete duplicate entries, correct misspelling and other errors, add missing data and provide consistency.

data ethical guidelines—guidelines that help organizations be transparent with the data, ensuring simplicity, security and privacy.

data feed—a means for a person to receive a stream of data such as a Twitter feed or RSS.

data governance—a set of processes or rules that ensure data integrity and that data management best practices are met.

data integration—the process of combining data from different sources and presenting it in a single view.

data integrity—the measure of trust an organization has in the accuracy, completeness, timeliness and validity of the data.

data lake—a large repository of enterprise-wide data in raw format. Supposedly data lakes make it easy to access enterprise-wide data. However, you really need to know what you are looking for and how to process it and make intelligent use of it.

data mart—the access layer of a data warehouse used to provide data to users.

data warehouse—a repository for enterprise-wide data but in a structured format after cleaning and integrating with other sources. Data warehouses are typically used for conventional data (but not exclusively).

data mining—finding meaningful patterns and deriving insights in large sets of data using sophisticated pattern recognition techniques. To derive meaningful patterns, data miners use statistics, machine learning algorithms and artificial intelligence.

data modeling—a data model defines the structure of the data for the purpose of communicating between functional and technical people to show data needed for business processes, or for communicating a plan to develop how data is stored and accessed among application development team members.

data scientist—someone who can make sense of big data by extracting raw data, massaging it and come up with insights. Skills needed are statistics, computer science, creativity, story-telling and understanding of business context.

data science—a discipline that incorporates statistics, data visualization, computer programming, data mining, machine learning and database engineering to solve complex problems.

data set—a collection of data, very often in tabular form.

database—a digital collection of data and the structure around which the data is organized. The data is typically entered into and accessed via a database management system.

database management system (DBMS)—software that collects and provides access to data in a structured format.

demographic data—data relating to the characteristics of a human population.

discrete data—data which is not measured on a continuous scale. Examples are binomial (pass/fail), Counts per unit, Ordinal (small/medium/large) and Nominal (red/green/blue). Also known as attribute or categorical data.

discriminant analysis—a statistical analysis technique used to predict cluster membership from labelled data.

distributed file system—a data storage system meant to store large volumes of data across multiple storage devices and will help decrease the cost and complexity of storing large amounts of data.

dystopia—a world where society has broken down and almost nothing works. (Compare *utopia*.)

empirical model—an equation derived from the data that expresses a relationship between the inputs and an output $(Y=f(x))$.

ETL (Extract, Transform and Load)—the process of extracting raw data, transforming by cleaning/enriching the data to make it fit operational needs and loading into the appropriate repository for the system's use. Even though it originated with data warehouses, ETL processes are used while taking/absorbing data from external sources in big data systems.

event—a set of outcomes of an experiment (a subset of the sample space) to which a probability is assigned.

exploratory analysis—an approach to data analysis focused on identifying general patterns in data, including outliers and features of the data that are not anticipated by the experimenter's current knowledge or preconceptions. EDA aims to uncover underlying structure, test assumptions, detect mistakes and understand relationships between variables.

external data—data that exists outside of a system.

F-test—A hypothesis test for comparing variances.

fit—the average outcome predicted by a model.

garbage in, garbage out—software engineering maxim that the data output is, at best, only as good as the data input. Sometimes abbreviated, GIGO.

GIGO—abbreviation for "garbage in, garbage out" (which see).

grid computing—connecting different computer systems from various locations, often via the cloud, to reach a common goal.

Hadoop—an open source software framework administered by Apache that allows for storage, retrieval and analysis of very large data sets across clusters of computers.

high performance computing—using supercomputers to solve highly complex and advanced computing problems.

histograms—representation of frequency of values by intervals.

in-database analytics—the integration of data analytics into the data storage layer.

in-memory computing—a technique of moving the working datasets entirely within a cluster's collective memory and avoid writing intermediate calculations to disk. This results in very fast processing, storing and loading of data.

intelligence—the ability to recognize identities, discern differences and similarities, and to analyze cause and effect, allowing for forecasting, planning and problem solving. Also thought to be sometimes involved with creativity. In humans, intelligence can sometimes be thwarted by destructive attitudes commonly referred to as egoism, leading to conditions like arrogance.

Internet of Things—the interconnecting of physical devices of all types through an electronic network. This may include devices like a smart phone, refrigerator, oven, lights and other domestic controls, plus vehicles, computers and other types of equipment. The purpose of these connections is for control, data sharing and management of all connected resources.

IoT—Internet of Things (which see).

IoT (Internet of Things)—the network of physical objects or "things" embedded with electronics, software, sensors and connectivity to enable it to achieve greater value and service by exchanging data with the manufacturer, operator and/or other connected devices. Each thing is uniquely identifiable through its embedded computing system but is able to interoperate within the existing Internet infrastructure.

juridical data compliance—use of data stored in a country must follow the laws of that country. Relevant when using cloud solutions with data stored in difference countries or continents.

key value databases—storing data with a primary key, a uniquely identifiable record, which makes it easy and computationally efficient to look up.

latency—any delay in a response or delivery of data from one point to another.

load balancing—the process of distributing workload across a computer network or computer cluster to optimize performance.

location analytics—location analytics brings mapping and map-driven analytics to enterprise business systems and data warehouses. It allows you to associate geospatial information with datasets.

location data—GPS data describing a geographical location.

log file—a file that a computer, network or application creates automatically to record events that occur during operation. For example, the time a file is accessed.

logistic regression—investigates the relationship between response (Y's) and one or more predictors (X's) where Y's are categorical, not continuous and X's can be either continuous or categorical. Types of logistic regression are:

- *Binary Logistic Regression:* Y variable takes on one of two outcomes (levels), e.g. pass/fail, agree/disagree.
- *Ordinal Logistic Regression:* Y variable can have more than two levels. Levels are rank ordered, e.g. Low/Medium/High, 1-5 preference scale.
- *Nominal Logistic Regression:* Y variable can have more than two levels. There is no implied order to the levels, e.g. Blue/Yellow/Green, Company A/B/C/D.

machine-generated data—Data automatically created by machines via sensors or algorithms or any other non-human source.

machine language—the lowest level of computer instructions in the language that the machine understands without need for translation. Most computer languages require interpretation (on the fly; script file) or compiling (before distribution; an executable file) to translate them into machine language. A set of ones and zeroes which the computer hardware can read.

machine learning—the ability of machines to learn from experience (sensors) or other inputs. This is a subfield of artificial intelligence (which see).

machine learning—a method of designing systems that can learn, adjust and improve based on the data fed to them. Using predictive and statistical algorithms that are fed to these machines, they learn and continually zero in on "correct" behavior and insights and they keep improving as more data flows through the system.

mapreduce—a programming model for processing and generating large data sets. This model does two distinct things. First, the "Map" includes turning one dataset into another, more useful and broken down dataset made of parts called tuples. Tuples may typically be processed independently from each other across multiple processors. Second, "Reduce" takes all of the broken down, processed tuples and combines their output into a usable result. The result is a practical breakdown of processing.

Massively Parallel Processing (MPP)—using many different processors (or computers) to perform certain computational tasks at the same time.

mean—the weighted average of data. The population mean is denoted by μ (Greek letter *mu)* and the sample mean is denoted by $\bar{x}$.

median—the middle value of a data set when arranged in order of magnitude.

metadata—data about data; it gives information about what the data is about. For example, where data points were collected.

mode—the measurement that occurs most often in a data set.

multi-dimensional databases—a database optimized for data online analytical processing (OLAP) applications and for data warehousing.

naïve Bayes—a classification technique based on Bayes Theorem with an assumption of independence among predictors. In simple terms, it assumes that the presence of a particular feature in a class is unrelated to the presence of any other feature.

network analysis—analyzing connections between nodes in a network and the strength of their ties.

neural network—models inspired by the real-life biology of the brain. These are used to estimate mathematical functions and facilitate different kinds of learning algorithms. Deep Learning is a similar term and is generally seen as a modern buzzword, rebranding the Neural Network paradigm for the modern day.

normal distribution—The most important continuous probability distribution in statistics is the normal distribution (a.k.a. Gaussian distribution). The normal distribution is the familiar bell curve. Once m and s are specified, the entire curve is determined.

NoSQL (Not ONLY SQL)—a broad class of database management systems identified by non-adherence to the widely used relational database management system model. NoSQL databases are not built primarily on tables and generally do not use SQL for data manipulation. Database management systems that are designed to handle large volumes of data and are often well-suited for big data systems because of their flexibility and distributed-first architecture needed for large unstructured databases.

null hypothesis (H0)—statement of no change or difference; assumed to be true until sufficient evidence is presented to reject it.

one sample T-test—statistical test to compare the mean of one sample of data to a target. Uses the t-distribution

operational databases—databases that carry out regular operations of an organization that are generally very important to the business. They typically use online transaction processing that allows them to enter, collect and retrieve specific information about the organization.

optimization analysis—the process of finding optimal problem parameters subject to constraints. Optimization algorithms heuristically test a large number of parameter configurations in order to find an optimal result, determined by a characteristic function (also called a fitness function).

outlier detection—an object that deviates significantly from the general average within a dataset or a combination of data. It is numerically distant from the rest of the data and therefore indicates that something unusual and generally requires additional analysis.

paired T-test—a test used to compare the average difference between two samples of data that are linked in pairs. Special case of the 1-sample t-test. Uses the t-distribution.

pattern recognition—identifying patterns in data via algorithms to make predictions about new data coming from the same source.

pig—A data flow language and execution framework for parallel computation.

population—a dataset that consists of all the members of some group. Descriptive parameters (such as ?, ?) are used to describe the population.

power (1-beta)—the ability of a statistical test to detect a real difference when there is one; the probability of correctly rejecting the null hypothesis. Determined by alpha and sample size.

predictive analytics—a subset of business analytics (which see). This provides a look into the future or possible futures. This allows managers and executives to make more precise decisions based on facts rather than opinions.

prescriptive analytics—a subset of business analytics (which see). This provides an idea of what our organization should do now and in the future to solve certain, well-defined problems and goals.

predictive modeling—the process of developing a model that will most likely predict a trend or outcome.

probability—the likelihood of a given event's occurrence, which is expressed as a number between 1 and 0.

probability distribution—A statistical function that describes all the possible values and likelihoods that a random variable can take within a given range. Probability distributions may be discrete or continuous.

public data—public information or data sets that were created with public funding.

Query—asking for information to answer a certain question.

R—an open source programming language used for statistical computing and graphics. It is a GNU project which is similar to the S language. R provides a wide variety of statistical (linear and nonlinear modeling, classical statistical tests, time-series analysis, classification, clustering, etc.) and graphical techniques and is highly extensible. It is one of the most popular languages in data science.

range—difference between the largest and smallest measurement in a data set.

real time data—data that is created, processed, stored, analyzed and visualized within milliseconds.

regression analysis—a modeling technique used to define the association between variables. It assumes a one-way causal effect from predictor variables (independent variables) to a response of another variable (dependent variable). Regression can be used to explain the past and predict future events.

residual—the difference between reality (an actual measurement) and the fit (model output).

robot—a machine, frequently one controlled by a computer, which can perform complex tasks, including things like self-diagnostics, self-repair and self-adjustment. Such machines utilize a form of artificial intelligence that can be specialized to a specific set of tasks, or theoretically, a more generalized AI that allows autonomous action, machine learning (which see) and an ability to program itself within designed limitations.

robotics—a field of science and engineering that involves multiple disciplines to produce robots (which see).

sample—a data set which consists of only a portion of the members from some population. Sample statistics are used to draw inferences about the entire population from the measurements of a sample.

scalability—the ability of a system or process to maintain acceptable performance levels as workload or scope increases.

semi-structured data—data that is not structured by a formal data model, but provides other means of describing the data hierarchies (tags or other markers).

semi-structured data—data that may include tables plus free-form text. Part of big data (which see).

sentiment analysis—the application of statistical functions and probability theory to comments people make on the web or social networks to determine how they feel about a product, service or company.

significant difference—the term used to describe the results of a statistical hypothesis test where a difference is too large to be reasonably attributed to chance.

single-variance test (Chi-square test)—compares the variance of one sample of data to a target. Uses the Chi-square distribution.

software—a set of computer instructions which provides some useful functionality, such as word processing, graphic design, calculations, projections and even artificial intelligence.

software as a service (SaaS)—enables vendors to host an application and make it available via the internet (cloud servicing). SaaS providers provide services over the cloud rather than hard copies.

software engineering—the discipline of writing instructions for computers that perform specialized tasks to achieve a specific purpose. Such engineering may be done in one of hundreds of computer programming languages, from low-level machine language or assembly language, to high-level (3rd generation) languages like Fortran, Cobol and C++.

Spark (Apache Spark)—a fast, in-memory open source data processing engine to efficiently execute streaming, machine learning or SQL workloads that require fast iterative access to datasets. Spark is generally a lot faster than MapReduce.

spatial analysis—analyzing spatial data such geographic data or topological data to identify and understand patterns and regularities within data distributed in a geographic space.

SQL (Structured Query Language)—a programming language for retrieving data from a relational database.

standard deviation—the positive square root of the variance:
- Population: ?
- Sample: s

stream processing—designed to act on real-time and streaming data with "continuous" queries. Combined with streaming analytics (i.e. the ability to continuously calculate mathematical or statistical analytics on the fly within the stream), stream processing solutions are designed to handle high volumes in real time.

structured data—data that is organized according to a predetermined structure.

structured data—data that resides in a table or set of tables. The most highly structured would be a normalized relational database. Part of big data (which see).

sum of squares—in ANOVA, the total sum of squares helps express the total variation that can be attributed to various factors. From the ANOVA table, %SS is the Sum of Squares of the Factor divided by the Sum of Squares Total. Similar to R2 in Regression.

terabyte—1024 gigabytes. A terabyte can store approximately 300 hours of high-definition video.

test for equal variance (F-test)—compares the variance of two samples of data against each other. Uses the F distribution.

test statistic—a standardized value (Z, t, F, etc.) which represents the likelihood of H0 and is distributed in a known manner such that the probability for this value can be determined.

text analytics—the application of statistical, linguistic and machine learning techniques on text-based data-sources to derive meaning or insight.

time series analysis—analysis of well-defined data measured at repeated measures of time to identify time based patterns.

topological data analysis—analysis techniques focusing on the theoretical shape of complex data with the intent of identifying clusters and other statistically significance trends that may be present.

transactional data—data that relates to the conducting of business, such as accounts payable and receivable data or product shipments data.

two sample t-test—A statistical test to compare the means of two samples of data against each other. Uses the t-distribution.

type I error—the error that occurs when the null hypothesis is rejected when, in fact, it is true.

type II error—the error that occurs when the null hypothesis is not rejected when it is, in fact, false.

unstructured data—data that has no identifiable structure, such as email message text, social media posts, audio files (recorded human speech, music), etc.

unstructured data—data that is entirely free-form. Business intelligence requires natural language software (a form of AI) to make use of such data. Part of big data (which see).

utopia—a perfect place where everything runs smoothly, including political, social and moral aspects. Literally, from the Greek for "no place," because most philosophers have viewed such perfection as impossible.

variance—the average squared deviation for all values from the mean:
- Population: 2
- Sample: s2

variety—the different types of data available to collect and analyze in addition to the structured data found in a typical database. Categories include machine generated data, computer log data, textual social media information, multimedia social and other information.

velocity—the speed at which data is acquired and used. Not only are companies and organizations collecting more and more data at a faster rate, they want to derive meaning from that data as soon as possible, often in real time.

veracity—ensuring that data used in analytics is correct and precise.

visualization—a visual abstraction of data designed for the purpose of deriving meaning or communicating information more effectively. Visuals created are usually complex, but understandable in order to convey the message of data.

Glossary References

1.   Augur, H. (2016, May). A Beginner's Guide to Big Data Terminology. Retrieved from http://dataconomy.com.

2.   Dontha, R. (2017, January). 25 Big Data Terms You Must Know to Impress Your Date (or whomever you want). Retrieved from http://datasciencecentral.com.

3.   NT, B. (2014, July). Big Data A to Z: A glossary of Big Data terminology. Retrieved from http://bigdata-madesimple.com.

4.   Analytics and Big Data Glossary for the Enterprise. (2017, March). Retrieved from http://data-informed.com.

5.   An Extensive Glossary of Big Data Terminology. Retrieved from https://datafloq.com.

About the Author

Mert Damlapinar has been a VP of Marketing & E-Commerce, an E-Commerce Digital Director, a Director of Sales, a Business Development Executive, founder of thre start-ups, and a Molecular Biologist. With extensive experience in biotech and CPG industries for over 18 years, he has traveled to more than 20 countries on 4 continents. He has won the Employee of the Year award, Best Sales Performance awards and was selected Most Scoring Player in college sports for 4 consecutive years. He has climbed the Great Wall and survived many yacht races and polo games. He has a bachelor's degree in Molecular Biology from Hacettepe University and a master's degree in Applied Business Analytics from Boston University. He completed graduate-level training in Machine Learning at MIT and executive-level education in Integrated Marketing at Cornell University. He and his wife share their home in Manhattan with an Italian Greyhound, a Lionhead Rabbit and a lifetime collection of books.

Connect

LinkedIn
https://www.linkedin.com/in/mert-damlapinar